W9-BSM-102

Secret Allies in the Pacific

Secret Allies in the Pacific

*Covert Intelligence and Code Breaking
Cooperation Between the United States,
Great Britain, and Other Nations
Prior to the Attack on Pearl Harbor*

by ROLAND H. WORTH, JR.

McFarland & Company, Inc., Publishers
Jefferson, North Carolina, and London

ISBN 0-7864-1136-8 (softcover : 50# alkaline paper) ∞

Library of Congress cataloguing data are available

British Library cataloguing data are available

Manufactured in the United States of America

Cover photograph ©2001 Corbis Images

*McFarland & Company, Inc., Publishers
 Box 611, Jefferson, North Carolina 28640
 www.mcfarlandpub.com*

To Loretta Mary Worth—
25 years of love, affection, and support

Contents

III. Other Covert Intelligence Sharing

IV. Suppression and Revelation
of the British Role

Preface

With a graduate paper behind me on some of the oddities of the Pearl Harbor attack of December 7, 1941, I had time to browse through the volumes of government investigations related to that assault. I was looking for nothing in particular; I merely had a general interest in the testimony and was seeking out those parts that might be particularly interesting to the postwar generation and help us better understand the attitudes and actions of those involved on the American side at Pearl Harbor.

This research ultimately bore fruit in a compilation entitled *Pearl Harbor: Selected Testimonies*, published by McFarland in 1993. To the extent that anything specific was in my mind beyond a general interest in intelligence gathering during the period, I was looking for anything related to the prewar total economic embargo the Western allies imposed on Japan. (Yes, another book: *No Choice But War*, McFarland, 1995. I don't believe in letting information go to waste.)

As I recall it, it was the second volume of investigations that contained the surprise. I missed the significance of Gen. Douglas MacArthur's affidavit the first time I glanced at it, but when it was repeated a page or two later it was as if I had been hit over the head with a pipe: *MacArthur was admitting to receiving all the "Ultras."* The British decryption efforts were "Ultra"; the United States had "Magic." What was MacArthur doing getting the British information? That sent me back to the first volume and I started over from scratch, now alert for every scrap of information I could find about Allied intelligence sharing (and code breaking in particular) in the Pacific before the outbreak of the conflict.

The irony I ultimately discovered was that the Americans had adopted the British nomenclature and that the general was applying later terminology to the information he had received back in 1941. In spite of this initial error, I discovered that there *was* a large amount of information on the British effort and the cooperation between the Allied governments. This book brings together for the first time this valuable but overlooked source of information on the matter. Admittedly it is much like a jigsaw puzzle: a piece here, a piece there, a small section there.

Assembling this puzzle produces not the entire picture, for there was a conscious American decision to downplay the British role. Yet a broad portrait of how the two governments interlocked their decryption programs emerges, and bringing this information together in one spot should be of interest both to any serious student of the events that led to the eruption of the Pacific War and to those interested in the code breaking programs in particular. Indeed, this information is of special importance because it was publicly available and, seemingly, universally overlooked. Furthermore, the testimony was taken under oath and within a few years of the events, while later writers have had to rely upon their memories from decades earlier. Contemporary British documentation, in contrast, has been hard to come by and repeatedly limited by British authorities.

The American investigations also reveal other forms of intelligence sharing of the era, and these are brought together in the current volume as well. Although a number of useful later sources have been utilized, probably a third or more of the information herein comes from this mine of facts, previously untapped for its usefulness in this area.

As a kind of literary bonus, the reader will discover that the famed Ultra Secret (the anti–German decryption program) was publicly revealed in the United States before hundreds of reporters decades before the British went public with the information. No less a personage than the former U.S. secretary of war did this—and it made so little impact on the memory of both the public and specialists that the British "admission" in the 1970s was universally taken to represent a previously unknown aspect of World War II history. And it was—unless one paid very careful attention to the testimonies compiled by the U.S. government.

Perhaps this is why it is always useful for a later generation to review previously well-worked sources of historical information. The very fact that decades have gone by may alert us to the significance of information that earlier researchers overlooked. This is not arrogance; it is simply an admission that we are all human beings and we do not always look beyond the immediate to matters that may be of great importance but peripheral to our direct concerns.

As indicated, the data from the U.S. government investigations provide the core of facts around which this book is built. Yet the firsthand accounts of participants have slowly become available, though far more often stressing European Ultra rather than Pacific. The information provided by participants has been supplemented by the probings of various scholars on related issues. The fitting together =of these two bodies of knowledge provides a more thorough picture of what was happening.

One challenge to the writer has been how to integrate the newer material with the testimony from the government investigations during and after World War II. As seemed most useful on a chapter by chapter basis, in some cases I have integrated the testimony with later evidence. In other cases, I have summed up the testimony and clearly distinguished what was discovered later so that the reader can better grasp how a partially painted landscape was ultimately filled out by what later became public knowledge.

Roland H. Worth, Jr.
August 2001

Introduction

American estimates of the likelihood of war with Japan and what the targets of the initial assaults might be were influenced by several factors.

A fair amount of material was publicly available through Japanese radio, newspapers, and magazines. In spite of strict censorship it was impossible to cut off all data that would assist foreign powers in evaluating the war-making potential of Japan.

Human contacts supplemented this. Some of those contacts were in Japan itself, where a few individuals shared with American diplomatic personnel certain economic and political data that came their way. Such sharing was limited for several reasons. For many it was a matter of strict patriotism, even if there might be doubts as to specific government policies. Furthermore, the Tokyo government discouraged friendships with foreign representatives and the secret police carefully watched diplomats and those who came in contact with them.

Economic information was significantly harder to hide than political and military, but Japan was an international trader, and in order to trade on any significant basis, at least limited amounts of information had to be provided and exchanged by the concerned parties. In the process it was easy for individuals to learn more than they were supposed to, even if no conscious attempt were being made to obtain or provide additional details.

Hence systematic debriefing of those who came in detailed contact with Japanese business provided an entrée into the practical functioning of that country's economy, its strengths and weaknesses, and its potential if war were to break out. George W. Bicknell, Assistant G-2 for the Hawaiian Department of the U.S. Army, touched upon these sources when asked where he obtained the information he utilized in preparing his reports:

> We used every available source. Our principal source for obtaining economic information and information about the Far East was from businessmen returning on liners or coming in on the clipper ships from the Orient, interviewing them, getting their opinions; interviewing any officials of the British or other national military organizations that came through Hawaii, as well as picking up the intercepts on all Japanese radio stations, reading the Japanese-language papers and obtaining some papers from the Orient and piecing all of that information together.[1]

From such mainly open sources—especially the press and radio broadcasts—it was no secret that the international situation was not only perilous but imminently explosive. Army Counterintelligence in Hawaii was given the responsibility in May 1941 of producing a biweekly "Summary of Contemporary Opinion." This was based on an analysis of Japanese press reports and data available from the army's own scattered sources, such as these interviews with businessmen. The issue of November 29 began with the underlined warning, "Our forces should be placed on the alert and stay there, due to the imminent possibility of an attack."[2]

This was good advice, but not practical for any sustained period of time with the limited resources the American forces had in Hawaii. The wear and tear on equipment was prohibitive for anything but short term alerts.

The army and navy were even more interested in directly relevant military data than in underlying economic-political information. Although a number of sources provided military data, 1940–1941 was especially significant because of the emergence of electronic means to uncover clues to potential enemy behavior.

For example, "traffic analysis" was very useful in locating the whereabouts and the imminence of action by the Japanese fleet. If a high amount of radio communication was suddenly "in the air" going to certain identifiable vessels, then a movement of some type was probable. Since certain destroyers were routinely assigned to specific aircraft carriers the detection of transmissions from these destroyers was a good—but not infallible—tip-off as to the location of the carriers they served. In the second half of November the number of identifiable transmissions from these destroyers plummeted. Those that were monitored pointed toward a presence in the Formosa or the Indochina area. Radio silence hid the fact in early December that half of the Japanese carrier fleet was on its way to Pearl Harbor.[3]

Even more important was the ability to break the Japanese codes and ciphers. The Army Signal Intelligence Service's successful cracking of the "Purple" diplomatic code was so amazing that those involved gained the nickname of "magicians,"[4] leading to the label "Magic" that was applied to their work. This was an invaluable source for the top diplomatic personnel of the United States and provided an uncensored source on Japan's actual state of mind as to war and peace questions.

Things were not going so well with the strictly military and naval systems. Back in June 1939, the Japanese had introduced an "Operations Code" that the Americans called the "AN" cipher and which was also known under the label of JN-25. It took until November of 1940 for translatable decryptions to be produced. No sooner was this done than in December of the same year a dramatically new variety of the system was introduced. Hence as 1940 came to a close there was a total blackout on the central cipher used by the potential foe. Even "HE" (the "Material Code System"), which was only utilized for low-grade supply and other routine matters, was not cracked for months.[5]

In this grim battle for knowledge superiority, the Americans were happy to gain whatever official or unofficial support they could obtain from Britain and powers aligned with her. The purpose of this book is to sketch the nature of this cooperation, how it was created and evolved, and what it was able to accomplish.

The cooperation was done in the deepest of secrecy. With war raging in Europe, it was obvious that anti-intervention forces would have a field day even if the cooperation were in the opposite corner of the world. They would be naturally suspicious that it was intended as an indirect manner of dragging the United States into the European conflagration. Even on strictly Pacific-only terms, the arrangement was open to challenge: The British were far more likely than the Americans to be the victims of any anti–western aggression in the Pacific. Why should the United States be obligated to save the British Empire?

After the war was over the British still preferred to keep their cooperation secret. Even to this day, the British government is unwilling to fully open the relevant archives for use by researchers. It took Great Britain almost 30 years to admit the existence of the European code breaking effort known as Ultra, and that admission came only when books were about to be published that, as part of different subjects, would discuss the work of Ultra and its contribution to winning the war. The British are even more reluctant to part with information on what we might, for convenience, call Pacific Ultra—the part of their decryption efforts aimed at Japan. So successful has the effort been to obscure Pacific decryption, that even today "Ultra" remains essentially synonymous with the anti-German effort of the war.[6]

Yet there is a surprising amount of information available in spite of official British reluctance to discuss the subject or to permit full access to its pre–Pearl Harbor data. The largest single source on Allied intelligence sharing in the Pacific prior to the war, however, is from the various American investigations of the responsibility for the Pearl Harbor fiasco.

Even in the more recent publications, we are still dealing with a jigsaw puzzle. Nevertheless, the American efforts provide hundreds of the pieces, even an incredibly candid reference to the existence of European Ultra—a reference made in the presence of an enormous crowd of reporters and listeners and which, somehow, made no lasting impression. By piecing together the data, we can gain a better comprehension of how cooperation and competition worked in a period when it was in all parties' interest to provide each other assistance while protecting their own prerogatives.

I
American "Magic"

Magic in Washington

Division of Responsibilities: Washington, Hawaii, and the Philippines

In retrospect it is easy to forget that the Washington unit of Magic had far greater responsibilities than merely breaking Japanese codes. It had the broad general responsibility of paying attention

> [t]o naval operations in the Atlantic Ocean and to the plans and intentions of foreign governments. In addition to the foregoing duties, the Washington Unit had another important function: Training personnel for the other units so that they would be able to "pull their weight in the boat" when transferred to duty overseas. For this reason, the Washington Unit had, at this time, the most experienced personnel (some with over ten years of C.I. [Communications Intelligence] duty) and the least experienced (ninety percent with less than one year of C.I. duty). The Washington Unit had been standing continuous watches since February, 1941.[1]

All three major installations in Washington, Pearl Harbor, and the Philippines had certain basic goals. "The mission of all three stations was in general to exploit all cryptographic systems employed by foreign powers and to develop what was then known as radio intelligence but is now known as traffic intelligence organizations, and to develop radio direction finder nets."[2]

As a broad generalization this was a quite adequate summary, but how did the emphases and tasks of the three stations actually differ in practice? Comdr. Laurence J. Rochefort explained:

> During the latter part of 1941, the station at Pearl Harbor was

assigned the specific tasks of attacking personnel code, administrative code, the code in use in the Marshall Islands area, and to exploit those systems. They were also directed to conduct research on all Japanese naval systems except the five-numbered system.

Cavite [in the Philippines][3] was charged with the exploitation of information contained in diplomatic systems and [the] numbered system.

The station in Washington was charged with the general control of all three plus Japanese diplomatic systems and such other systems as might have been directed by higher authority.[4]

Prioritization was essential due to the vast amount of data flowing into the three central decryption stations. Because of a shortage of manpower, it was impossible to handle simultaneously the flood of intercepts that came into any of the monitor control centers—at Pearl Harbor, the Philippines, or especially Washington (since all of them ultimately were sent there). Hence decisions had to be quickly made as to what was to get the emphasis, and a pre-arranged procedure was in place to handle such situations. Although Comdr. Arthur H. McCollum is speaking specifically of those texts received by mail from monitoring stations (due to the inability to get them in any faster), the principles would apply to other intercepts as well:

> … It is my understanding that priorities were first given on the basis of the code classification. In other words, the higher the code classification, probably the more important the information was. There was also the precedence of the dispatch, that is the urgency with which it was sent. Those were obtained from the normal procedure signs at the head of the dispatch.
>
> Then an attempt was made to decrypt them together, if we had the particular code table in which that code was sent. We did not always have it. Sometimes these codes would be received and we did not have the method or means of decrypting them until sometime afterwards.
>
> Once it was decrypted, or sufficiently decrypted to indicate some importance, it was handed to one of the translators who took a look at it to determine whether he thought it should be completely broken down for further decryptation. That had to be done because of the limited number of people capable of translating the language, and to make the very best use of the people we had.
>
> When we were working full blast, the way we were, oh, for

the month immediately preceding the attack on our fleet, great effort was made to get the stuff out of these negotiations right away, just as quickly as we possibly could. Now, that was dependent on the time of arrival at the decoding center, which was not of necessity directly related to the time of transmission from Tokyo, whether the code to decode it was available or not, and dependent upon the relative importance of it as determined prior to reading any of the contents.

Now, when you come then to a slack period, that is, when we weren't getting so many messages, they would go back and work on the old ones. The effort was to decode everything but to try to decode the most important ones first.[5]

The "freshness" (recentness) of the material could also vary significantly even when first received in Washington. There were not enough facilities available to permit the Far Eastern intercept stations to provide all data by radio retransmission to Washington. Hence a good amount of material (admittedly, sometimes duplicates of what was already available) came to the West Coast by the once-a-week Pan American clipper service from Hawaii. In some circumstances it might even be sent via ship, making the delay that much longer.[6] Even when radio facilities were available, material was sent by this means only if it was in a preapproved category on the list Washington provided.[7]

The Breaking of the "Purple" Diplomatic Cipher

In the abstract, the Japanese knew full well that others could potentially break their codes and ciphers. ("Codes" and "ciphers" represent two different methods of hiding one's message but they have come to be used as virtual synonyms and we use them in a similar fashion in the current work.) During the Washington Armament Conference of 1921–1922, some 5,000 of their communications were both intercepted and read by the Americans.[8] The publication of Herbert O. Yardley's firsthand account of how it was done produced great indignation in Japan and a widespread feeling that the Americans had taken advantage of their nation.[9] During the ensuing two decades machine systems that seemed to provide near invulnerability for the most important correspondence became available and were perfected.

In addition to the major hurdles imposed by the effective Japanese ciphers themselves, there was a major language barrier as well. There was a widespread conviction that foreigners could never truly master their language. Hence even if the ciphers could—somehow—be broken, the British and the Americans would still have great difficulty effectively getting much use out of the resulting data.[10] This worked as a major *dis*incentive for the Japanese to take as seriously as they should have the indications they received that penetration had been obtained.

There was, moreover, a considerable element of truth to the Japanese view of their language. As the sole French correspondent in Japan in late pre-war years and throughout the Second World War itself remarked, the language was "grammatically imprecise, illogical and complicated in syntax."[11] An American analysis of the time conceded that Japanese "amount[ed] almost to a cryptologic system" in and of itself.[12]

For example, if the word "kaisen" was decrypted from the cipher, it could have at least eight meanings. Three were references to war actions ("opening of hostilities," "sea battle," or "decisive engagement"); two were references to vessels ("barge" or "ghostship"); three were to totally unrelated images ("re-election," "itch," or "rotation").[13]

Such possible ambiguities in meaning could lead to considerable difference in how one rendered the texts into English. To this day there remains a controversy over whether the American translation of the decrypts were not guilty of a "harsher" rendering of the Purple diplomatic messages than the Japanese intended the texts to convey. Whatever limitations may well have existed, this certainly did not hinder grasping of the basic policy and policy shifts, however the nuances may have been missed or even misinterpreted.

Washington was especially concerned with breaking the Japanese Purple diplomatic code. William F. Friedman led the Army team to a successful penetration of that extremely difficult system, yet in retrospect he was willing to share generously credit with all those who worked with him:

> To the best of my recollection, the first complete translation was handed in some time in August [1940], it might have been the early part of August or the middle part of August. We had been working on the Japanese Purple system. This system had superseded a system known as the Red, which was also a machine cipher. But when the Purple system was first introduced it presented an extremely difficult problem on which the Chief Signal Officer asked us to direct our best efforts.
>
> After work by my associates when we were making very slow progress, the Chief Signal Officer asked me personally to take hand. I had been engaged largely in administrative

duties up to that time, so at his request, I dropped everything else that I could and began to work with the group. Naturally this was a collaborative, cooperative effort on the part of all the people concerned. No one person is responsible for the solution, nor is there any single person to whom the major share of credit should go. As I say, it was a team, and it was only by very closely coordinated teamwork that we were able to solve it, which we did.[14]

Those who stress Friedman's importance point out his unique and vital role. Friedman himself, however, was looking at the matter from a different standpoint, but one that has much validity as well: One person's genius can almost never accomplish the entire job. It may provide a critical conceptual breakthrough, but only as it is polished, worked over, and perfected by others does it reach its full potential. Such was the case with breaking Purple.

However laudable and desirable the Purple diplomatic intercepts were in and of themselves, a large portion of the available military manpower was being diverted from efforts to crack and translate the military ciphers of the enemy. Comdr. Laurence F. Safford estimated that in the five weeks prior to the attack, that while only 12 percent of the Navy's manpower was being used in Purple decryption efforts, a far more significant 30 percent was being diverted from its intercept capacity, and half of its translation potential.[15]

Pictures of German Enigma machines (not to mention functioning examples) survived the war. In marked contrast, this was not the case with the Purple machine. As one close student of the matter has written,

> A good many legends have grown around the building by Friedman and his colleagues of the machine which imitated the Japanese Purple device. It was, in fact, made from electrical equipment in short supply. It was not elegant, and from all accounts it appears to have replicated the Japanese machine not only in its ability to encipher and decipher, but in the showers of sparks which it sometimes gave off when operated.
>
> Strangely enough, the Americans who so brilliantly constructed this hardware from their theoretical conclusions were never to see how like or unlike the original their duplicate really was. As war broke out between Japan and the United States, the Japanese in the Washington embassy hammered their Purple machine to pieces. When a British regiment took over Japan's Berlin embassy in May, 1945, the Japanese, or the Russians, had already removed all cryptographic equip-

ment. The same was true throughout the Far East, including Tokyo itself, as the Americans began their occupation in the summer of 1945. A few broken metal parts were all that Friedman or his colleagues ever saw of Japan's Purple machine.[16]

Inter-Service Cooperation in Washington

The army personnel in Washington were from the Signal Intelligence Service and were under the command of Colonel Otis Sadtler. The navy contingent was from the Communications Security Section and answerable to Comdr. Laurence F. Safford.[17] In the nomenclature of the period the Washington decrypt operation was collectively called "Negat."[18]

Limited staff and a huge mountain of intercepts compelled a degree of inter-service cooperation that might not otherwise have existed. Col. Rufus S. Bratton, head of the Far Eastern Section of Army G-2, pointed out that this sometimes resulted in one service providing the text of the intercept and the other the actual English translation or even *both* of the services providing part of the English translation. In regard to one particular intercept Bratton noted, "I don't know who intercepted it, but it was a naval translation. For your information, sir, the Army and the Navy divided this material. There was so much of it that in order to process it and get it out where it could be used the Navy took certain parts of it and the Army took certain parts of it, and the results were interchanged so that we both had all the material all the time."[19]

Col. Safford also explained the army-navy cooperation to the same army panel of investigators:

> The communication intelligence organization of the Navy and the S.I.S. [Signal Intelligence Service][20] of the Army were working in cooperation on this matter for over a year. We had divided up interception of Japanese messages to insure that no circuits were left uncovered and that we had a minimum of duplication consistent with adequate coverage. We exchanged the messages between the interested services. Then there was arrangement made on the diplomatic messages that the Army processed them on the even days of the month, and the Navy processed them on the odd days of the month, but both services got copies of the translations and handled their own dissemination of intelligence from that point.[21]

This system was not imposed on the two sides, but was the result of negotiation between the two services.[22] The two military branches also agreed that the translated decrypts would be circulated outside their ranks on a similar divided responsibility basis: In this case, even numbered months were the army's responsibility (February, April, etc.) while the navy handled the odd numbered ones (January, March, etc.)[23]

The cooperation existed only so far as the diplomatic traffic. Collaboration did not exist when it came to other ciphers. The U.S. Navy saw no need to share the results of their work on the Japanese naval systems; nor did the army share the fruit of its effort to crack Nippon's army systems.[24] This was only natural: The navy did not anticipate gaining anything much of value from the army ciphers nor the army from those of the Japanese navy.

On the other hand, there could be cases where one provided a tip-off useful to the other service: If the Japanese army was launching a massive offensive in China, these troops would be denied to any invasion force heading southward. Likewise, if there was silence in regard to such plans and the Japanese navy was moving in a detectable direction, its likely targets would provide at least some warning to the U.S. Army that sooner or later—probably sooner—land forces would be disembarked as well.

In spite of the isolation of the two services in regard to naval versus army codes, the two recognized the need the other had for raw material from which to work. Hence when Manchuria was invaded in the early 1930s, the Navy (Marine) monitoring station at Peking recorded all army transmissions. These were funneled through the War Department to the army's decrypters for their use.[25] No inquiries were made as to the result[26]—perhaps out of concern that the navy would be asked questions as to its own findings that it preferred not to answer.

Limited Personnel and Space

Just as personnel were not adequate for the large workload, the physical quarters were also very limited. The overcrowding of the navy is vividly revealed in Col. Safford's description of how difficult it was to find a place for confidential discussions. Of the alleged winds execute (war-warning) message he recalled that, "Kramer says that we walked down the corridor together to his office, discussing the message. It was my custom to talk over ultra secret matters with Kramer, walking up and down the corridor. We were so horribly overcrowded. My office had about five people in it and his had an equal number. We had to go out in the corridor to get any privacy."[27]

In spite of the limited manpower available on both the army and navy sides, the two services decrypted and translated a huge volume of diplomatic traffic. In the six months preceding Pearl Harbor, they averaged around 300 a week—7,000 all total.[28] The number of Purple intercepts naturally varied from day to day but during November of 1941 it ran approximately 26 a day.[29]

The successes with Purple came at a price: extreme emotional wear-and-tear on the personnel and the neglecting of lesser diplomatic ciphers. As one of the participants later explained,

> The agency was simply too small and too exhausted.... Our eyes were red and glazed; exhaustion and dream consciousness had overcome us months before the event.... Had these [critics] been among us and seen how buried we were in stacks of messages through the "Purple" machine which had ... priority, they would not wonder that we failed to process and translate a few messages [in the consular code].[30]

As the result, messages in the lower priority consular code received little attention. In retrospect this was to cause considerable embarrassment and controversy. In particular, the "bomb plot" message that laid out a grid for reporting ship locations at Pearl Harbor stood out blatantly. This message also resulted in regular updates sent to Tokyo as to the ships in and out of port.[31] Yet within the modest manpower resources available in Washington this (or a similar retroactive embarrassment) was inevitable. *Something* had to have a lower priority.

Ironically, Pearl Harbor's cryptanalysts could have done the job equally well, but they were under orders to zero in on their unsuccessful assault on the JN-25 cipher.[32] Although the bomb-plot related messages would not have been a guarantee that Pearl was going to be the target of attack, common prudence would have certainly resulted in a higher level of in-port alertness—especially when superimposed upon the skittishness of the local command structure when faced with uncertainty as to the location of the Japanese fleet.

The navy and the army had their own numbering systems for intercepts. Their respective identification numbers both appear at the bottom of most (but not all) of these documents.[33] The navy's numbers began with JD-1 at the beginning of the year and, in the case of calendar 1941, reached to about JD-8000 by the end.[34] Although this provides a relative chronology of their date, it is not an absolute one. "You will find many places in the file where messages were inserted out of turn, out of their order of translation," investigators were told.[35] For one thing, "[t]he most impor-

tant messages in the minor systems often were out of turn, delayed two
or three days behind the more important messages," since the latter were
tackled first.[36]

The navy carefully segregated these files from all other intelligence
data. "[T]hese translations of intercepts were not permitted in the Navy
Department files. This is a special file kept in—all the files were in Captain
Kramer's safe."[37]

Distribution of the "Magic" Intercepts

As the outbreak of war edged closer, the method for handling the
decrypted and translated Japanese diplomatic communications was
altered. Here one key officer responds to questioning on the matter:

> Admiral Hewitt. How were these messages evaluated as to
> their importance and what distribution was made?
>
> Captain Safford. They were translated in the translation
> sections of the Navy Department unit and the War Department
> unit and the senior translator decided which were of relative
> unimportance, not worth writing up smooth, mostly con-
> nected with financial matters and visas and things like that;
> and the others were all typed smooth and turned over to
> Military Intelligence and Naval Intelligence, respectively.
> Originally the two intelligence organizations had prepared
> briefs or memorandums giving a summation or a paraphrase
> of the messages and they were distributed to the higher
> officials in the War and Navy Departments and to the
> Secretary of State and to the President.
>
> In the Navy Department the people that saw them were,
> specifically, the Chief of Naval Operations and his aide usu-
> ally saw them; the Assistant Chief of Naval Operations, the
> Director of Naval Intelligence, the Director of Naval
> Communications and the Director of the War Plans Division.
> The Secretary of the Navy also saw them and usually his aide
> saw them. The Naval Aide to the President saw them and
> took them in to the President.
>
> In the War Department they went to the Military
> Intelligence, Chief Signal Officer, Director of the War Plans
> Division, and the Chief of Staff, War Department, aid[e] also
> to the Secretary of War.
>
> Later on, in November, when things became critical, at
> the request of the President and after conference agreement
> between military Intelligence and Naval Intelligence, the sys-

tem of summaries and briefs was dropped and the original messages were prepared in folders and each day the folder was taken through. By agreement, all dissemination to the White House was handled through the Navy Department, and in return all dissemination to the State Department was handled through the Army, but the two things were duplicates. Anything the Navy was sending around, the copy was sent to the Army, and anything the Army was sending around, a copy was sent to the Navy; and they put on a serial number. Ours were JD-1 and the Army's were SI-X, with a serial; so they were substantially duplicates unless something went wrong.

In addition, it was the habit to put notations on the bottom as to references, and Kramer, when he took his stuff around, everything that was referenced to anything bear[ing] on this subject was put on the off side of the page, so that you had the message on one side and the references on the other, the left hand side, of the folder. Then, anybody seeing them had a complete picture. And Kramer went with them and stood in the doorway or outside and if there was any doubt, he could be called in to explain further to anybody who was interested in the subject. Kramer also went to the White House, I believe twice. Normally he would explain things to the Naval Aide to the President, and the aide would depend on his memory to answer any questions the President might want to ask. The President insisted on seeing the original messages because he was afraid when they tried to condense them, some one would change the meaning.[38]

The distribution system was one that evolved over a long time and went through periods of both expansion and contraction. For more than four months during 1940, as the first Magic Purple decrypts were being produced, they were shared with only 13 individuals in the entire U.S. government. Conspicuously missing were both the secretary of state and the president himself! There was a deep-rooted distrust of many of Roosevelt's advisers and considerable concern whether security would be adequately maintained on anything sent directly to the White House.

In late January 1941, it was grudgingly decided that to deny the chief executive officer and the chief diplomat of the nation access to these materials might be unconstitutional. Hence on the 23rd the president and the secretary of state also began to receive the data.[39] This small group of 15 men has rightly been labeled by one historian "the privileged few"[40]—the data went no further. The potential danger of a compromise of security was believed far, far greater than any benefits of broader dissemination.

In early May 1941, there was a panic when the Japanese came to suspect that their codes were being broken.[41] The groundwork was laid the preceding month when Sumner Welles, the American undersecretary of state, provided decrypt-based information to the ambassador from Britain. This information was forwarded to the ambassador's superiors in London. Unfortunately it was in a code that the Germans could—and did—break. The wording was sufficiently explicit that the Germans were certain the Americans had made a major breakthrough in cracking Japanese communications. They promptly provided a warning to Japanese officials.[42]

This was not all the evidence the Germans had. The German charge d'affaires stationed in the American capital sent this warning to his superiors (emphasis added): "As communicated to me *by an absolutely reliable source*, the State Department is in possession of the key to the Japanese coding system and is therefore also able to decipher information telegrams from Tokyo to Ambassador Nomura here regarding Ambassador Oshima's reports from Berlin."[43] This explicit warning—one wonders just who the source might have been—was diluted when Oshima, the Japanese ambassador in Berlin, passed on the warning. According to the message he was given it was "fairly reliably established" that the "code messages" were being read and therefore, that "drastic steps" needed to be implemented to correct the danger.[44] The shift from "absolutely reliable source" to "fairly reliably established" is fascinating in its own right, especially since the Germans also had Sumner Welles's message passed on by the British. Perhaps the Germans were trying to protect their informant or their own code-cracking capacity from being compromised.

Although the Japanese themselves quickly dismissed the possibility that any high security ciphers (such as Purple) were affected, there was the feeling among important U.S. military leaders that further restrictions on circulation of data were essential to avoid the danger that the situation would be repeated. Intra-military circulation was certainly within their control, and both the army and navy chief commanders in Hawaii (Gen. Short and Adm. Kimmel, respectively), were permanently removed from the list of those to receive the decrypts.[45]

More immediately explosive was the denial of the raw decrypts to the president. The rationalization for this was that a decrypt had been found in the trash basket of one of FDR's top advisers. Raw decrypts were only provided Capt. John R. Beardell, who was permitted to summarize them for the president. Likewise sanitized summaries were permitted via the State Department. It took weeks before FDR realized the full extent of what had been done and it was not until November 12, 1941, that he again had regular access to the decrypts themselves.[46]

The denial of such access probably most offended Roosevelt's sense of propriety and position—after all, he *was* the president of the United States. On the other hand, it is highly unlikely that he felt he was being denied vital information. Unlike Churchill, who insisted upon a steady flow of Ultra data and receipt of the most interesting decrypts, Roosevelt had a far more hands-off attitude toward the Magics. This attitude lasted throughout the war. On February 12, 1944, Secretary of War General Marshall commented in a message to Roosevelt, "I have learned that you seldom see the Army summaries of 'Magic' material."[47]

Decades later, there remain bitter disputes as to how the final 14 point Japanese message to Washington was actually handled and who received it and when. These controversies (and a number of others) are all of great intrinsic interest, and have been dealt with (often at length) by historians and theorists of all stripes. Since we are primarily interested in sketching the broader picture of American and Allied decryption work in the Pacific before the war, these matters are of no importance to the present study.

Even so, there were obvious and serious problems with the distribution procedure being officially followed by the Magic decryption program: No one individual or office had the responsibility of systematically integrating the newly obtained information with older data in order to assure that potentially vital shreds of intelligence would not be overlooked. Information is of little or no value unless it reaches the hands of those best able to understand the full ramifications. Hence we have the paradox that "[i]n protecting the Magic secret those in control limited its usefulness. Instead of showing the messages to lower-ranking analysts who might have been more sensitive to their implications, they circulated the intercepts for the most part only among those with the power to make policy decisions."[48]

On an ad hoc basis, individuals involved in the handling of the translated intercepts, as well as the government recipients, attempted to recall, remember, and incorporate this information on an individual basis. But all these were busy men. It was a practical impossibility for them to retain in their memories all that had been said and, even if possible, this knowledge would have distracted them from their more immediate and public government duties and obligations. What they only sporadically received was an analysis of how the latest communications affected what was already known. In short, the brilliance exhibited in *breaking* the codes disappeared when it came to *effectively handling* the information.

2

Magic in Hawaii

Evolution of the Code
Breaking Program in Hawaii

Lieutenant Thomas H. Dyer established a cipher unit in 1936 at the direction-finding station at Heiia, Hawaii. This is a bit of an exaggeration; actually Dyer himself constituted the entirety of the new program. Two years later an additional direction-finding/monitoring unit was established at Wahiawa, Hawaii. A central office to handle the resulting data was established at Pearl Harbor itself.[1] This was on the second floor of the 14th Naval District headquarters at the main Navy yard.[2] When Lt. Comdr. Thomas B. Birtley, Jr., took over responsibility for Hypo (the identification label for the Hawaii-based operation), Dyer continued his own work in a subordinate position.[3]

Until early 1940 the navy's decryption program in Hawaii had been organizationally separate from the monitoring system that provided the raw material and other communications related information. Rear Adm. Claude C. Bloch, who took over as Commandant of the 14th Naval District (i.e., Hawaii) in April 1940, recalled how he combined both aspects of intelligence work into one location:

> We had a unit at Pearl Harbor, when I arrived, composed of communicators and intelligence people, Japanese language students, and they were separated into two units and their information had to be coordinated, and all the information we got from that intelligence, by radio intelligence and such other information as we got from that unit, was transmitted to Cavite and the Navy Department.... When I arrived, I was dissatisfied with the organization and I organized it into

one unit known as "Combat Intelligence"[4] where they were under one head, which unit consisted of radio direction finders, radio interceptors, and all the other things they had with one officer in charge.

In the middle of July, 1941, when we had the facilities, we put them in one big room in the basement of the office building, a secure place, with their own channels of communications to the radio stations and radio direction finders, and so on; I always did my best to augment the force by getting more men and better men.[5]

Actually "hands on" running of the program was in a subordinate's hands. In the spring of 1941, the brilliant Comdr. Joseph J. Rochefort assumed command of the decrypt and intercept programs.[6] With Rochefort lobbying for the move with his superiors, Hypo moved into the basement of the headquarters of the 14th Naval District. This both functioned to enhance security as well as gain for it an air-conditioned working environment—a rarity in those days.[7] With the new Rochefort provided name "Combat Intelligence Unit," it soon went to a 24-hour-a-day operation in which each person worked six days on duty and then had two days off. The remainder of the year it completely ceased operations only on the three major national holidays of July 4, Labor Day, and Thanksgiving.[8]

Although formally attached to the 14th Naval District, its internal priorities were set by the Magic unit in Washington "as to the type of work they wished us to work on."[9]

Comdr. Safford recalled that the unit's function was the immediate one of protecting American forces from surprise attack. The Pearl Harbor unit focused on "the dispositions and plans of naval forces in the Pacific Ocean and the surveillance over Japanese naval communications. We expected that this would prevent the Fleet being surprised as the Russians had been at Port Arthur.... These duties did not include surveillance over diplomatic communications of any sort."[10] Indeed, "[t]hey hadn't been assigned any diplomatic circuits since about 1932."[11]

None of the decrypted intercepts were shared with Hawaii at all for local evaluation,[12] during the second half of 1941. While those in Washington were well aware how dangerously the negotiations had degenerated in the final month before war, those officers responsible for the security of Pearl Harbor received only the more limited summaries and guess-estimates that Washington chose to share. At least in retrospect, the local commanders felt that the lack of this hard data grievously compromised their own evaluation of the closeness of war.

Not only was Hawaii out of the loop for the diplomatic intercepts, it lacked the essential equipment being used to crack it in both the Philippines and Washington. Capt. Theodore S. Wilkinson recalled that the code-cracking program run by Rochefort at Pearl Harbor "did not have the facilities for the purple code, nor originally facilities for any code. Later he was asked by the department to specialize on one or two codes...."[13] Before a different investigatory panel, Comdr. Safford testified at greater length as to the specific types of code-breaking work that occupied the Pearl Harbor team:

> Pearl Harbor's main mission was an attack on the Japanese flag officers system. This particular code and cipher had been in effect since about 1 December 1940 and remained in effect for some time after Pearl Harbor. We were also attacking this code with another group in the Navy Department and, I believe, the British were working on it. We never succeeded in a solution.
>
> From about 1926 to December, 1940, most of our knowledge about the Japanese Navy came from this code. We thought it the most important system the Japanese Navy was using and we had our most skilled and most experienced officers and men working on it. After the attack on Pearl Harbor, about December 10th, the Hawaiian unit discontinued their attack on this code and put all their attention on a lesser system of the Japanese Navy. We continued attack on the flag officer cipher back in the Navy Department, until the system went out of use.[14]

In his postwar memoirs, Layton dates the shift to the lesser code (JN-25) a week later.[15] This lesser code, however, was very important in its own right: It was used to transmit operational fleet movement orders.[16] Postwar estimates by Rochefort and others closely related to the project indicated that only about 10 to 15 percent of JN-25 was readable in the month prior to Pearl Harbor.[17]

For a small scale operation, the local contingent was unusually well trained. "The personnel of this Unit had about four or five years of C.I. experience on the average. The officers included our best, and six or seven had other previous C.I. duty in the Asiatic C.I. unit."[18]

During the summer and fall of 1941 the responsibilities of the unit expanded. Comdr. Rochefort was reassigned there in the early summary of that year.

> I might say, General, that when I first went there it had no name whatever. It was called the "radio unit" of the district

but we changed it after I went there and called it "combat intelligence," and then enlarged it to include such things as providing situation maps for the Commander-in-Chief [Pacific Fleet], and plots of all vessels in the Pacific, and so on, and so forth; and generally we consisted of an intercept station, a radio-direction-finder station, and in the crypto-analytical units in Pearl Harbor, proper.[19]

The threefold division of the unit's work, mentioned so briefly in the last sentence, was spelled out in more detail in Rochefort's testimony to the Hewitt Inquiry (emphasis added):

The station at Pearl Harbor consisted in the main of an *interception unit*, which was stationed at Aiea [sic; Heeia] radio station in charge of Chief Radioman Langford; a *mid-Pacific direction finder net* with stations at Dutch Harbor, Samoa, Pearl Harbor, and Midway. These were controlled in Pearl Harbor under the supervision of the then Lieutenant Commander Huckins. The *decryptation unit* was responsible for the attack, exploitation, translation, and dissemination of all intercepted traffic. I was in direct charge of that section as well as directly in charge of all sections.[20]

Before a different inquiry he spoke in a little more detail about the Hawaii-based monitoring unit. "We had what we termed the 'intercept unit,' which during 1941 was located at Heeia, at an old naval radio station." It "is just beyond Waialua over on the other side" of Oahu, explained Rochefort. Since his listeners were a little confused by his terminology, he elaborated further, "It might be understood a little more clearly, sir, if we called it a monitoring station. I believe that is what the FCC [Federal Communications Commission] calls it—a monitoring station. In other words, we intercept any traffic that is going, either way."[21] Many years later, Layton pointed out the great difficulties this imposed upon the program: Because of the lack of a teleprinter link, someone—sometimes even Rochefort—had to daily undertake the 60 mile round trip to obtain the latest intercepts.[22]

Physical Premises and Workload

Station Hypo moved into its underground headquarters building facility in the summer of 1941. " 'The dungeon' as it was known," Lt. Comdr. Edwin T. Layton recalled after the war, "did not have windows, and the air-conditioning system was notoriously temperamental." It had only one entrance and this was constantly protected by an armed guard.[23] It was a place where work, seemingly, could never get done—yet was routinely grinding out vast amounts of information. As Layton described it after the war,

> To outsiders like myself, who had the necessary security clearance to get past the armed marine door guard, the Hypo "dungeon" was organized chaos. Over his desk the enigmatic Captain Dyer had hung a sign reading, *You don't have to be crazy to work here—but it helps!* Under the glass on his desk resided what was reputed to be the best collection of pin-ups in the Pacific Fleet, which added its own touch to the unbelievably cluttered appearance. But Tommy Dyer knew exactly where everything was on it. A new yeoman once made the mistake of tidying up the legendary "Dyer's desk" and it brought down Dyer's wrath after he was unable to locate a critical decrypt.[24]

By March of 1941, Hypo had begun to receive then modern IBM tabulating equipment that enabled it to dramatically speed up its pace of decryption efforts.[25] Describing the situation just before the 1942 Battle of Midway, Layton portrays the vast amount of data that was able to be processed with the help of the then state-of-the-art equipment: The intercepts hit 500 to 1,000 daily. Even the most trivial item had to be at least briefly examined to assure that little was overlooked. The five digit groups of each message were entered onto IBM cards. Long messages could take up to 200 of these and the cards had to then be fed into IBM machines for processing. By the time of Midway, these hit the three million cards a month level, which pushed the limits of available storage capacity, not to mention ingenuity in explaining why in the world the military required so many.[26]

> The printouts produced from the tabulating process, from which the Japanese messages could be translated, were piled up on desks, floors, and every available space. Each analyst working on current decrypts needed his own stack of acco binders containing the printouts of past messages for reference.... What saved the whole system from collapsing was the team's overall easygoing lack of hierarchy and its remarkable ability to recall and relate details of decrypts made months later.[27]

With an appropriate reduction in volume the same pressures, difficulties, and turmoils existed in the operation of Station Hypo prior to the Japanese attack as well. An elaborate filing system was utilized to help in both the decryption and interpretation. Donald M. Showers, who began work with Hypo in early 1942, described it in a postwar interview:

> We typed the translated decrypts onto a five-by-eight card, the entire message: call signs, date-time groups, frequency of transmission when known, and then the text. We underlined everything that was meaningful. Then we used a multilith duplicator to make twenty or thirty copies of each, depending on the number of underlined items. The cards were then placed in racks of open boxes in date sequence with a special set for each underlined item, such as abbreviations and designators. When one of the cryptanalysts recalled some earlier decrypt, I would break out a stack of cards for the day in question and search through them by the underlinings. Each of our recoveries was valued from A to D, according to reliability.[28]

Hypo's Cipher Targets: Flag Officers Code and JN-25: The Japanese Fleet Operational Cipher

Hypo's assigned decryption target (in contrast to its role of monitoring and forwarding other intercepts) was in regard to the elusive but high status Flag Officers Code. In contrast, Cast (the sister program in the Philippines) had responsibility for tackling the fleet operational cipher of the Japanese Navy. At this point, the story becomes entertwined with Cast, the decision of Washington to divide responsibilities in this manner, and the involvement of the British in the effort.

Due to the vital importance of the fleet operational code (JN-25) both before and during the war, we need to digress and explain its nature and thereby give a better idea of what an abstract term like "cipher" (in contrast to "code") meant in actual practice. The cipher was composed of two parts. Initially there was a five-digit number. Depending on the combination selected, this would represent one of 33,333 different phrases or words. Then one would go to a second table of five digit numbers. According to the prescribed starting point on the list, one would add the two sets of numbers together and that would be the number Morse coded. For example, if the actual number for the desired word was 54211 and the additive was 43126, then 97337 was transmitted.

The additive for each and every number set would change per the pattern in the prearranged list. A further complication: American-style math, when faced with adding the digits 9 and 1, would make the final digit a zero and "carry" a "1" into the next math column. Following Chinese procedures of the era one would *not* carry forward the "1." To translate the text into usable language, the receiving individual first deducted the additive according to the reference list issued him and then consulted the basic number/word list to determine the actual word being conveyed.[29]

This was the basic system used throughout the variants (JN-25A, JN-25B, etc.): the underlying numeral/word list remained identical. *Only the selection of additive number combinations (and the starting point on the list) varied.* These additive lists were issued in 100-page collections and periodically replaced.[30]

At the beginning of each communiqué was a plain text notification of the beginning point. For example, one might receive 0849318. This meant that the recipient turned to page 84 of the additive list in effect. He looked across the top margin of the page until his eyes hit the number "93," and then he looked down the page till he found "18" in the left hand margin. In the hypothetical example we provided above, when the two columns came together he would find this initial number would be 43126.[31]

In theory, the Morse coder was supposed to change the beginning point on each and every message. In real life, the tedious process of adding numbers together and transmitting meant there was a tendency—especially when volume was large—to fall back time and again on a given day to the same starting point. Hence when the Americans or British were fortunate enough (as was often the case) to receive a number whose plain text encryption beginning point was the same—0849318 in our example— that provided a group of messages in which one knew that the following additives would *always* be in exactly the same order whether the message was received on that or a subsequent day, so long as that particular additive list was still in effect.

Let us say the message was a 100 words long. If one could successfully break and read the text, then one knew that when one received a future JN-25 that began with 0849318, one had 100 of the additives *and* the meaning of the number/word correlations that was produced when one removed the additive from the total. That was minor when one considers there were 33,333 word/phrases on the underlying word/number list. On the other hand, the more places one successfully penetrated the additive list and the underlying word/number correlations, the easier future work became.

The additive book was altered every six months, so one had that length of time to master the existing system.[32] When each new book was issued—the new "key," as it was called—the work had to begin all over.

In early March 1941, the FEBC (the British anti-Japanese decryption program, which will be discussed later) provided Cast with a copy of the cipher system used for operational orders of the Japanese Navy (JN-25), at least to the degree to which it had so-far penetrated it.[33] Adm. Thomas C. Hart, commander of the Asiatic Fleet, desired for Cast to be given primary or sole responsibility for continuing the effort for the American side. Initially the Navy Department rejected this, informing the admiral that it intended to shift the responsibility to Hypo in July.[34] This decision was reversed in April.[35]

This resulted in the six men at Cast with the necessary qualifications unsuccessfully banging their heads for the remainder of the year against JN-25, while twice that number of men at Pearl Harbor (with the assistance of up-to-date mechanical equipment) consumed their equally futile weeks attempting to break the cipher used for flag officers.[36] What made the situation even worse was that the supply of flag officer intercepts was tiny (less than three a day) while by the end of the year there were thousands of JN-25 intercepts,[37] thereby giving a far larger sampling to work from which would have assisted decryption efforts.

Only on December 17, 1941, did Hypo gain permission to tackle JN-25; within four months it had made major breakthroughs. By early May of 1942 Hypo was about to read approximately 90 percent of the text of any given message.[38] One of the unanswerable questions of history is whether if Hypo had been given the responsibility in July—as originally scheduled—it would have been able to piece together enough direct or indirect nuggets of information to have forewarned the United States of the attack.[39]

What is conspicuously absent in our above discussion is Hypo's lacking any decrypt responsibility for the far more well known Purple diplomatic code. The tool which Pearl Harbor lacked and which—in retrospect—most angered its staff was a machine with which to "crack" and read this correspondence. By September 1941, Bletchley Park (center of Britain's decrypt programs), had all of three such machines, and the only one sent to the Pacific who located in the Philippines.[40] Why not build more machines? The parts had been requisitioned through the War Production Board by the fall, but the request was moving nowhere quickly.[41]

Any one of the existing machines (not to mention those not built because of snags in the government bureaucracy) could have provided

Pearl Harbor access to this data. Hypo's members were convinced that it might have provided them an invaluable tool to avoid the successful assault on December 7. In a postwar interview Edwin T. Layton, the chief intelligence officer for the Pacific Fleet argued that it came down to the extra insight that comes from looking at data from a different perspective:

> We at Pearl Harbor were the ones who had first seen the militarization of the mandated islands early in 1940 when ONI hadn't made that deduction on the basis of the same information. I'm sure that had we seen messages that had to do with Pearl Harbor, then there would have been a different evaluation of those items of intelligence. There's an old Indian saying that the snake in your corner is the largest. This is true in intelligence. If you receive intelligence that has to do with where you are, you give it greater significance. In the late autumn of 1941, Washington was too involved with the shipping war in the Atlantic to take proper notice of intelligence that related to the Pacific. Had "Magic" decrypts been available to us, they would have at least alerted us to the possibility of an attack on Pearl Harbor.[42]

There is much that appeals in this analysis. On the other hand, the Philippines *did* have a purple machine and it did nothing to increase their level of preparation.[43] Furthermore, if Kimmel had sent his fleet to sea before the attack—upon the suspicion that it was imminent—it would most likely have sailed southwest from Hawaii, since the closest Japanese military installations were in that direction and, therefore, constituted the most likely point of attack.[44] As war broke out, Kimmel's fleet was caught in port. On the other hand, if it had been at sea it would probably have been in the wrong location to ambush the approaching rival fleet.

Although Hypo was aware that the high level diplomatic correspondence was being read, only one person (recently arrived from Washington) knew what it was actually called. In an effort to alert Hawaii as to its dangerous situation, Comdr. Safford sent out a message received in Hawaii on December 3rd that referred to it with unprecedented directness:

> Circular twenty four forty four from Tokyo one December ordered London, Hongkong, Singapore and Manila to destroy Purple machine. Batavia machine already sent to Tokyo. December second Washington also directed destroy Purple, all but one copy of other systems, and all secret documents. British Admiralty London today reports embassy London has complied.[45]

When Admiral Kimmel saw this, he inquired what a Purple Machine was. The Fleet Intelligence Officer (Layton) was asked, but he didn't know. Passing the query through the Hypo organization, they came across the one person who knew to what the term actually referred.[46] Kimmel read the code destruction as simply another of the preparatory steps to war that were occurring on an almost daily basis.[47]

Hawaii's Fleet Locater Network

Although Dutch Harbor and Samoa reported to the Hawaii Fleet Locator Network, it only functioned as elements of the fleet location aspect of the intelligence unit at Pearl. They had no intercept capacity. As Rochefort informed the Army Pearl Harbor Board, "I didn't get anything from Dutch Harbor and Samoa, General. They only had either three or four radios, and they were merely a direction-finding unit, that was all, and they were supposed to be trained direction-finder men; but that's about all they were good for."[48]

Guam was technically under the control of the Asiatic Fleet based in the Philippines but sent its reports back to Pearl; it also operated a direction finding station as well.[49] Guam—"Station Baker" ("B")—was established in 1929 and moved to a new location a few miles away in 1934. With no cryptanalysts and only eight enlisted men as staff, most of its equipment was out-of-date even prior to the immediate pre-war period.[50]

"It was not a communications or intelligence unit. It was an intercept unit at Guam," Lt. Comdr. Layton explained to the Army Board.[51] In 1937 these installations were established as part of "what we called the 'Mid Pacific strategic direction-finder net,' which were all high-frequency direction finders...."[52] By correlating the direction of a given signal from these four sites one could pinpoint (relatively speaking at least) the source of the monitored signal from the Japanese fleet. Its potential went far beyond this for it was equipped "to tell the Commander-in-Chief and any other interested parties where certain units of *any* nation, other than our own—and our own, if so directed—were" (our emphasis added).[53]

The information from the four sites flowed "into the office which was located in the administration building in Pearl Harbor, and was evaluated there with other information, and was disseminated to the Commander-in-Chief of the Pacific Fleet (based at Hawaii, RW) by means of a daily bulletin, which included locations of enemy vessels and estimates and evaluations regarding future operations."[54] If anything of "any importance was determined" the information was automatically relayed to a predetermined list of individuals, including the commander-in-chief of the Asiatic Fleet (in the Philippines) and to the chief of Naval Operations in Washington.[55]

There was some confusion among certain senior navy brass as to the degree to which Pearl Harbor could penetrate the Japanese codes. Some were convinced that it possessed the ability to read the diplomatic traffic, but the truth was that the only Purple machine in the Pacific had been dispatched to the Philippines instead.

What may have contributed to this exaggeration of Pearl's abilities was likely the result of its able traffic analysis, which enabled it to make highly perceptive guesses as to what was going on without being able to read the actual text of many intercepted messages. When Rear Adm. Leigh H. Noyes was questioned about the matter he pointed to this as the explanation for Rear Adm. Richmond K. Turner's earlier misstatement that Pearl Harbor possessed that decryption capacity:

> [H]e is speaking of what we call radio intelligence, which is the activity that Captain Rochefort has been discussing. It does not involve knowing the contents of the messages. It involves direction finding, to find the location of ships, the analysis of the transmissions they monitored, and call signs on messages in code, which, although you cannot read, you can form a good estimate of what the ships are doing from the call signs and the direction alone. This is called traffic analysis.[56]

In other words if the ships had been moving in a certain direction from intercept to intercept, one could hazard a fairly good guess that they would continue to move in that direction. If one knew from other sources that the Japanese forces in a certain location were in need of reinforcement and these naval units were moving in that direction, the odds were increased that they were heading for that particular destination. Sometimes one did not even have to obtain an intercept from an important warship to know its location. If one knew that such and such a destroyer always attended a certain aircraft carrier and one obtained a message from that destroyer, one had effectively located the carrier as well.

In actual practice, great skill and sometimes a great deal of luck entered the picture. As Edwin T. Layton, intelligence Officer for the Pacific Fleet's commander-in-chief, explained to the Roberts Commission:

> It is very difficult in this nature of intelligence to say where a man is from his traffic. If he receives it by the broadcast

method he can be at sea, but he is sometimes in port. When carriers are not heard from, if they do not originate traffic, they are most likely in port, because there they are on low-frequency low-power circuits that cannot be heard, or on the ship-shore circuit, which is very low power, and sometimes they have a direct wire to the beach. While of course the traffic originated for them from without their area is still received and still on the air, that condition exists.

That condition also exists a good part of the time, and it is only when they originate traffic themselves at sea that direction-finder bearing can be taken to ascertain their general line of bearing; and with the direction-finder net—for instance, Oahu and Cavite and Guam—a fairly good strategic cut is made as to their location; also, when they are at sea, by the type of their traffic; whether it is a tactical traffic or administrative traffic—that is, they use their own tactical calls or their own administrative calls—one may deduce and surmise the type of exercises they are involved in, and also, from the type of traffic they have had before that, what is their immediate objective.[57]

As noted, even when one could not read the messages, the volume (or lack) of radio traffic combined with knowledge of the point of origin or destination permitted deductions to be drawn as to the current dispositions and potential intents of the Japanese navy. At Pearl Harbor a daily report was prepared analyzing this data. The report of December 6 (describing the pattern of communications on the 5th) noted that communications were "very heavy with a great deal of old traffic being transmitted. Messages as far back as 1 December were seen in the traffic. This is not believed [to be] an attempt to maintain a [deceptively] high traffic level but is the result of confusion in traffic routing with uncertainty of delivery." Four major points of origin were noted: Tokyo, the port of Ominato in Japan, the port of Takao in Formosa, and the Japanese naval complex in Saipan. "Practically all of Tokyo's messages carry prefixes of high authority."[58]

Many of the intercepts were, indeed, genuine. A large number were, however, intended to be misleading about Japanese naval locations and intent and clearly the interpretation by Pearl Harbor indicates much of their purpose was fulfilled. To further confuse the American side, several carrier radiomen whose distinctive Morse code sending style was likely to be recognized by the Americans—their "fists" as it was called—were retained in Japan to send out parts of the traffic. This way, it was reasonably hoped, the Americans would expect the carriers the radiomen worked from were still at port in the Inland Sea and not moving to attack positions.[59] There were misgivings from the traffic analysts at Corregidor that this deception might be going on, but without more concrete evidence it could only remain a dark suspicion rather than regarded as a probability.[60]

Non-Decryption Sources of Intelligence in Hawaii

The successful decryptions that occurred were not ends in themselves; they were means to an end, an element in painting the location and intents of the Japanese military throughout the Far East. This source was supplemented by data obtained from other sources in the Far East and codified into reports, primarily for internal Naval consumption. Through either caution or bureaucratic reluctance to share data (or simple lack of relevant information), the input from other government agencies was modest.

Admiral H. Kent Hewitt summed up the minimal information obtained in framing a question for Rochefort:

> Now, you stated in your previous testimony that your sources of information, in addition to the work of your own unit, were the other two combat intelligence units and other government agencies, such as the FBI, the Army, and the FCC at Honolulu. You also stated that the information furnished by these latter agencies was of no value prior to December 7th, and stated before the Court of Inquiry that the collaboration of these agencies was on a personal basis. Will you explain what the relationships were with the FBI, the Army, the FCC, and the other intelligence agencies with whom you dealt?[61]

Rochefort elaborated further on the limited usefulness of these resources in his response:

> With regard to the FBI, I met with Mr. Shivers, the agent in charge, on frequent occasions and discussed the general situation, particularly pertaining to Japanese in Hawaii, but did not discuss any ultra matters. Mr. Shivers on his part kept me informed as to what he was doing, possibly with some limitations.
>
> The relationship with the Army dealt primarily with the G-2, Colonel Fielder, and was similar in nature to that carried out with the FBI.

The relationship with the FCC was limited to technical matters, particularly those pertaining to direction finding, location of unauthorized stations, and other similar matters.[62]

Japanese Language Training for American Officers

Passing attention should be given here to the efforts of the U.S. military to provide a cadre of officers trained in Japanese. As part of its preparedness for all contingencies, a number of navy and marine officers received Japanese language training in Japan itself. This training began as early as 1910 and continued to nearly the point of American entry into the Pacific War in December 1941.

The men involved were assigned to the Naval Attaché's office at the U.S. Embassy in Tokyo. From 1935 on the dozen language trainees no longer had diplomatic immunity; this change was initiated by the United States in order to justify denying the status to the four times larger contingent of Japanese nationals undergoing alleged language training under the aegis of Japan's embassy in Washington.[63]

The navy contingent of trainees was pulled out on Labor Day of 1941 as a security precaution because of the potential for war. The army's trainees, however, stayed behind. They were interned (although they technically did not have diplomat status) along with the regular diplomatic personnel when war broke out. They were permitted to leave when the diplomats were repatriated in 1942.[64] The individuals who underwent this on-the-spot language training played important roles in intelligence work during the war.[65]

An infusion of talent from this and other sources enhanced Pearl Harbor's operation. Capt. Wilkinson speaks of how in the spring of 1941 (he misdates the event since they had not yet departed Japan), "Captain Rochefort, then Commander, was sent out, and half a dozen former language students who had recently been evacuated from Japan because of the growing crisis were sent to join him, and he had perhaps 20 or 30 enlisted men. They were working mainly on the radio intelligence proper."[66]

Magic in the Philippines

The Public Image:
The Philippines as Cutting Edge
of American Defense

Admiral Thomas C. Hart, resident commander in chief of the Asiatic Fleet, knew full well that if war broke out his resources were modest and the situation tenuous at the very best. In his public utterances and private communications with the U.S. government, Gen. Douglas MacArthur was the exact opposite: He was convinced that if the Japanese made the fatal mistake of invading the Philippines it would be a disaster for them. Two years before the war, with Gen. MacArthur still in temporary retirement in the Philippines, he was interviewed by Theodore White of *Time* magazine. He dismissed the Japanese army as "not even second class."[1]

This public mind frame remained his stance when he was recalled to active duty and given the task of coordinating the defense of American and Philippine forces against possible invasion. In October 1941 he informed the visiting commander of British forces in Singapore that he could hold *all* of the Philippine Islands, not just Luzon where the capital was located.[2]

Not only could an invasion be decisively defeated, Gen. MacArthur was skeptical whether a significant invasion effort was even feasible. In a December 6 conference with both Adm. Hart and British Vice Adm. Tom Phillips, he conceded that it would require another four months to reach his full defensive potential. Even so he was confident that "the inability of an enemy to launch his air attacks on these islands is our greatest security.... [T]he inability of the enemy to bring not only air but mechanized and motorized elements leaves me with a sense of complete security.[3]

MacArthur's boundless enthusiasm won over many in the War Department.[4] Later, in private, President Roosevelt even went so far as to blame the general for misinforming him as to the major problems faced in the Philippines. "If I had known the true situation," he complained to one admiral, "I could have babied the Japanese [negotiations] along quite a while longer."[5] MacArthur was a brilliant general and his later successes blotted out his overconfidence and failed strategy at the beginning of the conflict. A different general, without the later opportunity to redeem himself on the battlefield, would have been remembered quite differently.

Station 6: The Army Contribution

Commanded by Major Joe T. Sherr, Army Station 6 consisted of 16 enlisted men and two officers, all attached to the 2d Signal Service Company of the Signal Intelligence Service of the U.S. Army.[6] It was located at Fort McKinley, just outside the capital city of Manila.

Because of the humid conditions, its mechanical equipment was constantly breaking down. It finally reached the point that one individual had to be permanently assigned to the repair work. To solve this problem, the recommendation was made that the facility be air conditioned; the proposal was literally greeted with laughter. The requisition was rewritten as a request for "de-humidification" equipment, was approved, and by October 1, 1941 the system was in operation.[7]

One difficulty faced by Station 6 was its limited supply of Japanese-reading or speaking personnel. It happened that a few months before Pearl Harbor, several Nisei (second generation Japanese-Americans) were sent to the Philippines after training by the FBI to act as spies against Japanese infiltration.[8] When war broke out they were loaned to Station 6 to monitor non-coded Japanese broadcasts. They also did additional duty translating captured documents and questioning prisoners of war.[9]

Station 6 played an important role in monitoring for Purple messages and assuring the navy had the maximum possible coverage of such communications. As we will see below, there were built in problems with how the system actually functioned.

Cast: The Navy Contribution

The Magic operations in the Philippines were divided between the two services. The navy's was typically described as being at Cavite (Cavite Bay). (To be more exact, Cast itself was actually located at Monkey Point, Fort Mills, Corregidor, in a specially built tunnel constructed in 1939 and 1940.)[10] The army's work was carried on either at Manila or Corregidor, depending upon the exact date one has in mind. In testimony the three sites of Cavite, Corregidor, and Manila tended to be used indiscriminately as descriptions of the location of the intercept and decryption work of the two services.[11]

The purpose of Cast, of course, was preparedness for all contingencies through the accumulation of the maximum possible body of knowledge. As one of its ranking officers testified,

> Our mission, Admiral, was to maintain a unit for study of enemy fleets and communications in order, first, to keep track of their peacetime intentions; second, to prevent against a surprise attack, insofar as possible, or an attack without a declaration of war; and, third, to keep as well up as possible on the organization, methods and so forth [of the Japanese fleet], sir.[12]

The operation began with minimal capacities. "Originally there were no facilities at Cavite for decrypting diplomatic traffic," observed Adm. Noyes, "it all had to be forwarded to Washington. I might say that starting in 1939, when I first came, what little we were doing was not of immediate importance and mail was used almost entirely for forwarding of the intercepts."[13] These were conveyed "in the Japanese" code itself in which they had been intercepted.[14]

Work priorities shifted with the passage of time. "During 1940 and early 1941, this Unit was mostly concerned with Japanese diplomatic communications, but in October or November, 1941, it shifted its main attention to Japanese Naval communications."[15] Special attention was given in 1941 to "the naval system known as JN-25, which was the system containing the greatest volume of Japanese dispatches."[16]

The diplomatic code J-19 was also assigned to the unit.[17] Comdr. Safford stressed that even though Purple was the more difficult cipher to penetrate *initially*, once it had been broken, it was only reasonably difficult to *keep* it broken as its regularly scheduled changes occurred. In contrast J-19 was a perpetual headache. "The J-19 at this period was solved by cryptographic analysis. That had to be done over again each day, and it really took more time and effort to keep abreast of the J-19 than it did the 'purple' once we had the machine reconstructed."[18]

With the expansion of duties came the expansion of staff, but with the limited manpower resources these were not always ideal personnel. At its maximum, just prior to Pearl Harbor, the unit consisted of 51 enlisted men and 10 officers, with Lt. Rudolph J. Fabian as its commanding officer.[19]

Although some very skilled individuals were assigned, this was far from uniformly the case. When the Asiatic Fleet intelligence officer was looking for seven new yeomen to add to the complement soon after 1941 began he called in the typist Yeoman Robert E. Dowd for an interview. He asked little beyond Dowd's smoking and drinking habits, and the next thing Dowd knew he had been assigned to Cast.[20]

When he discovered that he was supposed to help break enemy ciphers he was amazed. "I didn't know," he recalled later, "that ships communicated except by flag, by semaphore, and by signal. I was a cryptographer?"[21] With the relentless "logic" that is historically famous in military commands, he was handed the hitherto unbreakable JN-25B and told to try his hand at it. When he naturally failed he was transferred to operating the machinery that assisted those who actually knew what cryptography was about.[22]

The latter brings us to the technological resources that helped Cast overcome some of its limitations due to limited manpower and training. In 1940 Cast obtained a Red machine that could break the diplomatic code named after that color.[23] During the spring of 1941, the unit received its Purple machine, which permitted it to break into the highest classified Japanese diplomatic communications.[24]

In addition to personnel for the intercept aspect of the operation and handling various support operations, the navy "had seven officers and nineteen men" available for actual decryption by the time of Pearl Harbor.[25] "The personnel of this Unit had about two or three years of C.I. experience on the average, and the officers were young, enthusiastic, and capable," government investigators were later told.[26]

In spite of their zeal and training Capt. Wilkinson pointed to at least three ways in which the Philippines group inevitably played second fiddle to the central Washington headquarters: 1) a lesser number of intercept stations providing reportage; 2) less manpower and, especially "experienced manpower"; 3) an inability to read as many codes. "In many codes [they] couldn't touch them, but in the so-called purple code [they were] to a degree able to translate."[27]

Regardless of their limitations, the responsibilities of the unit gradually increased. As Comdr. Safford recalled,

> The unit at Corregidor had been intercepting messages in the Japanese "purple" code and other diplomatic codes for several years and continued to do that up to and including December 7, 1941. Their main attention was on the local Asiatic circuits for the information of the Commander-in-Chief, Asiatic Fleet, but very late in November, 1941, they were given the additional duty of covering the Berlin-Tokyo circuit because we couldn't get adequate coverage from all the other stations combined. These were forwarded to Washington and weren't touched locally.[28]

The Navy's "Purple" Capacity

About "March 1941 one [Purple] machine became available"[29] and Adm. Leigh H. Noyes played a crucial role in convincing Adm. Harold R. Stark to send it to the Philippines instead of Pearl Harbor.[30] At first this seems odd since Pearl had a higher caliber staff. Noyes insisted that it was *not* a matter of favoritism for Adm. Hart's command over that of Adm. Kimmel in Hawaii.[31] For one thing, he noted, "I knew perfectly well that they could decipher the diplomatic traffic and send it to Honolulu."[32] Of course, in retrospect this was not done. Washington certainly had no grounds for criticism of Hart over that lapse since Washington itself cut off its supply of decrypted Magic texts well before hostilities broke out.

Of greater importance was the belief that because of its location and the peculiarities of communication via the airwaves, it "was the best place to intercept Japanese traffic and receive information...." In short, Noyes continued, "it was the best listening post for us."[33]

On a lower echelon, the decision was sometimes posed in very different terms. Lt. Comdr. Alwin D. Kramer recalled that "the prime reason for ever having set up a cryptanalytical unit at Corregidor ... was to keep the commander in chief, Asiatic Fleet, at that time Admiral Hart, as fully apprised as possible of political, military and other developments of like nature in his sphere."[34] The same motive would exist for installing the machine at Pearl though, of course, the Philippines were far closer to the most probable sites for the outbreak of hostilities.

Another reason (though it would have been equally true if the equipment had been located in Hawaii) was to take some of the work load off the Washington end of the operation. "The object of putting the machine at Cavite, which was the best listening post we had, was to cut out the transmission between Cavite and Washington, let them decrypt the messages there, throw out the unimportant ones, or to ML the important ones to Washington, depending on the importance."[35] These messages were then forwarded in decrypted form.[36]

Those messages they were unable to crack were simply forwarded in their original undecrypted form.[37] Of course these would be forwarded in an appropriate, highly secure *American* cipher[38] via radio transmission.[39]

Indeed, the first duty of the Philippine army and navy collaboration was to immediately forward the most important intercepted messages and only then begin the local effort to tackle their decryptation. "All purple traffic intercepted and certain other traffic in the red and J-19 codes were immediately enciphered and sent to Washington. That is whether we read it later or not."[40] Essential to breaking into any of the traffic was the obtaining of the latest "key," the daily change in the underlying encrypting of the message. The Philippine operation "was not responsible for the recovery of the keys necessary to read it. That was done in Washington and forwarded back to it."[41]

The Navy Intercept and Fleet Location Network

In order to provide a source of regular intercepts to work on, the navy had a modest amount of equipment to utilize. The head of the Navy's program in the Philippines recalled, "I had twenty-six radio receivers, ranging from low frequency to high frequency, had a set of business machinery and the appurtenances necessary for the interception of both high speed and low speed enemy transmissions."[42] Since not all frequencies could be simultaneously monitored, "we covered certain circuits from which we could get most of the information we desired, sir, and the greatest volume of material."[43]

To cooperate in Pacific-wide efforts to locate the source of actual transmissions (and, hence, the vessels themselves), Lt. Fabian possessed a direction finder.[44] This was located at Corregidor.[45] Reporting to it was "a small intercept and finder-station on the Island of Guam."[46] Administratively, it was under the Asiatic Fleet, with its headquarters in the Philippines,[47] but with its reports being funneled to Hawaii where its most important data on fleet movements were regularly shared with the commander-in-chief of the Pacific Fleet.[48]

Of more immediate value to local defense was the capacity to intercept communications from Japanese military aircraft. Taiwan was the probable jumping off point for any major aerial assault and by monitoring its transmissions and how the site of broadcast shifted during the flight, about an hour's warning could be obtained before the fighters were over the Philippines.[49]

It is unknown whether the system was operating on December 8 (7th Hawaiian time) and detected the incoming flight that destroyed Gen. MacArthur's defensive and offensive aerial capacity.[50] If the flight had been detected, it would have been the system operators' immediate responsibility to inform Adm. Hart, who presumably would have personally relayed the report to Gen. MacArthur. (This assumes that the admiral was aware of how time consuming was the normal Cast procedure of passing communications to MacArthur; commanders are often woefully uninformed of the details of such matters.)

The general feeling at Cast was that MacArthur's G-2 did not have the foggiest idea what the data they provided really meant or what might be done with it.[51] So it would probably not have shocked them that if the data somehow *did* get passed to MacArthur's command on a priority basis, his people might still ignore, minimize, misinterpret, or even dismiss its significance.

Limitations and Difficulties of Army-Navy Cooperation

The relationship between Gen. MacArthur and Adm. Hart was "correct" but each was constantly on the alert for breaches of the "proper" army-navy relationship and alterations of the existing understanding of the duties and responsibilities of the two services.[52] Perhaps the most dramatic example of this was MacArthur's decision to declare Manila an "open city" (i.e., free of combatants) on December 25, 1941. He had not discussed this with Hart, who had planned on continuing to base some of his meager naval resources in the city. Nor was it feasible for Hart to remove all of the material in the short time frame the general had announced of less than 24 hours.[53]

In Hawaii, the two military services were also zealously protective of their respective prerogatives. However, there was at least a greater willingness of the two service commanders to meet on a social level. They played golf twice a month and had a weekly meeting to discuss shared concerns.[54] However much the arm's-distance relationship allowed mis-understandings to develop, unlike in the Philippines it had no impact upon the decryption program. That responsibility was strictly a navy oper-ation in Hawaii.

In contrast, in the Philippines both services had a significant com-mitment to such work and a closer cooperativeness would have been of benefit to both branches. To make this feasible, the army would have had to relocate its facilities at Corregidor to avoid the time delay in trans-mitting data between the two locations. Until the very outbreak of war this was simply not feasible from the standpoint of inter-service military politics and commander egos. Even so, the situation had become so intol-erable that at least modest efforts had already been made to remove some of the worst hindrances to cooperation.

In early 1941, the directors of Naval Intelligence, the chief signal officer, and the chief of Army G-2 in Washington met to discuss means of improving inter-service cooperation in the Philippines. Instead of send-ing army and navy intercepts to Washington and having needed materi-als re-relayed to the other party back in the Philippines, they were given "the authority to exchange locally."[55] Although this certainly improved the local situation, a key participant in the decision conceded that the pri-mary "object was to improve the system of getting the diplomatic infor-mation to Washington, rather than for the local value."[56]

On March 25, 1941, a Navy dispatch to the Philippines informed the commander-in chief, Asiatic Fleet, and the chief of staff of the United States Army in the Philippines of the details of a "proposed" plan "of coordinating." It noted, "Details to be worked out locally. Foregoing is additional to forwarding of intercepts to Washington by both services."[57]

What inter-service cooperation translated into in practice was that the army's Station 6 received all the diplomatic intercepts but only a trickle of reports on anything the navy considered to be within its jurisdiction. Refield Mason was the fleet intelligence officer for the Asiatic Fleet and later explained how "cooperation" actually functioned:

> The Army was furnished daily a copy of all diplomatic trans-lations that had been made by the unit at Corregidor. The purely naval matters, when our intelligence came from purely naval traffic, inasmuch as there wasn't any translating going on as a matter of fact, they weren't furnished any copies of either dispatches that we sent to CincPac or Washington or received from them, but I conferred quite frequently with the head of the intelligence department in the Philippine Army Department and always provided at least—I can't be too

specific on the point of how frequently, but quite frequently—
our estimate of the locations of the Japanese fleet. As I recall
now, I didn't give him the source of this information but graded
it as "doubtful" or "possible" or whatever we thought of it.[58]

This is true, as far as it goes, but does not adequately stress the time
delays caused in the navy and army utilizing geographically separate
installations. Station 6's primary work was on intercepting Purple messages. Whatever Purple and other diplomatic intercepts it received were
then transferred into an American cipher for forwarding to Washington.[59]

Copies of the untranslated messages were—eventually—shared with
Cast as well. "Eventually" does not refer to any policy of accidental or
intentional obstruction on the army's part—it was the result of the divided
locations of the two units and the security precautions considered as essential. Although only 30 miles away in Manila Bay, Corregidor, due to its
isolation, did not make for ready access.

For example, a Monday intercept would be delivered on Tuesday to
the dock for hand delivery to the captain of a military harbor vessel, who
then delivered it to waiting Cast personnel at the dock at Corregidor. If
everything went right, it would be broken, read, translated, and typed
into English.

On Wednesday, the decrypts would be returned to a Section 6 messenger at the docks on Manila Bay. Later the same day these would be
hand delivered to Brig. Gen. Richard K. Sutherland, MacArthur's chief
of staff. If there were items that Sutherland thought would interest or be
of value to his superior, he sent the messenger into MacArthur's inner
office with the materials.[60] As a participant in the program later recalled,
"Sundays and holidays usually delayed delivery another day because the
Navy usually took these days off."[61]

Oddly enough, Col. Charles A. Willoughby, Gen. MacArthur's chief
intelligence officer, was not authorized to receive the decrypts. Perhaps
equally odd is the treatment of Col. Spencer B. Aiken. He was specifically
requested by MacArthur and transferred to the Islands to serve as his
chief signal officer and had helped establish intercept stations earlier in
his career. He even knew of the presence of a Purple machine with Cast.
Yet he had no responsibilities at all concerning that work.[62]

Evacuation of Cast and Station 6

The capture of any of the personnel of Cast or Station 6 could easily lead to the compromise of the entire American decryption program.

No matter how intense an individual's bravery, no one could guarantee the immunity of an individual from giving in to the stresses of imprisonment and outright torture. Furthermore, the talents of these men were literally priceless since there were so few of them available. The navy was quicker to recognize this than the army. It gave the timely evacuation of the personnel of Cast a very high priority,[63] while the army (see below) delayed fatally longer.

Recognizing that there was no guarantee that all personnel would successfully survive the move, Cast was divided into four groups. Within each were men with the varied talents required by a cryptographic unit so that any one of the four groups would be able to conduct, wholly on its own, at least a limited intercept and decryption program.[64]

On February 5, 1942, the first 17 men and officers were removed aboard the submarine *Seadragon*. The sub had received an uncertain amount of damage during the bombing of Cavite, and only emergency repairs had been possible. Officially, it was deemed seaworthy so long as it did not submerge more than 60 feet. Of course, in the case of aerial assault, this was dangerously shallow. Nor did the crewmembers seem to trust it even that deep.[65]

Fortunately the Japanese never bothered it, and probably never detected it. The submarine unloaded the passengers at Java, where they assisted the Dutch decrypters. Japanese military pressure was so intense, however, that they soon had to be moved once again by sub to Australia.[66]

On March 6, Gen. MacArthur himself finally yielded to the president's orders and escaped via PT boat. Five days afterward 30 additional decryption personnel (two of the three remaining groups) were evacuated aboard the submarine *Permit*.[67]

The 21 remaining staff continued their decryption efforts until the final hours of the American resistance in Bataan in early April. With the American forces on Bataan facing the necessity of surrender later that day, the few remaining men were ferried out to rendezvous with the *Seadragon* in the early pre-dawn hours. In spite of a lengthy depth-charge assault they also made it successfully through the Japanese naval forces.[68]

When all four groups were reunited in Melbourne, they and the Australian navy specialists in the same field created the Fleet Radio Unit (FRUMEL, the MEL for Melbourne). FRUMEL was the source of valuable intelligence data for the remainder of the Pacific War.[69]

If the navy had stood by its men, both out of corporate loyalty and because of recognition of their invaluable talents, the Army was a far different story. Station 6 joined Cast on Corregidor on Christmas Eve.

Unlike the navy, the army dangerously delayed the departure of its personnel even as the ultimate loss of the Philippines became unquestionable.

The first Station 6 men did not leave until March 27. When Corregidor capitulated, six soldiers were still there. Though they endured considerable deprivation and even torture, the Japanese never guessed their true importance and, therefore, never singled them out for the kind of special attention that could have exposed the carefully guarded secret of Magic. Even so only one of the six survived the war.[70]

Cooperation and Exchange of Information with Magic in Washington, Hawaii, and the Philippines

With major efforts underway in three different widely dispersed locations, some arrangements for cooperation and coordination were essential. Washington would obviously have priority and as headquarters have the ultimate say in decisions on the matter. In actual practice how did cooperation work? Did it increase or minimize the actual information available in the field? To a great extent questions such as these can be answered by piecing together the information provided in piecemeal fashion during the government investigations of Pearl Harbor.

General Exchange of Missed Messages and Message Parts and the Effort to Maximize Security on All Forwarded Information

The area of broadest cooperation lay in compiling as complete a list as possible of all diplomatic and military messages and their texts. This was not a simple matter at times, since some monitoring stations would not pick up messages between specific sites at all, others only sporadically, while those which *could* readily intercept might be able to pick up only a part of the text while a distant location had copied the remainder.

Comdr. Arthur H. McCollum, chief of the Far Eastern Section of the Office of Naval Intelligence, pointed to the efforts to overcome this difficulty: "There was a regular exchange between all the stations and Washington, and vice versa, sir. Everything that we got [in Washington], they had a system of checking up on, to see whether they got it, and possibly they did have the fill-in" in any specific case.[1]

Oddly enough, this up-beat scenario was immediately followed by an implicit admission that the system did not always work even when another post did, indeed, possess the sought communication: A senator suggested that, in regard to the particular message under consideration, "Then we should find some message if we inquire from the Philippines about this [missing] second part, should we not?" McCollum responded, "They can check through the numbers to see whether they have it or not; yes sir."[2]

But if the system had achieved as complete a success as McCollum had implied, would not Washington *already* have possessed a copy of the missing text *or* a notation that none had been obtained from any source? In all fairness, in a system as large as Magic and under immense time and limited personnel pressures, such bureaucratic "misses" were inevitable. Perhaps the amazing thing is that they were as limited as they were.

As noted in the previous chapter, all diplomatic and other intercepts were promptly forwarded to Washington in their original language. Maintaining security on this vast flow of data was imperative, as well as was limiting how many even knew of its existence. Any message that quoted a Japanese intercept (either in its original language or translated form) or which clearly alluded to the very existence of such documents had to be encrypted by a specially authorized individual. The process was described by Admiral Noyes:

> Each office of the Navy Department had officers authorized to release messages and we only insisted that a message be authenticated by the authorized officer. We had one very strict rule. The basis of all our handling of these enemy intercepted messages was the extreme importance of allowing no inkling to reach the Japanese that we could read their messages. That would have ruined everything.

We had a strict rule and endeavored to carry it out that nothing should ever appear in any kind of ordinary Navy traffic which referred to the fact that we could read any Japanese messages. We had a special cipher, a special security cipher, which any reference to Magic was supposed to be in, in which it was supposed to be decrypted, and I or some of my subordinates were the only ones that released messages in that system.

I would have released in the system, if anyone wished to, I would have been directed by the Chief of Naval Operations or requested by the Director of Naval Intelligence, or by War Plans, to transmit the messages in this form, and any one of those forms, I would have immediately sent them in cipher. If they could express it as intelligence without referring in any way where the information was to be obtained, for example, the expression of "reliable source," that doesn't give away the secret, they could have been sent in ordinary naval dispatch.[3]

According to Noyes, Washington would have preferred *never* to have sent anything out of the capital that referred to the successful American effort—not even in this especially secure code.[4] Since this was a manifest impossibility the most that could be done was to insist consistently that the explicit references to Magic be limited to this cipher and to protection against the possible compromise of that code. Three possible dangers were especially pronounced, and steps were taken against all: the sending of too great a volume in the code, the accessibility of it by too many officers, and the ease of access to actual translated intercepts.

The concern about length grew out of the need to protect the system from Japanese penetration. "[P]articularly in any long message, it is the greatest opening to a cryptanalyst to break a cipher or code...." Hence the effort to keep "the traffic down ... in this particular cipher."[5] Or as Noyes said a little later, "A large amount of traffic is one of the worst things that can be done, one of the worst offenses that can be committed against the security of any means of communication."[6]

True as all this was, such an effort could reduce the volume in but a limited way. All *incoming* Japanese intercepts relayed by radio *had* to be entered in the cipher. (Noyes fails to mention this obvious difficulty.) All that could be done was to limit the *outgoing* transmissions in number and, especially, in length.

The two other dangers could be summed up in the words "potential security leaks." The more people utilizing the cipher the greater the danger an individual might intentionally or (more likely) accidentally give away the secret of what was going on. "The cipher was not used," Noyes stressed, "even by my own communication watch officer. We had a special watch who were the only ones that could read the cipher. When messages came in this cipher, the regular communications watch officers had to send it down to the special watch to be translated. They never saw it."[7]

Just as the security of the cipher itself needed to be protected, an additional potential security risk lay in the need to preserve the translated intercepts. If the wrong person were to have access to these the secret might also be exposed. This was protected against by the physical segregation of the records from the regular files. "Anything that referred to the purple code should not have appeared in the ordinary Navy filing system. It should have been done in a special channel which was kept entirely separate from this ordinary sort of stuff," Adm. Noyes informed the congressional investigation.[8]

Washington–Philippine Cooperation

As noted in the previous chapter, Washington provided the crucial daily keys to penetrate the diplomatic codes and assistance on other technicalities that would help the effort in the Philippines. From its own translated Magics, the decryption team (and ultimately Gen. Douglas MacArthur) had considerable access to the status of current negotiations.

Since Hawaii was not working on Purple, it had none of this firsthand knowledge after the decision was reached to no longer provide decrypts for the Pacific Fleet commander. Beyond this, the Philippines were left as uninformed as Pearl Harbor: The decrypts they had not worked on were not returned in translated form. Whatever direct information they had of the negotiations came strictly from the messages they themselves rendered.

The Corregidor "slant" to Washington's interest (inevitable since the Philippines had the Purple machine and Pearl Harbor did not) was brought out precisely in Comdr. Safford's summary of the situation:

> We also had a very free and continuous exchange of technical information between the two units, by which I mean the keys for the "purple" machine and keys for another system which we called Jig-19, and any other information which would help either unit in its performance of duty.
> With regard to communications between the Navy Department and our unit at Pearl Harbor, there were comparatively few.[9]

A little later he reiterated the same basic point, "Corregidor and the Navy Department exchanged by radio information on the 'purple' machine and on what we called the Jig-19 system and other diplomatic systems, but Pearl Harbor was not addressed in these messages."[10]

Washington-Hawaii Cooperation

At the point when Pearl Harbor was still receiving selected decrypts, these were commonly intermingled with other sensitive information and conveyed by commercial plane. The navy had "a special arrangement with Pan American by which the pilot carried in a locked box, to which he did not have the key, messages for Honolulu."[11]

This means of communication was periodically supplemented by the use of special couriers to hand-convey messages on non-Magic related matters. Layton recalled the procedure he had once used to insure security on a letter he was sending stateside. "As I recall it, I wrote the letter in pen myself with no copies and had it sealed, gave it to the flag secretary of the commander in chief, who in turn gave it to an officer courier passing through and going by air to the United States and to Washington for hand-to-hand delivery to Captain McCollum." As to receiving his response, "It came back via the locked box on the Clipper, which has previously been described here as a secure means of delivery of highly important and highly secret material."[12]

As to decryption efforts, intercepts were forwarded to Washington (in an American cipher), as already noticed. As to the ciphers Pearl Harbor was assigned, technical information was exchanged, "There was [information sharing] in so far as it pertained to the projects they were assigned."[13]

The official justification for not sharing translated intercepts themselves lay in intra-navy jurisdictional boundaries. The Hart Inquiry was informed,

> The C.I. Unit in Washington had no authority to forward to the C.I. Units in Pearl Harbor or Corregidor, or to the Commanders-in-Chief direct, any information other than technical information pertaining to direction finding, interception, and so forth. The dissemination of intelligence was the duty, responsibility, and privileges of the Office of Naval Intelligence as prescribed in the Communication War Plans approved by the Chief of Naval Operations in March, 1940.[14]

The perceived need to cite at length the *legal* authority for the decision suggests more than a little retroactive suspicion that the decision had been a wrong one.

Philippine-Hawaii Cooperation

Just as Washington cooperated fully with the Philippines in regard to technical issues involving interception and decryption, the Philippines did the same in regard to Hawaii. Safford was asked whether "all three units [Washington, Corregidor, Pearl Harbor] kept in close touch with the results they individually obtained." His affirmative answer simultaneously carefully hedged the degree of cooperation, "Yes, sir, as far as it pertained to the *technical work* they were doing, but *not otherwise*"[15] (emphasis added). An example of such information sharing is "the receipt from Washington of the frequencies then employed by the Japanese in making voice broadcasts."[16] Such advisement would increase the ability of Pearl and its subsidiary stations to intercept the various types of Japanese communications.

The curbing of the distribution of translated Magics did not impede the provision of significant amounts of *other* types of intelligence information that would permit the chief intelligence officer of the Pacific Fleet to keep his Pearl Harbor-based commander-in-chief up-to-date with information from less "sensitive" sources. For example, when procedures worked as they should have, fleet movement information or other major intelligence was forwarded to Pearl either from Adm. Hart or his own Asiatic Fleet intelligence officer.[17]

Lt. Comdr. Edwin T. Layton, who occupied the position of the Pacific Fleet's chief intelligence officer, listed "the Communication Intelligence Organization which had sections at Cavite [etc]" as one of a number of military and civilian government sources he utilized in providing daily intelligence briefings for his superior, Adm. Husband E. Kimmel.[18] If "an important dispatch was received" later in the day, requiring a prompt briefing of Kimmel, that information "generally [came] from Cavite."[19]

Admiral Bloch, commandant of the 14th Naval District, spoke in terms of a generous sharing of information. The cumulative data obtained from all sources "was transmitted to Cavite and the Navy Department. They had a private circuit or private channel, they talked to us and we to them telling them what we were getting, and the material was correlated and sent out. This was our principal source of Japanese intelligence. We also got the intelligence that was collected at Cavite."[20]

In his postwar memoirs, Layton specifically dates the last Magic diplomatic intercept as having been received in July 1941.[21] Yet in spite of the official exclusion of Pearl Harbor from receiving the Philippines' Magics, it appears that at least a limited—*very* limited?—number of Magics were transmitted south to the Pacific Fleet.

Senator Ferguson inquired of Layton, "Did the Philippines send you any of their magic that they translated?" "The one I referred to specifically," Layton responded, "was from Com. 16, which was in the Philippines, setting up the five winds and the two winds hidden word codes."[22] "It came to us in or by this special intelligence high security channel for transmitting this so-called magic purple messages." It was forwarded in English. This was the only translated intercept that Layton could "recall at the present time" having received from the Philippines.[23]

Presumably Layton had in mind the bitterly controversial *four* winds message that would tip off the imminence of war and misspoke when he described it as "the five winds" message. Although Comdr. Rochefort, in charge of the intercept operation at Pearl Harbor, was certain that others were received, the only specific text he could recall "would be the receipt of the so-called 'winds' message from Cavite on or about November 27th.... By 'winds' message, I mean the message which established the procedure for indicating war."[24]

The inability of both Layton and Rochefort to recall any other texts argues strongly that the number of Philippine provided intercepts must have been very limited, especially in the last months before war. Of course, there may have been an unofficial forwarding of a large number of *summaries* of the Magics rather than the texts themselves. This would explain their conviction of having received a number of Magics while being able to make explicit reference only to one.

Breadth of the Monitoring System and Its Locations

Necessity of Widespread Monitoring Sites

One factor that made the Japanese codes a natural target lay in Japan's need to communicate by means that made many messages interceptible by the hostile Western powers. Much German communication could be carried by ground wire. In vivid contrast, there was precious little Japanese communication (outside occupied China or individual islands of Japan) that could utilize this mode of communication on a regular basis. Even when land wires were available there was no guarantee they would function correctly. These difficulties hindered Allied communications as well. A British operative described the problems encountered a few years into the war in India. The telex line between two British intercept stations functioned splendidly—"for twenty seconds and then went on strike for days."[1]

Furthermore, the vast geographic scope of the Japanese conquests required a greater reliance on less secure aerial communications. By "1942 Japan occupied or controlled an area with an outer radius some 3,000–4,000 miles from Tokyo, compared with a German radius, excluding U-boats, usually under 1,000 miles from Berlin."[2]

The very success of the American decryption program easily obscures the hard work that went into obtaining the raw data that made the system work. As already noted, intercept stations existed in the Pacific. Various feeder locations routed their intercepts through Pearl Harbor, and both Pearl Harbor and the Philippines ran their own monitoring stations that fed data stateside. Additional monitoring sites in North America reported directly to the Washington headquarters.

No one site could patrol all frequencies nor all broadcast sites that it was desirable to monitor. Hence a division of labor was essential due to the very bulk of radio traffic.

As the congressmen investigating the Pearl Harbor attack examined certain of the intercepts, it concerned them that not all were forwarded from the monitoring sites the day they were received. Comdr. McCollum, chief of the Far Eastern Section of the Office of Naval Intelligence, explained to them the technical reasons why this was sometimes the case and mentions, in passing, the regional filtering centers through which the monitors passed their data:

> These dispatches were intercepted at a great many intercept or pick-up stations located in various parts of the world. On[c]e they were picked up, the pick-up station had no personnel qualified to either decode or translate any of this material. They only had operators who were skilled in taking the Japanese equivalent of our Morse code. Those dispatches, therefore, from any given pick-up station, when received, were sent to a center, depending on who was the control center— either Washington, Pearl Harbor, or Corregidor.
> They might have sent it either by radio, teletype, or by mail. Radio and teletype facilities were not always available.[3]

Comdr. Safford was asked whether missed messages were a common phenomenon. He responded, "It happened often enough to be very distressing. It was not at all uncommon to have a hole in messages, sometimes it was the first part missing, sometimes it was the last. It was usually at one end or the other rather than the middle."[4]

Even the best located intercept station was subject to the strange and unexpected vagaries of reception that permitted an unlikely post to receive a given message while the most predictable one did not "hear" it at all or received only a garbled intercept. A memorandum written by Comdr. Safford noted that, "A complete exposition of radio wave propagation would be very lengthy and out of place. It is sufficient to say that the radio frequencies used between Japan and the United States were quite erratic in performance, and that long distance radio communications in an East-West direction are more difficult and less reliable than those in a North-South direction."[5]

Another difficulty came from what Safford called "interference," presumably atmospheric conditions.[6] This problem was completely unpredictable and could dramatically reduce or increase a given station's intercept ability.

In other cases, parts of the same messages were, for one reason or another, transmitted from different transmitters. "Sometimes they were allowed to send one part of a message over one circuit and another part of a message would go over another circuit and due to some combination we could get the one and not the other."[7] McCollum may have had the same problem in mind or the difficulty created when a single transmitter divided one long message between two separate and interrupted transmissions: "We frequently would pick up one part of a dispatch. In other words, this was one transmission and then the other would be sent in another transmission, and not infrequently you would pick up one part sent as one transmission and not get the other part sent as another transmission, sir."[8]

The fact that some transmissions would inevitably be missed was used as a goad to spur maximum performance at each site. Because there was no way to guarantee complete interception "we kept on telling our stations to that effect. We were endeavoring to get as much as we could but we could not guarantee a hundred percent performance."[9]

General Marshall mentions the usefulness of multi-locations in the context of one of the most famous intercepts, that breaking off negotiations:

> The messages on which the magic is based were collected throughout the Pacific. I should imagine, though I am not the best witness on this, that the largest portion of the collection occurred in the Philippines because of its proximity to Japan and its ease of interception, but it sometimes occurred, as in the instance I believe the record will show on the fateful message which gave the 1 p.m., December [as the time for the delivery of the final Japanese diplomatic note], it was intercepted in the Puget sound region rather than out in the Philippines or out in Hawaii.[10]

Specifically, it was the Bainbridge Island, Washington, intercept station that caught the missing segment.[11]

Efforts to overcome the problem of partially or wholly missed intercepts resulted in the expansion of the duties of the Philippine station. "We finally had to call on Corregidor to cover the Berlin-Tokyo circuits as the combined efforts of intercept stations in the East Coast, West Coast, Hawaii and England could not provide better than about fifty (50) percent coverage."[12]

Statistics limited to the week before war broke out reveal how the more limited the number of stations, the more limited the chance of accomplishing complete interceptions. "During the period 1 December–

7 December 1941, the Navy Department received (70) Japanese diplomatic intercepts from Corregidor as compared with seventy-three (73) from Bainbridge Island, twenty (20) for all other U.S. Navy stations, and ninety-three (93) for all U.S. Army stations."[13] Without such radio intercepts there was, effectively, no Magic. Japanese military dispatches were not about to be handled in such a way as to allow even the most daring pro-American sympathizer access to them—even in the crypted fashion.

When it came to diplomatic messages there was slightly more flexibility. "[O]ccasionally land wire or cable" copies were obtained. "Some were photographs of station copies as they passed through the various commercial communication facilities, but roughly ninety-five percent were obtained by radio intercept of the U.S. Army and U.S. Navy at various points."[14]

In our preoccupation with the Allied successes in the field, it is important to remember that every Allied code and cipher was potentially vulnerable to penetration as well, though the Germans were the primary beneficiaries rather than the Japanese. Indeed, if the Axis had won the war the books being written would be about their successes and how they contributed to the ultimate outcome.

A British scholar who sums up several of the great Allied successes feels compelled to admit:

> Unhappily, the dictators seem to have been as well informed of the Allies' proceedings as the Allies of theirs. Count Ciano continued to receive intercepts of some British diplomatic telegrams. The codes used by Mr. Robert Murphy in the Mediterranean, broken by the Germans, gave away American contacts with General Weygand and probably caused his dismissal by the Vichy Government.
>
> If the Americans were greatly aided in the crucial battle of Midway island by deciphering the Japanese signals, the cryptanalysts of the Axis scored a much more significant success in reading the cypher mainly used for Atlantic convoys between February 1942 and June 1943. They studied carefully, for example, the Admiralty's daily signal about the supposed whereabouts of the U-boats. Moreover, the Germans were monitoring some of the telegraphic exchanges between Ankara and London, and between London and Moscow.
>
> British methods, reflected Goebbels, were extraordinarily careless: "I can only hope that this is not the case with our own secret communications as well; for if the British knew in detail about us everything that we know about them it could have very grave consequences."[15]

As Ultra and Magic verify, the Allies *did* know as much and what was most important they hid far more effectively. But with a little more effort and good fortune on the opposing side, the outcome might have been dangerously different, at least in Europe.

American Monitoring Sites in the Western Hemisphere

ARMY

As of the attack on Pearl Harbor, the army had several monitoring stations. In the United States there was one at Fort Hancock (New Jersey), the Presidio (San Francisco), Fort Sam Houston (Texas), and Fort Hunt (Virginia). There was an intercept station at Corozal in the Panama Canal Zone as well.[16]

The monitoring installation station at Petaluma, California (north of San Francisco) targeted Japanese Army transmissions between Tokyo and Manila.[17] When it detected transmissions it forwarded the broadcast frequency and likely times of transmission to Manila, where individual army personnel had the mind-numbing responsibility of jotting down the crypted materials that would make absolutely no sense to them and whose meaning they would never be told.[18]

NAVY

A few details are especially worth notice concerning several of the navy's monitoring and intercept stations.

(1) *Washington, DC.* Oddly enough a 20 foot wide concrete-block addition on top of the Navy Building in Washington itself contained a monitoring unit which was alert to all diplomatic transmissions. Training of new personnel was also carried out in this small facility. Because of this unusual location, those who completed the program had the nickname of the "On-the-Roof Gang."[19] Between 1926 and the opening of war in 1941, 150 sailors were sent through the course as well as 26 Marines.[20]

(2) *Cheltenham, Maryland.* In 1941 this was regarded as one of the navy's five most important intercept stations.[21] Although the station was located in the state adjoining the District of Columbia, a teletype system was installed in late 1941 that permitted immediate relay of intercepts to the Magic operation in Washington itself.[22]

(3) *Bar Harbor, Maine.* Bar Habor was incorporated rather late in the pre-war years into the monitoring system. It came on line only after several Far Eastern locations (Hawaii, Guam, and the Philippines) were already functional.[23]

(4) *Bainbridge Island, Washington.* In 1941 this was another of those locations regarded as on the list of the navy's five most important listening posts.[24] At least by late November of that year, a teletype system permitted the "instantaneous" relay of intercepts to Washington.[25]

(5) *Dutch Harbor, Alaska.* The direction finding station at Dutch Harbor was opened in 1940.[26] This small five person group was ordered approximately two weeks prior to Pearl Harbor to pay special attention to possible broadcasts from the Japanese Combined Fleet. (It had "vanished" and the American side naturally wanted to know its location as a possible indication of where and when war action might erupt). Tom Gilmore, one of the monitors, recalled how futile the effort was: "During that two-week period ... not one of us ever heard a word on those carrier frequencies."[27] (No great surprise: anything else would have been a violation of the strict orders under which the fleet was operating.)[28]

One conspiratorial interpreter of the period—who had done elaborate research—cites another individual assigned to the installation who claimed that on December 6, the enemy fleet was monitored some 270 miles to the southeast. Since the Japanese fleet at that time was more than double that distance away, whatever was detected was clearly something else.[29]

American Monitoring Sites in the Pacific Temporarily in Use in the Inter-War Period

We have discussed a number of intercept and monitoring installations in the context of the Philippine and Hawaii central coordinating centers for Magic. Although these were the ones in operation as of late 1941, the U.S. military had attempted to create and operate earlier centers as well, which the changing face of available financing, international politics, and war had required to be moved or abandoned. The ones in Peking and in Shanghai are of special interest.

(1) *Peking.* In 1927 the Marine detachment in Peking began to be the primary monitoring site for Japanese military movements in Asia.[30] By the middle 1930s, Japanese Army advances in the region played a major role in consolidating the monitoring effort back in Shanghai.[31]

(2) *Shanghai.* This was the original site known as "Station E," from which in the 1920s the U.S. Navy listened to Asian military communications.[32] The Japanese threat to Shanghai was so serious by late 1940 that the monitoring unit was pulled out of China entirely.[33]

This move was a major blow to the monitoring system. As a radioman participant in the monitoring system, Clarence P. Taylor recalled:

> They were limited at Corregidor. You could get some of the traffic out of Tokyo to the net, but they would be limited to some of the southern stations like Amoy picking up the net. In Shanghai, most of the time, we could copy every station on the net and, if we missed a message, somebody else had missed it [too] and it would have to be relayed to them ... and then we would get it. As I say, we had them cold, 100%. We got every dot and dash, almost, that was sent on that net.[34]

These locations are referred to in only the sketchiest and most passing terms in the government investigations of the events leading up to Pearl Harbor. Lt. Comdr. Krammer briefly alluded to the setting up of "a cryptoanalytical unit at Corregidor *and at other times in certain places in China*...."[35] Safford testified that "There had been an intercept and direction finder station at Shanghai, but it was evacuated to Corregidor in December, 1940."[36]

II
The Allied Effort

Decryption Efforts of the Secondary Powers of the British Commonwealth: Canada and Australia

Canada

BIRTH OF THE INTERCEPT AND DECRYPTION PROGRAM

Decryption work was carried on in Canada by the Examination Unit of the Army's Signal Intelligence. Herbert O. Yardley, head of the famous group that pioneered modern code and cipher breaking—the "American Black Chamber" (1919–1929)—worked for it on various codebreaking endeavors beginning in late 1940.[1] A combination of factors ultimately forced the Canadians to fire Yardley. First there was the American lobbying of the British due to resentment at Yardley's "betrayal" of American decryption programs that operated during World War One and immediately thereafter. The second factor was the determination of British Security Coordination (operating out of New York City) to have its own independent capacity to decrypt the Nazi spy network messages coming out of South America. Yardley refused to share the cipher keys, thereby making him the mortal enemy both of BSC as well as its superiors in intelligence in Britain itself.[2]

Crunched between Anglo and American pressures, the Canadians found the presence of Yardley untenable. His role destroyed the possibility for maximum cooperation with the British, who were far ahead of them in the field. As the result, they reluctantly yielded and fired Yardley. Ironically his last day on the job was Saturday, December 6, 1941.[3]

CANADIAN SOURCES OF COVERT INFORMATION
AS TO GERMAN INTENTIONS

Monitoring work first began at Rockcliffe Airport at Ottawa.[4] An additional station was built at Hartlen Point (near Halifax) and became operational in early 1941.[5] Appropriately enough, in the interest of inter-service cooperation, one post was run by the navy and the other by the army.[6] Supplementing these were a few listening stations run, oddly enough by the General Post Office,[7] as well as a large number of civilians who owned short-wave receivers of their own and were willing to partic-ipate in the program.[8] These various locations attempted to copy any suspicious voice broadcasts and forward them for analysis.

The Halifax station is referred to in the U.S. government investigations about Pearl Harbor. Comdr. Safford informed the joint committee how "the British were operating a monitoring station at Halifax...."[9] Whether they were able to intercept a winds execute (giving forewarning of the beginning of war) hinged upon "whether the operators were capable of copying the Japanese Morse code. That is something that I do not know for any station outside those the United States navy controlled."[10] Later in his testimony Comdr. Safford corrects the nationality of those running the facility: "the *Canadians* were guarding those Japanese stations the way we were," attempting to intercept any possible winds execute (emphasis added).[11] Since the station would have been tied in with the world-wide British system we can see how it could have been referred to either as a British *or* a Canadian station.

As Yardley's staff grew (though it remained small in absolute numbers), it was especially interested in crypted communications from South American sources being broadcast or otherwise transmitted to Europe.[12] Curiously, his Canadian group was breaking certain ciphers with which both the Americans and British were having great difficulty.[13]

Two transatlantic cables ran from the United States to Europe but had only "transit lines" through Canada (so-called because no Canadian originated telegraphic traffic was funneled into it).[14] The original pre-war censorship rules forbade tapping these lines. The potential value of such material, however, caused the Canadian military to reverse its policy late in 1939. To avoid protest, this tapping was kept a tightly guarded secret.[15]

CANADIAN SOURCES OF COVERT INFORMATION
AS TO JAPANESE INTENTIONS

The only telegraph cable to the Far East from North America ran through Vancouver, B.C. As early as 1939, the Canadian government felt free to monitor and copy any communications going this route that they thought might be useful to them.[16] In turn, this material was forwarded to MI5 in Britain when it was deemed of potential value to the British.[17]

The United States initially tried to keep word of its Japanese decryption program out of the hands of the Canadians. During the summer of 1941 the possibility that such a program was being carried out produced a lively internal discussion among the Canadians who were debating whether to attempt such an effort themselves. Yardley emphasized to his coworkers that it was virtually hopeless to expect any type of confirmation, "Even between friendly governments, there's very little cooperation in such things. One government would be so afraid of its sources of information, it would hesitate to let another government know it was breaking down certain codes and ciphers."[18]

Later things loosened up a bit. Although Brig. Gen. Sherman Miles pleaded forgetfulness as to most information related to cooperation with the British system, even he recalled the effort to channel Canadian intercepts into the American system:

> We gave them [the British] the means of intercepting [i.e., a Purple decrypt machine], and I also had some discussions during that year 1941 with the British military attaché and the Canadian military attaché, because certain of these messages were being intercepted by Canada, but not any other part of the British Empire. The Canadians did not have the means of breaking them nor did they know anything about the technical details of decoding. We were very anxious, however, to get from them any messages that they could pick up out of the air which, for any reason, we could not or the British could not.[19]

When questioned whether there might be written records concerning such matters, Brig. Gen. Miles responded, "The whole question was treated with great secrecy, and these conversations I spoke of between the British and Canadian Military Attache and myself were always verbal conversations, not reduced to writing."[20]

In the summer of 1941 the Canadians were basically traveling in the dark about what was happening on the United States side of the border as to cipher breaking. They suspected but they did not know. The availability of Yardley's talents was pivotal in convincing the Canadians to try to expand their own efforts into the area of cracking Japanese communications. Domestic input was readily available. In addition to sources already mentioned, the Japanese had a legation located in Ottawa and copies of its messages were available from the telegraph office for work by the Examination Unit.[21]

By early October, the first successful decrypts began to come out of Yardley's office.[22] True, these were in only low or medium grade ciphers,[23] but the Canadians took quite justified pride in accomplishing this with so few people and without outside help.

Some of the decrypts consisted of consulate reports on Canada's preparations for war. One reported in detail the discussions in Parliament concerning weapons production in the country and included specifics on the number being produced.[24] Another concerned Canadian troops being sent to the Far East.[25] Yet another contained a summary and evaluation of Canadian attitudes toward Japan as reflected in newspaper coverage and editorials.[26]

Incoming messages from Japan to the consulate provided data about how Tokyo evaluated the looming war danger. The most ominous of these were not decrypted, however, until shortly after the war broke out.[27] What made the Canadian government positive that war was about to erupt was a *German* decrypt sent from a Nazi spy network in South America. It reported to Berlin that a major Japanese convoy was on the move south toward Indo-China. This report was attributed to an unidentified source that the network regarded as thoroughly reliable—though carefully noting that this meant only that the report was given in good faith rather than expressing certainty in its absolute accuracy.[28]

This news fit in extremely well with a British dispatch from Singapore also referring to such a massive convoy, though the actual numbers of reported war craft diverged significantly.[29] The two reports (one from a friendly and one from a hostile source) made the government certain that war would erupt very quickly.[30] So confident was the prime minister of this that he was spending Sunday working with his staff on the text of a declaration of war at the very time the report of Pearl Harbor reached North America.[31]

Australia

DEVELOPMENT OF ITS INTERCEPT AND DECRYPTION PROGRAM

Although it is easy to lose sight of the Australian program because of the dominant role played in decryption by England, it deserves attention in its own right as well. Numerically (and not surprisingly) it was described immediately after the war as "a small C.I. [combat intelligence] organization,"[32] which makes inherent sense in light of Australia's relatively light population.

In 1940 the Australian government had established its own independent signals intelligence operation, which was quickly composed of individuals with both academic and military backgrounds.[33] The decision to take this step grew out of the availability of Comdr. R. E. Nave, who was a native Australian and who had spent many years breaking Japanese codes for the British.

His entry into that work began with service at the British Embassy in Tokyo from 1921–1923 in order to master Japanese. After a few short years of other duties, he was shunted into code-breaking endeavors of various types, which continued to be his focus throughout the remainder of that decade and all of the 1930s.

When 1940 arrived, he was stationed with the British Far East Combined Bureau (FECB) at Singapore, continuing the work in which he now had vast experience. Because of health problems, however, in the early part of 1940 he decided to take sick leave in his home country. While he was there, a former compatriot at the British embassy in Tokyo discovered his presence. Well aware of Nave's talents, he made the necessary proposals and encouraged Nave to obtain British permission—essential because he was a serving officer of the Royal Navy—to take leave of his British duties. Instead, he would help create a full fledged special intelligence section for the Australian government itself.[34] The "Bureau" was the unofficial name Nave attached to it.[35]

The Australians operated four listening posts in Australia itself: at Darwin, Canberra, Brisbane, and Melbourne.[36] Melbourne was the first to be set up, in 1939, before Nave entered the program and the commitment to a major effort had been made.[37] Prime targets for the Australians' attention were all communications going in and out of the Mandated Islands of the South Pacific,[38] islands that were transferred from Germany to the control of Japan in the aftermath of World War I.

The Australian operation was, by its modest size, unable to compete as anywhere near an equal with Bletchley Park in Britain. Even so it was able to independently crack one code being utilized for communications between Tokyo and the Japanese embassy. They shared the "key" into the system with both FECB and the Americans, as part of their contribution to the joint work.[39]

They could also point to at least two major independent intercepts and decryptions. One came in September 1941, when the consulate of Japan was ordered to make arrangements with some other diplomatic installation to assume its duties in case war broke out.[40] Another was the instruction of December 4, 1941, to the consulate to destroy all their ciphers and codes,[41] a sure warning that war was imminent.

The Australians were in regular communication with the British FECB operation in Singapore as well as providing data to the Dutch operation in Java.[42] They were under orders *not* to share directly that data with the Americans but to funnel it through the FECB. The British Dominions Office had issued a very strict instruction on the matter, "Information from most secret sources should not be passed direct to Untied States observers but will be exchanged through the Far East Combined Bureau at Singapore."[43]

Whether unofficially before the war or as the result of discussions during the war itself, the United States was aware that FECB was supposed to have acted as a clearing center for Commonwealth originated information, not only for data going *to* the Americans, but also for data coming *from* them. As Comdr. Safford recalled, "The Australian C.I. Unit had liaison with the Singapore C.I. Unit, including exchange of translation and keys except for the purple and red machines. The winds 'set-up' message ... were in J-19. Singapore sent translations to Corregidor ... and undoubtedly sent these same translations to Australia."[44] Furthermore, he added, "[i]n December 1941 they were intercepting Japanese diplomatic radio traffic and reading messages in the J-19 system."[45]

Although acting independently of the United States effort, the Australians joined in the monitoring effort to intercept any war-imminent winds execute message. According to John E. Marsten, one of the legal counsels for the joint committee, the committee had "communications from ... the Australians" stating or indicating this.[46] Comdr. Safford wasn't sure whether the monitoring was for voice broadcasts or Morse code messages,[47] which probably was intended to mean that they had the capacity for both.

A STRANGE CASE OF AUSTRALIAN OBSTRUCTIONISM

Such prohibitions of direct communication did not exist regarding intelligence data received from nondecrypted sources. For example, the Dutch provided information directly to the Australians and the Australians also passed information on to the Americans. In a very strange case shortly before war broke out, the Dutch had done just that and the Australians declined permission for the local Americans to pass on the report until a startling number of hours had passed.

Specifically, on the 5th (local time; the 4th U.S. time) Dutch intelligence sources became convinced that war was imminent. Presumably because of the ambiguous attitude of the United States about providing iron-clad commitments of specific reactions, the Dutch apparently provided this information first not to the United States but to their nearer geographic neighbor, Australia. The Dutch undertook preliminary military preparedness measures and urged the Australians to do the same.

Since American Col. Merle Smith died during the war, his assistant, a Lt. O'Dell, was eager to put the record straight after the war that the delay had been due to Australian obstruction, not American negligence:

> There was a cable that was sent on the fifth of December to the Commanding Generals of the Hawaii and Philippine Departments concerning the movement of a Japanese task force in the South China Sea. The information had come to the Military Attache through the Australian Government, Air Chief Marshall Sir Charles Burnett, who called Colonel Merle Smith and myself to his office.... We were called over on Thursday afternoon about 5 o'clock.... Air chief Marshall Sir Charles Burnett, myself, and Colonel Merle Smith and Commander Saom, who is the Naval liaison officer from the Dutch East Indies. The information was primarily in regard to the Netherlands, through the Indies, that principally concerned itself with the movement of a Japanese task force in the South China Sea.
>
> However, within an hour after we had gotten there some additional information came in, the exact nature of which I wasn't told at the time, but when we went out, Colonel Merle Smith had me prepare a cable which he revised to send out and the principal part of that other than the movement of this convoy was that the Dutch had ordered the execution of the Rainbow Plan A-2.... It provided for specific occurrences they would counteract by certain other action.
>
> In other words A-1 would have been some other direction expected attack. A-2 was from a particular direction, and they

ordered the execution of this A-2. That was significant
because the plan called for joint operations for the Australians
and the Dutch, and to the best of my knowledge, our Navy
if nothing else.[48]...

This was to go into effect only in case of war and here the
Dutch had ordered it. That was the definite information that
it had gone into effect. There was a bit of flurried excitement
with that, and Sir Charles Burnett asked us not to send that
cable and Colonel Merle Smith, although impatient to send
it, said that he would wait 12 hours at Sir Charles Burnett's
specific request.

In other words, they didn't say they would let that cable go
out, but I dare say they probably would have stopped it if we
had tried to launch it.[49]

Col. Rufus S. Bratton was read this testimony by the congressional
investigative committee and asked whether he had ever discovered why
the Australians had insisted that the communiqué be delayed. "I was told
that the Australian authorities wished to take the matter up with their
own parliament before they released the information to us," a statement
which his questioner took to mean "until they could have a Cabinet meeting."
Bratton embraced this interpretation, "I think that was it, sir. That
is my recollection."[50]

Assuming that there were not deeper reasons behind the delay, this
calculated obstructionism suggests that the Australians themselves were
not fully convinced as to the best reaction. Certainly, they also had made
commitments to the Dutch but had the situation truly so deteriorated that
it was now time that explicit war-committing actions had to be taken?

This is not to deny that the matter of informing the cabinet played
a role. Indeed, for the military or the prime minister to unilaterally undertake
action and to be unable to convince the cabinet of the propriety of
the decision would have provoked a major government crisis. Resignation
would be the ultimate horror, the specter of a possibly divided government
a more immediate one.

O'Dell himself saw in this delay a sensitivity to the political repercussions
of the news: If it was not forwarded immediately, the military
could be given a hard time over its own political leaders not learning of
it before the Americans:

The reason for the delay was that there was a War Cabinet
Meeting at which Sir Charles Burnett was to report this
information to the Australian War Cabinet which was meeting
in Melbourne that evening, and he went from his office
to the War Cabinet meeting.... [Y]ou see, we were there over

an hour, over two hours, that afternoon, and the information was dribbling in spurts, and we had that and it was only when we were getting ready to go, which was around seven o'clock, that the War Cabinet meeting was called. I shouldn't say before six thirty, at the time we came out there, it wasn't scheduled. They called this emergency meeting and at that time when we had prepared the cable and were getting ready to code it, Sir Charles Burnett requested very specifically that it not be sent, that we hold it up until he had informed the War Cabinet. In other words, he hadn't told his own government yet.[51]

Even so, the need to unify the Australian government so it could present a united front was a political fact of life *regardless* of when the war-warning message was forwarded. The Americans were hardly likely to act in a particularly provocative way in the short term for they were as undesiring of a Pacific War as the Australian government itself. Indeed, the American government would need to go through a similar period of analysis before committing itself to a reaction. Hence the consideration that could have proceed simultaneously was delayed a long 17 hours (not the original 12 requested). When it was finally possible to issue a communiqué, Col. Merle Smith sent this one out to both the War Department and the commanding general of the Hawaiian Department, pointing out both the Dutch report and the Dutch-Australian response:

> Based on Dutch intelligence report (unconfirmed here) of naval movements from Pelau objective Menado and/or Ambon, Dutch ordered execution plan A-2 and suggested RAAF [Royal Australian Air Force] reciprocal movement be directed Laha Ambron and Koepang. So ordered pm yesterday including flight Catalina to Rabaul task reconnaissance Buka and northwest passage Australian Army reinforcements Ambon Keopang subject to request Dutch East Indies. This message held 17 hours by ... Government eight a.m. Dutch reported advancing plans to be on Keopang not now considered necessary. Eleven am chief of Air Corps desired proceed with all aircraft forward movements. Manila informed.[52]

Even after the required delay "the Australian Government wasn't too happy about our sending this out.... I mean they realized that it was inescapable, and we had to keep our government informed, but—" leaving the sentence hanging.[53]

O'Dell explained that to speed up the arrival of the report at top command levels stateside, it had been sent to Hawaii with "the request to repeat it to Washington." This was a departure from the normal communications procedure, which would have delayed the transmission even further.[54] Ironically, it was not received and decrypted until 7:58 p.m., Washington time—the evening war erupted.[55]

Decryption Efforts of the Secondary Independent Powers: The Dutch and the Chinese

Dutch East Indies

Because of its possession of the oil-rich Dutch East Indies, the Netherlands had a natural interest in gaining the maximum knowledge of Japan's plans in order to play its own modest military cards as astutely as possible. This first led to its own effort to assault the Japanese ciphers and then led to willing cooperation with the other Western powers in this and other intelligence gathering efforts.

THE DECRYPT TEAM

The program was headed by Col. J. A. Verkuyl, who was assisted by Capt. J. W. Henning in overseeing the Dutch "Kamer [Room] 14's" decryption program. This was originally a small three-man unit set up in 1933 at Bandung in the Dutch East Indies. The following year this army operation was supplemented by the creation of a two-man navy unit located at Batavia (the contemporary Jakarta).[1]

Kamer 14 was located at Bandung Technical College. Although there was growth in the pre-war years, it remained a small operation. As the eruption of hostilities grew nearby Kamer 14 was about to recruit 50 of the college's math and engineering students to assist its understaffed efforts.[2]

In spite of their small numbers, they enjoyed considerable success at their work, all out of proportion to their resources.[3] The British FECB at Singapore began receiving decrypt and other intelligence data from the Dutch East Indies in late 1940.[4] At least conventional (rather than decrypt) intelligence data was provided to the Australians as well. As hostilities broke out, through their liaison in Australia the Dutch provided information about invasion fleets heading south for Malaya[5] and, later, of another fleet heading for Sumatra.[6]

Although the triumph over Purple was successfully hidden from the Japanese, Nippon was quite convinced that upon occasion less secure codes were being penetrated. Lt. Comdr. Kramer referred to a code canceled by the Japanese in 1940 or 1941 due to the suspicion that either the British or the Dutch had penetrated it, "A code which we designated as AJ-12, in my recollection, I have not seen the message since those days, I remember Japan canceling arbitrarily, because as I recall that message, they suspected that the British and the Dutch, I believe, were reading that system."[7] A memorandum prepared by Comdr. Safford refers to the fact that "the Dutch in Java were also reading J-19...."[8]

After war broke out, the Dutch in Java were able to provide direct assistance to the Americans as a temporary refuge for its cryptographers. When Lt. Rudolph Fabian landed with 16 other of his Cast crewmen on February 11, they received a generous and enthusiastic welcome from Kamer 14 and its expanded body of helpers. Although the local noncommissioned officers assigned to assist them knew little English, a number did have a working knowledge in at least one of five or six different languages. The overlap with those known by the Cast team enabled the necessary information to be passed from the Americans to the Dutch NCOs and vice versa.[9]

Fabian was careful (as an elementary security precaution) to assure that the American decrypts stayed securely away from these new work associates.[10] Perhaps because of the expanded body of individuals involved in the program, the Dutch were not as security conscious as one would have expected. Charlie Johns, one of the Americans under Fabian's command, was startled to observe one particular "Dutch intercept operator. He was sitting there copying Japanese. His family was there with him. I guess they'd make up his message blanks and things like that. Papa was looking over his shoulder."[11]

The American stay ended on February 21. The *Snapper* safely evacuated the American unit to its new duty assignment in Australia.[12] When Japan invaded the East Indies for its oil, the Dutch decoders were successfully evacuated, with Darwin, Australia, their immediate destination. Some continued their work there while others joined the Americans in similar work back in the United States.[13]

THE DIPLOMATIC USES OF INTERCEPTED DATA

A major part of Japan's decision for a southern thrust—rather than a northern strike into Russian Siberia—hinged upon the ready accessibility of desperately needed petroleum from the Dutch East Indies. Even with a fully assured supply, there was no certainty that the military would not demand a southern strike; without the assurance of an adequate supply an invasion of the Indies was virtually guaranteed. It was as essential to Japan's economic and security requirements in the 1940s as Middle Eastern oil has been to that of the United States in recent decades.

The Dutch knew that intense pressure would be upon them to permit greater oil export than they preferred to grant, Japanese expansionism having thoroughly soured them on anything that would even tacitly encourage it. Yet they *had* to provide at least enough to avoid "provoking" a direct retaliatory action for which the Japanese could cite Dutch "intransigence." Hence when Kamer 14 was able to break successfully the diplomatic codes used for conveying Japan's internal instructions to its diplomats, the Dutch knew what the Japanese considered as "desirable" versus "essential." This allowed the Dutch to follow a negotiating strategy that limited their concessions to the inescapable.[14]

After war began, the string of incredible Japanese victories in the Pacific left no doubt that Java was doomed—and sooner rather than later. Intelligence officers of the Dutch considered the desperate ploy of rebroadcasting those intercepts they had received—rebroadcasting them to entirely different commands than they were intended, in the hope of sowing confusion and throwing at least a small monkey wrench in the tidal wave coming their way.[15] Decryption specialists from both Australia and New Zealand urged them not to do so, contending that any advantages achieved would likely be far less than the confusion it would cause the Allies in determining the next likely actions of the foe.[16]

THE FOUR WINDS SET-UP MESSAGE:
THE DUTCH AND THE BRITISH

Much of the discussion concerning the Dutch work in the field revolves around the four winds message. Coming out of the give and take before the government investigators were several expressions of the opinion that Dutch possession of the message setting up the winds message indicated that there was likely a direct British-Java linkage independent of the Americans regarding such interceptions. Comdr. Safford recognized that the British might have provided the message, but he seemed to lean to the possibility that the Dutch had accomplished it themselves: "They knew about the original message, either got it direct or possibly the British sent it to them or we presumed they got it themselves."[17]

Lt. Comdr. Kramer was also unsure how the Dutch obtained the text but was inclined to a British source. Indeed he was surprised that the Dutch had been undertaking decryption work before the war. "[T]o my best recollection this is the first instance that I was aware that the Dutch were working on this traffic.... I might amplify my previous answer by stating that although it was obvious that the Dutch had differences on the subject [with the U.S. in interpreting the significance of the winds execute], my first reaction was that very likely the British at Singapore had furnished it to them."[18]

As he thought on the subject longer during his testimony, he remained inclined to the British playing the key role: "My recollection is that at the time I was under the impression that in all probability the British at Singapore had given that information to the Dutch, although there was a possibility that the Dutch themselves were engaged in this cryptanalytical work."[19]

Friedman, head of the army's Purple-breaking program, seems to imply that certain traffic went in the opposite direction, *to* the British and that some of it, in turn, was passed on to the Americans. "The only thing that I do know is there exists in the files one or two messages [related to Pearl Harbor] which came from British sources out in the Far East. If you remember, the British had some relations with the Dutch in the East Indies."[20]

A potential problem in this approach lies in the text of the message that the War Department was provided from Batavia, Dutch East Indies. This went beyond the implicit danger of the text used by the United States and the British and made the threat irrevocably clear-cut: "Code intercept: Japan will notify her consuls of war decision in her foreign broadcasts as weather report at end. East wind rain United States: North wind cloudy Russia: West wind clear England with attack on Thailand Malay and Dutch East Indies. Will be repeated twice or may use compass directions only. In this case words will be introduced five times in general text."[21]

If the Dutch were merely being provided the translated decrypt why would it read so much harsher then the British version? Kramer's explanation is that this was *interpretation* more than translation:

> Senator, I have no first-hand knowledge of how this message was handled, but on that point I should like to remark that the British translation furnished to the Asiatic Fleet, Admiral Hart, I considered a precise and accurate translation now of those Japanese circulars; that from a present scanning of these documents I do not consider it unusual that the Dutch considered this thing as referring to a war decision so far as the Dutch were concerned since, as I recall it, the expression used with regard to the Netherlands East Indies was the Japanese word "koreauku," which means "occupation."[22]

That the Dutch would interpret the message as threatening invasion makes excellent sense in light of Lt. Comdr. Kramer's own concession of the reading of the underlying Japanese text. Unfortunately the Dutch forwarded this to the Americans *as if the actual text* and, as such, the divergence only makes sense if *they themselves had translated it*. One could argue that they had altered the British version in order to pressure the Americans as to their (Dutch) exposed position.

Yet how could they dare do that in light of the danger that the British were sharing their translation with the Americans as well? (After all, the United States was far more important as a potential war-ally and they were hardly likely to share decrypts with a lesser power and leave out the most important one.) It would seem more likely that the text represents the translation of the Dutch themselves, either working from their own intercept or from an original language text provided by their British friends.

THE FOUR WINDS SET UP MESSAGE:
THE DUTCH AND THE AMERICANS

Elliott R. Thorpe was ordered to the Dutch East Indies during the summer of 1941. He served there as the army's military observer as well as being in charge of all lend-lease arrangements with the Indies. In his dual position he also functioned as the conduit for passing on Dutch decrypts of the Japanese communications to the War Department in Washington.[23]

One especially grabbed his attention. No less than the commander of the Dutch army in the Indies, Gen. Ter Poorten, violated normal protocol by personally delivering an intercept to him. After requesting the secretary to leave, the general locked the door to the room, and informed the American, "I have something here I believe of great importance to your government." That "something" was the message that Tokyo had sent to its ambassador in Bangkok setting up its winds war warning alert.[24]

It informed the diplomat that in the event of hostilities and the breakdown in communications, that a warning would be sent buried in a weather broadcast. If war was to begin against the Americans, the code would be, "East Wind, Rain." Thorpe shared this with the American consul general, Dr. Walter Foote. Foote thought the message was nowhere near as significant as either the Dutch or American army officers had supposed. Indeed, he desired to postpone taking any action at all on it, but Thorpe insisted upon sending it out that very evening.[25]

The message was transmitted by cable as a security precaution. Although one never could be absolutely certain whether a wireless message might be decrypted, there seemed no chance that the Japanese had tapped into the cable lines.[26] The whole proceeding clearly annoyed the local consul. The next morning, Foote made this clear by sharing with Thorpe his own message to the State Department. In it he downgraded the importance of the winds message.[27]

Thorpe continued to forward intercepts that the Dutch considered especially significant. Altogether, he forwarded four in early December that pointed to the potential for imminent hostilities. For reasons never explained to him, the final one—sent on December 5 local time; December 4 in the U.S.—resulted in a strict instruction not to forward any more such documents to Washington.[28]

The Four Winds Execute/Implementation Message: Did the Dutch Intercept It?

We already saw that the Dutch team shared with the United States its intercept setting up the four winds message as a warning of war. This leaves the other question, of whether they actually *intercepted* a winds execute, i.e., a message with the actual warning phrases. They certainly did monitor for it. John E. Marsten, one of the legal counsels for the joint committee, referred to the fact that the committee had "communications from ... the Dutch regarding the monitoring for the Winds 'Execute' message...."[29] Comdr. Safford was unsure whether they were listening for Morse code transmissions or merely for voice broadcasts.[30] Either way he was convinced that they did not receive a genuine execute—which is not to exclude false executes, such as those received by the Americans, messages that *almost* matched the required wording.

Safford based this conclusion on discussions with those in a position to know. "When he came back to the United States I talked with him to see if he could recall any further information on the subject. Mr. Foote said that he was positive that the Dutch in Java had not received the execute on the winds message."[31] Nor was this his only source. "I have it from two sources now; an officer who was there serving in liaison with the Dutch and Mr. Foote."[32] He does not identify this intelligence liaison man (probably Thorpe, discussed above) but the fact that he could speak authoritatively on the subject implies both a high security clearance and having had at least partial access to the Dutch intercepts.

Although the question of whether the United States intercepted a winds execute message is one of the most contentious issues surrounding the Pearl Harbor attack,[33] it has long been my suspicion that the importance of the issue has been vastly over-rated. As one analyst has put it,

> It would have warned that Japan was about to go to war with the United States. That conclusion, given the strained state of U.S.-Japanese relations, should have come as no surprise. In any event, it would not have precluded other strategic options for Japan—Japan did in fact strike simultaneously along an extended front ranging from Malaya to Hawaii. Most important in terms of the controversy over Pearl Harbor, "east wind, rain" would have contained no hint that the Japanese were about to open the war with a surprise attack on the U.S. fleet in Hawaii.[34]

If such crucial information had not been provided by a winds intercept, why should even the most warmongering interpretation of Roosevelt's intentions have led one to conclude that the president either personally or through his subordinates suppressed it—whether coming from American, British, or Dutch sources?

As to the Dutch, all their interceptions and decrypts were burned in March of 1942 to avoid them falling into the hands of the Japanese.[35] Hence we can never have *direct* proof if a four winds execute was or was not received—or, for that matter, that any even more compelling evidence of war was in Dutch hands.

On the other hand, a 1960 account of the group's work, prepared for the Dutch Military Archives by former Capt. Henning (a top and pivotal member of the pre-war Java based team), stated that there was no evidence directly pointing to an attack on Pearl Harbor. In contrast, traffic

analysis had clearly indicated that there was a large buildup of the
Combined Fleet in the Kuriles,[36] but this seemed most amenable to the
supposition of a sneak attack on Russia's port of Vladivostok.[37]

NON-DECRYPT INTELLIGENCE SHARING
WITH THE UNITED STATES

Regardless of to what degree this may have occurred, we are certainly on safe ground in saying that intelligence data from non-cipher
sources was also being forwarded. Three late November intelligence
reports issued by the Pacific Fleet Intelligence Officer Layton utilize or
evaluate Dutch-provided information. In one dated November 22, 1941,
the war nerves of the Dutch Indies show through quite clearly:

> Dutch authorities in the NEI [Netherlands East Indies] have
> received information that a Japanese Expeditionary Force
> which is strong enough to constitute a threat against the NEI
> or Portuguese Timor has arrived in the vicinity of Palau. If
> this force moves past a line through Davao-Waigea-Equator
> the Governor General of the NEI will regard it as an act of
> hostility and will consider war to have begun.[38]

Concerning the "Reliability Rating" of this report, Layton simply
provided a question mark. An American evaluation of the claim (dated
November 23, 1941) cast considerable doubt on the earlier report. Available
information "does not indicate the presence of units" other than those
usually in the area "and no unusual concentration of that force." On the
other hand there was an indication of a buildup in transports and that the
Dutch feared this might be preliminary to more threatening action.[39]

On the 25th the ultimate Dutch source came to light: "The U.S.N.
Shipping Adviser in Batavia reports that the Dutch report concerning
the Japanese Expeditionary Force near Palau originated from the Dutch
army in Timor. Portuguese Timor was named as the objective of the
Expedition. The information was classed as doubtful and no further
confirmation has been obtained." The word "no" is underlined twice by
one of the original readers of the report.[40]

Lt. Comdr. Layton probably had this skeptically received report in
mind when he testified before the Army Board:

> I would like to mention that we had in accordance with this
> a message from the Dutch who said that they had these secret
> sources which told them the Japanese were going to move in
> on Dutch Timor and possibly even Portuguese Timor, and
> asked us if we had any information of that move. We told

them we had nothing whatsoever, but there was some indication that some Japanese forces would soon proceed to the Palau area, but whether or not they had aggressive intentions against Timor we could not confirm.[41]

Of course, additional data was being derived from the intercepts as well. Many of the decrypts and non-decrypt reports were of modest significance in and of themselves, indicating, for example, movement of Japanese forces from one location to another. When the number of vessels involved was large enough or when sufficient separate though smaller movements were happening simultaneously, there was the possibility of deducing a military move about to occur.[42] But even here professional judgment and experience had to be brought to bear as to what the actual targets would be, the degree of danger involved, and the probability of enemy battlefield success and how quickly it would occur. "Hard" data was only the beginning; without adequate and skilled interpretation its usefulness was extremely limited.

China

Geographically and from the standpoint of population, China deserved recognition as a world power. This desired respect was denied on the international level because China's government was not only corrupt, but far worse it was inefficient and ineffective and dared not tolerate an army that could become a potential threat to those holding the economic and political reins. Rather than finding a way of coopting the army into a basis for its power, the military forces were simultaneously regarded as both essential yet ultimately unreliable. As a result of such factors, China appeared to the rest of the world as a crippled giant, to be pitied far more than respected.

For the Japanese, who had been developing the desire for overt control in the region for decades, Chinese political and military weakness represented an opportunity for expansion in an area where large gains were both possible and where none of the militarily strong international powers would feel the need to openly intervene. Hence, we must classify China—in this period—as among the secondary powers in international status and influence.

Yet secondary or not, it was literally on the battleline with an expansionist Japanese military and represented a potential source of information if corruption, security, and ego concerns could be adequately met.

The Dutch East Indies (and the mother country of the Netherlands for that matter) paled into insignificance in size and manpower compared to China, and yet it would prove a source of useful data. Might not China do the same?

Knowingly or not, it did so through the presence of American and British monitoring stations that fed intercepts into the systems of those two powers. But here we are more concerned with the potential for more overt cooperation.

YARDLEY AND THE CHINESE

The United States attempted to covertly tap into the Chinese decryption program through Herbert O. Yardley, the former U.S. expert in the field who was working under contract with the Chinese government in Chungking. Maj. David D. Barrett was an assistant military attaché for the American government in that city. Under the name of "Herbert Osborn," Yardley had traveled to China, and as the months rolled by Maj. Barrett became increasingly suspicious that the mysterious Osborn might be the former crack intelligence leader of the U.S. government. In September 1939, Maj. Barrett sent a message to Military Intelligence in Washington and asked whether Yardley was still in the United States.[43]

Although G-2 (Military Intelligence) had already known that Yardley was in China, he was still in bad odor in Washington due to his having revealed American secrets in his exposé of his earlier work in the field. Furthermore, the United States was definitely pro-China even though it was careful to avoid unduly antagonizing the Japanese in the process; it had been deemed best simply to let Yardley carry out his work and not disturb him, to act as if in ignorance of his presence.

By the time Maj. Barrett's message reached Washington, the War Department's earlier attitude was under reconsideration. Key individuals had begun to wonder whether Yardley might represent an asset it could utilize once again. Barrett's message arrived at a crucial point, and he was instructed to "inquire if results of his work can be made available to you." Recognizing the explosive nature of the subject (in regard to both China *and* Japan) he was instructed, "be guarded in your radio messages about this matter even when in secret code." One major method of doing this was never mentioning him by name.[44] If the United States was attempting to read the Japanese codes, it would be certain the reverse was the case as well. Worse yet, if somehow the Chinese stumbled onto what was happening, the diplomatic repercussions could have been profoundly embarrassing.

For his own safety, Yardley had to be discreet as well. His superiors had warned him about dealing with foreigners of any type. They were far from thrilled with his even dealing with Chinese—unless they were his direct coworkers. Curiosity was aroused as to why Maj. Barrett was attempting to meet with him, and Yardley (always a good improviser) responded that because he was an American citizen and because of the on-going war, the embassy wanted to keep in contact with him and its other citizens living in the country.

With this as cover, the two were able to meet for the first time in February 1940. Yardley described his ongoing health problems and referred to his efforts to intercept more of the Japanese communications. Maj. Barrett inquired as to whether information on the subject could be provided. Yardley responded with a request about exactly what type of materials were desired. At their next meeting Maj. Barrett had the answer: the ciphers used by the Japanese army in the field.[45]

Yardley was agreeable. Indeed, he would attempt to expand his access to such information. He would provide everything relevant to American interests on a continuing basis. On the other hand, the risk was great—a claim no one would challenge. Although Yardley estimated the material would be worth at least $100,000 to the United States, he was willing to settle for far less. They were to find a position for Edna Ramsaier and pay her $6,000 a year—$2,000 for her and $4,000 for a year to be held for him. She had been his assistant in the "Black Chamber" World War One code breaking days, and felt confident she could earn her salary; the remainder of the money would be for the risk he was taking.[46]

Unknown to Yardley, due to the slowness of communications, Ramsaier had been hired for crytopology work less than a week before. Even so, the conditions were enough to sour G-2 on any further involvement with Yardley.[47] The fact that the Signal Intelligence Service had cracked the Purple diplomatic code may have played a role as well. Yardley's reputation as a loose cannon who might write yet an *additional* exposé likely weighed heavily on their minds as well.[48] He had done it once; why not again?

A meeting was arranged with Maj. Barrett's superior, Maj. William Mayer, who had military attaché rank. Yardley provided a report originally sent to his own Chinese superior describing the work of the cryptographic program under his authority. In the period since he had arrived, the report asserted that 19 ciphers had been broken. It noted that a detailed analysis had been made concerning how each of these had been penetrated. Yardley offered Maj. Mayer these analyses.[49]

Maj. Mayer doubted whether he would actually be able to provide them. Perhaps even more important, the major doubted whether he could accomplish it without Chinese knowledge due to the level of surveillance that was maintained upon him. The final and decisive vote against involvement became practicality. Hence neither Mayer nor his superiors were willing to accept the offer.[50]

However one may interpret the underlying motives behind Yardley's maneuvering, at this point he came up with a proposal that was clearly self-serving. With his Chinese contract virtually completed, a decision had to be quickly made whether to sign on for a longer tour of duty. Yardley came up with a scheme to enhance his bargaining position and the amount of money the Chinese government would have to pay him. He informed his superior that Maj. Mayer had told him his talents were urgently needed in Washington. Yardley then asked Maj. Mayer to back up his story, and Mayer bluntly refused. When the Chinese general approached Maj. Mayer, Mayer politely informed him that the American military had not requested Yardley to return to its service.[51]

Happy at the strengthening of his own negotiating position, the Chinese leader then promised that arrangements would be made to turn over to the Americans cryptographic materials on an ongoing basis. This, however, would have to be on an unofficial basis between the general and the intelligence officer.[52]

Was it a discreet effort at requesting a bribe? (A common phenomena in the Chinese wartime society of the day.) Maj. Mayer had his suspicions and relayed both the offer and his doubts up the chain of command. Col. J. A. Crane was the officer directing the military attaché section and his response was, "If he should voluntarily make any of the material available to you, of course you may accept it but with the clear understanding that it is not on a reciprocal or purchase basis."[53]

Yardley had still not recovered his health and any systematic work was constantly being interrupted by Japanese bombings. In July 1940 he left on a plane to begin his trip homeward. Nothing appears to have ever come of the Chinese proposal to share information systematically.

INTELLIGENCE DATA PROVIDED THE UNITED STATES

If the Chinese did not provide crypographical data—and the Americans were even more emphatically averse to doing so in the reverse direction— that did not prevent them at least occasionally sharing other types of intelligence information. Indeed reports from such sources led to the distribution of a high level warning in July 1941 that war with Russia was imminent. As Adm. Kimmel testified,

> On July 3, 1941, the Chief of Naval Operations sent me another dispatch. This reported that the Japanese Government had issued orders that certain Japanese vessels in the North Atlantic and Caribbean areas pass through the Panama Canal to the Pacific. Under these orders all Nipponese merchant vessels would be clear of the Caribbean and North Atlantic areas by July 22. It related information *from unusually reliable Chinese sources* [emphasis added] that within two weeks Japan would abrogate the neutrality treaty with Russia and attack. The dispatch concluded as follows:
> "That present strength and deployment of the Nip Army in Manchuria is defensive and the present distribution of the Japanese Fleet appears normal, and that is capable of movement either north or south. That a definite move by the Japanese may be expected during the period July 20–August 1 is indicated by the foregoing."[54]

Brigadier General Sherman Miles, a high ranking intelligence officer in the army, spoke before the Army Pearl Harbor board of how extremely limited was the direct military information that could be garnered from Japan itself. On the other hand, "We were getting a good deal of information from what might be called the borders; in other words, China, and even the part of the Continent occupied by the Japanese. The Koreans would get out once in a while and we would get some information in that way [also]."[55] Miles did not make plain whether this information was forwarded by local government officials or was the fruit of direct contact by American attachés.

Chinese helpfulness in obtaining data about the workhorse of Japanese combat aviation—the famous Zero—deserves special emphasis. In September 1940, it was first introduced into combat in China. Reports from Japanese pilots captured by the Chinese supplemented the Chinese's own ill-experience at its hands. This data, forwarded to the Americans, provided initial insight into the handling characteristics and capacities of the aircraft.[56]

In May 1941, a largely intact Zero was recovered from its crash site by the Chinese. A detailed analysis was prepared and shared with the U.S. naval attaché in Peking.[57] Although this data received a good circulation among U.S. Navy pilots, the full danger of the Zero did not fully impress the military leadership until after the Pacific war began.[58]

Bletchley Park and the British Far Eastern System

Bletchley Park and Its Operations: An Overview of What U.S. Investigations Revealed by 1945

Just as the Americans were busy monitoring Japanese language diplomatic and military broadcasts, so were the British. In like manner, they were zealously attempting to crack the secret of these various ciphers, both in cooperation with the Americans (next chapter) and on their own.

Although various testifiers speak of an exchange of information between "London" and Washington, "London" is an euphemism for Bletchley Park. Originally the British decryption effort *had* been located in London, but at the time of the Munich crisis it was permanently moved to its new and safer quarters.

Senator Ferguson inquired where the place was located that was responsible for "the so-called tracking [of] the code, so far as the British were concerned; was it in London?" Miles responded evasively, "I believe it was in London, sir."[1] Col. Henry C. Clausen also was vague about the location of this central depository of Far Eastern intercepts, "I also, Senator, got from the British, from their secret place, corresponding intercepts when I was in England."[2] He also refers vaguely to "the British in their file of intercepts" and how that certain of these duplicated those the joint committee already possessed.[3] The British record keeping system was sufficiently thorough that they felt confident in reporting that they lacked the long sought genuine winds execute:

I had that specific question put to the British people, and they investigated for me and gave me the report that there was no evidence of an execute message, but they did have two suspicious messages of that type that they would run down, and when I got back to Washington, I had them run these down through our super-duper agency that connected with the British and they got some information from out in the Far East, but they were not the ones that you and I would consider an authentic winds intercept.[4]

The fact that they "got some information from out in the Far East" indicates that archives had been maintained both in the field and at home.

Also in Britain itself were one or more monitoring stations. Comdr. Safford never specifies how many stations existed there, but he does mention their role in filling "holes" in the message interception system: "As I have stated earlier in my testimony, we had to call on Corregidor to cover the Tokyo-Berlin circuits as the combined efforts of intercept stations on the East Coast, West Coast, Hawaii, and England could not provide better than about fifty percent coverage."[5]

Just before he made this generalization, Comdr. Safford referred to a specific example of how monitoring work based in England came to the rescue of American Magic: "Part 2 of the very important part 3 Tokyo to Berlin, number 985, JD serial 6943, that was dated about the 1st of December, were missed, but the first and third parts were copied solid. Incidentally, this came from England and not from this country."[6]

Comdr. Safford was uncertain as to how many Britain-based individuals were "capable of copying the Japanese Morse code"—in contrast to their ability to understand the spoken language.[7]

The British operated a monitoring station in Canada as well. At least one liaison man provided Magic by the British had experience at that station. "The British were operating a monitoring station at Halifax, which I was told about by a British officer who spent about two weeks in my section in the spring of 1941. He was a liaison officer."[8] Of special interest is that this occurred more than six months before the outbreak of war.

In the Far East, the British operated a monitoring group in Hong Kong. This continued in operation until after the outbreak of war. A December 4, 1945 communication from the American ambassador in London to the secretary of state mentions the possibility that Hong Kong had intercepted a winds execute. If it did, however, it was only after the actual eruption of hostilities.

The Foreign Office has just informed us that while their

inquiries are not yet finished, up to the present no evidence has been found that any "wind" message was received before the morning of December 8, 1941, the day following the attack on Pearl Harbor. The Foreign office says that there was relayed to Singapore from Hongkong a broadcast by the Japanese which contained messages in code and which was received in Singapore six hours following the attack on Pearl Harbor. The text of the Japanese code is not available yet but if desired we will ask the Foreign Office for more particulars.[9]

The main British operation was located in Singapore. Hence in the case of the possible winds execute, Hong Kong forwarded its intercept to that location. The Singapore personnel could not only understand spoken Japanese but Japanese Morse code as well. Comdr. Safford brought this out in his discussion of British monitoring for the winds execute:

> I do not know that provisions the English may have made to monitor for this message in London and whether there were in England any operators capable of copying the Japanese Morse code. They had such operators at Singapore and Singapore was listening for the winds code, but I have been assured by a British officer who was in Singapore at the time Pearl Harbor was attacked, and who later came to Washington, that the British listened in vain for the winds message at Singapore, and when the attack at Pearl Harbor did come, they were just as much surprised as we were.[10]

Safford was unaware whether the British were monitoring for the execute on Morse code channels alone, or also on voice transmissions.[11]

From these remarks, we can see that some intriguing pieces of data were already available to the public by the time the U.S. congressional investigation of Pearl Harbor was completed in 1945—data whose significance was overlooked for decades. Using this as a jumping off point, let us now examine what postwar studies have uncovered about how the BP-based system operated. In the following chapters we will discover additional allusions to how this British system cooperated with the Americans and others.

Bletchley Park Itself

Bletchley Park was an estate located about 50 miles northwest of London. It lay mid-way between Cambridge and Oxford, permitting easy access to both universities' academic communities. It was purchased by the government for the Government Code and Cypher School (GC&CS) in 1938. With war a real possibility with the Nazi regime in Germany, it was anticipated that bombing of London would be so severe that it would be impractical to carry on such sensitive work from urban locations.[12] With the personnel, all of its pre-war records were moved to the new location.[13] Even though the Czechoslovakia crisis of that year was temporarily defused by the British capitulation at Munich, the CG&CS remained at its new home.

Because of its physical location the GC&CS-run decryption program is often called "Bletchley Park." It was also referred to by various of its personnel (or users of its decrypts) as War Station Room 47, Station X, and Mousetrap.[14] Because there were 2,000 WRNS (Womens Royal Naval Service) personnel attached to operate the "bombes" that were used to test various possible decryption solutions for the ever changing German Enigma, the Navy hierarchy was upset with the other appellations. It insisted that its people refer to it by the naval description, *HMS Pembroke V*.[15]

Once assigned to BP (another, and more obvious, appellation that was often used) one was there for the duration of the war. Although living off the premises was essential due to the number of personnel involved, transfer to some other government project was virtually impossible. A review committee had responsibility for such cases. Although it was more than willing to be sympathetic to the human element behind a petitioner's request, due to security concerns only in the rarest of cases was an exception made.[16]

In 1939 some 150 individuals were carried on the official payroll. This included individuals directly involved in decryption as well as all their staff (which included typists, clerks, etc.).[17] By the end of 1942 the numbers had increased to around 3,500.[18] Typical estimates are that by the first months of 1945, that figure had mushroomed even further to in excess of 10,000 personnel—though that estimate includes those working in all aspects of the program and not just those assigned to Bletchley Park itself.[19] Others place the number as low as in the 7,000s[20] or as high as 12,500.[21] For comparison, American Magic by this time had over 50,000 individuals involved in the various aspects of its effort.[22]

As the program grew larger, fewer knew what was actually taking place. Many were on the margin of the project and had no idea that their work was contributing to the breaking of the German and Japanese ciphers. Even those with some knowledge of what was going on had little or no conception of how varied and extensive was the success of the program. The "need to know" principle was rigorously—even *super* rigorously—observed.

Even so, a considerable number of individuals who were not directly involved in the decryption itself were needed to provide input that permitted the undertaking to milk its decrypts of the maximum possible information. A participant in the German part of Ultra described how it worked in regard to his own particular area of responsibility:

> We members of Hut 3 lived in a series of concentric circles. The tightest of these was Hut 3 itself together with Hut 6 and the Naval Section. This was the circle in which we could talk with complete freedom about what we were doing.
>
> The circle bulged slightly outwards to include those in London who were also on the Ultra list. There were, for example, a number of people in Air Ministry Intelligence who would be on the telephone to us several times a day. Most of them were men and women recruited like ourselves into war service in departments which had not existed, or barely existed, before the war. At the level of Wing Commander or Group Captain and above they were regular RAF officers, but below that level they were almost all wartime recruits with whom we were in constant touch and whom we got to know personally quite well.
>
> It is impossible to imagine Hut 3 without the scrambler telephone. Its invention meant that we could discuss the latest detail or puzzle with colleagues in the Air Ministry in the same way as we discussed these matters among ourselves in the 3A office.
>
> The second circle was BP itself. Outside the sections ... a few senior persons knew all about Ultra. The rest did not and they were the great majority of BP's inmates.[23]

To shift back to Far East Ultra in particular, so tight was the security that after the program began its growth, even a personal participant was unaware of how many Japanese codes were being tackled at one time. All he normally knew was what he and his immediate coworkers were laboring on.[24] In contrast to the Japanese efforts, those working on the German Enigma enjoyed considerable more leeway in discussing their work with those not directly involved.[25] Considering how limited even *their* leeway was (see extract above) this tells us a great deal about how strict were the limitations on cooperation that were imposed.

Development of British Japanese Language Capabilities

In the 1920s, the Government Code and Communications School's Japanese language staff consisted of a modest two specialists assisted when possible by a liaison officer provided by the navy.[26] An official alliance existed at this time between the Japanese and the British navies, and from both the traditional and practical standpoints one would have anticipated a desire to maximize the number of those skilled in the language of the other to facilitate communication, as well as to be prepared in case strategic policy reversals resulted in current friends becoming future foes.

In spite of this only a dozen officers were capable in Japanese, and much of the higher "brass" was opposed to increasing their numbers because they were convinced that the emphasis upon foreign language mastery diverted their talents and abilities from their proper navy-centered interests.[27] The British army had a far more constructive attitude on the matter: From 1903 to 1937 about 130 of its officers successfully mastered the language of their former ally who was now evolving into a potential enemy.[28]

As the war danger increased, it became necessary to recruit talent from those of a non-military background. During the expansion phase of Japanese Ultra, a disproportionate number of its personnel were recruited from Cambridge University.[29]

Japanese Decrypts as a Source of Information on German Intentions

Even in the last years of the 20th century, it was not uncommon to read writers and scholars speaking of "Magic" as if it were strictly Japanese language material and "Ultra" as if it only involved German decrypts.[30] Actually Ultra personnel targeted both major Axis powers.

"Boniface" was the original codeword for Enigma decrypts. This was later changed to "Ultras."[31] A specific terminology evolved to describe the Japanese decrypts in particular. Properly speaking, the English called their Purple intercepts BJs (for British-Japanese), but the nickname Black Jumbos came to be attached to them as well.[32]

British Ultra, centered at Bletchley Park, is most famous for its successful cracking of the theoretically unbreakable Enigma code used by the Germans. Ironically, Ultra's ability to penetrate the Japanese ciphers also provided useful information for the anti-German war effort as well. Since the Japanese embassy was sending back regular reports to Tokyo, British access to these messages provided another source of data from within Germany itself. Data concerning German military attitudes and plans were of obvious inherent value in evaluating the foe's war-making ability and intents.[33]

At times the reports provided data of even more immediate relevance. For example, they gave clear early evidence as early as mid-July that the powerful German thrust into Russia had lost its momentum and was in danger of stalling.[34] The Japanese ambassador and his staff traveled widely and had access to much data about Germany's efforts to defend Europe against the coming Allied invasion. Their reports further enhanced British and American insight into what they were up against when they launched the Normandy invasion in June 1944.[35]

Army Chief of Staff George C. Marshall was astutely aware of how useful the Japanese decrypts were for those involved in planning the war in Europe. He wrote in 1944 that the reports of the Japanese ambassador in Berlin represented America's "main basis of information regarding Hitler's intentions in Europe."[36]

Knowledge of technological innovations that would be becoming available in the European Theater was one potential additional side benefit. The Japanese had several skilled Scientific Intelligence officers stationed in Europe, and their reports provided an insight into changes that were being attempted by the Germans in improving existing weaponry and developing new forms.[37]

So far as the Far Eastern theater went, the reports provided data about what might be facing the Allied forces in that region at a later date. The Germans, for example, shared with their oriental ally models of anti-submarine listening devices and radar systems.[38] The British noted, however, that the Germans seemed to have a standing policy of *not* providing their cutting-edge versions, but only those that were already in well established use.[39] In the opposite direction, the British discovered the Japanese providing information on their own airborne radar to the Nazis.[40]

Decrypts as a Source of Information on Japanese Intentions

Both the Americans and the British were putting considerable resources into the decryption program—and each was making significant successes. Indeed one Australian historian argues that "it is not generally realized that in the period before Pearl Harbor the British had as much, if not more, success than the Americans with the Japanese naval codes."[41]

At least some who entered the British program after Pearl Harbor, however, were convinced that the Americans—with only occasional exceptions—processed the material much faster, broke the ciphers more promptly, and communicated the results to command levels more efficiently.[42] This may, in part, represent defensiveness over the British program's much more modest size and lack of offensive capacity in the Pacific to utilize the data that was recovered.

The rapid successes of the Japanese forces in the Pacific played havoc with the Bletchley Park end of the British system during the first half of 1942. The breakdown in reliable communications resulted in material only dribbling in. When the first group of trainees who had learned Japanese in a six month crash course reached Bletchley Park in August of 1942, they discovered that the only more-or-less current intercepts reaching BP were the few dozen from Flowerdown, located near Winchester, England. Even these were delivered by courier and an interval of days existed between interception and arrival at BP. A teleprinter finally removed the delay in September of the same year.[43]

The situation as of August was described by one of those new trainees in these words (which also implies something of the very limited personnel resources available domestically during 1941 as well):

> The Naval Section was under [Frank] Birch. The Japanese part of it, under [Hugh] Foss, was forty strong, and was housed at Elmer's School, a short distance from Bletchley Park proper. There were two Japanese translators already in place, Lieutenant-Commander Keith, and Mr. Nichol. Accommodation was tight, but by squeezing up even more tightly they managed to find a small room in which the six of us were installed.
>
> We were introduced all round, and then went in to Keith for instructions. He said that there were about a thousand encrypted Japanese naval messages intercepted every day, of which some seven hundred were in the general system, JN 25.... A fraction of these reached Bletchley within days—in fact under forty a day, intercepted at Flowerdown in the United Kingdom....
>
> Some of the remainder were in due course forwarded by bag from elsewhere. He said that current material was handled expeditiously at Washington, Kilindini (the port of Mombasa, then the headquarters of the Eastern Fleet), and

Melbourne. The Bletchley party had up to that point, he said, achieved nothing. Whenever they began to attack a problem, the solution arrived from another center and they turned to something else.[44]

By the end of 1942, however, BP was well on its way to recovery. At that point Bletchley was successfully reading several thousand Japanese intercepts a day, a similar number of Italian intercepts, and around 4,000 German ones.[45] Furthermore, it is important to note that the decryption difficulties were only at the BP end of the communication chain—the above memoir makes quite plain that successful penetrations were regularly being made at other locations. [46]

Although FECB had to destroy the mass of its records to avoid them falling into Japanese hands when Singapore fell,[47] their materials had already been provided to BP as they came in and were broken. Not unexpectedly, Bletchley Park itself maintained archives of all intercepts. Hence when the inquiry was made by the U.S. War Department about what messages the Japanese embassy in London might have sent out in early December, the British were able to give an exact count. In a War Department memorandum given to the joint congressional investigation it was reported,

> Pursuant to your request the War Department has made inquiry of the British concerning the number of coded messages sent by the Japanese representatives in London subsequent to December 2, 1941.
> The War Department has been informed that two coded messages were sent by the Japanese representatives in London on the 3rd of December 1941 and one coded message on the 5th of December 1941 and one coded message sent on the 6th of December 1941 and all four messages were sent on the code system known as PA-K2.[48]

This raised the question among the congressmen as to whether the embassy had followed its instructions to destroy all of its codes. Comdr. Safford explained that there was no contravention of their instructions in the course they had followed:

> There were two systems that were exempt from destruction. One was PA-K2, and the other was LA, neither of which were considered by ourselves as secret, and we presumed the Japanese did not consider them secret.... [PA-K2] is a minor system which had been in effect for a very long time, and was used for matters of negligible importance, but they presumably wanted to keep up with the newspapers, minor money matters, visas, things like that.[49]

Bletchley Park and the Russians

The existence of either European or Pacific Ultra was never shared with the Soviets by the British. Even so, as the war went on certain summaries concerning the European situation based on data from Enigma intercepts were prepared and forwarded. For example, in April 1941, Ultra-based data on the massive German build-up on the Russian frontier was forwarded to Moscow in summary form and attributed to a British agent.[50] The British representative did not grasp the significance of the report and reworded the message, thereby diluting its impact, before passing it on to a deputy foreign secretary.[51] In the months between the invasion and the end of the year, only a few Ultra-based reports were provided to Moscow, although there was a large amount of intelligence information forwarded from other sources.[52]

Yet the Russians knew of Bletchley Park's work at least by 1942. In that year they planted their own agent (whose spying was only discovered decades later) and through him they received certain intercepts and summaries of German communications.[53] Although the British provided the Russians with intelligence data throughout the war, they were cautious as to how much and how specific and did not want the Russians to know of the successes of BP. There was a combination of reasons for this. To begin with, the Russian codes were notoriously breakable. There remained strong and justified ideological suspicions of Russian reliability (and vice versa—if one wishes to look at it from the Communist side). Furthermore, BP's intercepts demonstrated skills that, if the Russians did not know existed, might be more easily utilized against them where and when needed. In the short term, they were allies, but what of the long term?

The Joint Army-Navy Far East Combined Bureau (FECB)

As late as the Munich crisis, the British army and navy were unable to agree to any regional pooling of their decryption efforts in the Middle East.[54] In vivid contrast, as early as the 1920s the two had agreed to establishing a joint monitoring station in China.[55]

In the mid–1930s, the two services formally set up the Far East Combined Bureau (FECB) in Hong Kong to monitor and break Japanese military communications.[56] This action was the result of an intra-military compromise. The British army wanted Shanghai to be chosen since its major intelligence operation was centered on that city; the navy preferred Singapore, presumably because of its importance and prestige as a naval installation. The two sides compromised on Hong Kong.[57]

With both its leadership and administration handled by the navy, there was considerable disgruntlement both from the army and the air force that their special needs were being neglected while a disproportionate amount of time, personnel, and resources were being devoted to intelligence data primarily of value to the navy.[58] Not that the army itself fully developed even those resources under its own exclusive control. In particular, its Secret Intelligence Service, though active throughout the Far East, did not successfully set up the kind of in-depth organization that could have been invaluable when war broke out and various areas were conquered.[59]

At the FECB itself the entire work of intercepting and decrypting was carried out by navy personnel. The air force and army had only liaison officers present.[60] We have something of the chicken and egg question as to which came first: the "neglect" of army-air force interests or the lack of adequate personnel to assure that the needs be met.

The head of FECB was officially the chief of Intelligence Staff. Since there was the natural desire to keep his identity and work secret, the cover identity was that of the captain on staff of the HMS *Sultan*.[61] The FECB operation as a whole was semi-seriously mocked by its participants as the "Loony Bin,"[62] presumably because of the intense pressures upon the participants due to the nature of their work.

In spite of the unit's earlier years in Hong Kong, in 1939 the bulk of the FECB personnel were moved to Singapore.[63] Because of its powerful fortifications, it was deemed a far more secure base that could withstand any threat that would be thrown at it. (A ground assault was the contingency it was not prepared for and which ultimately enabled the Japanese to seize it.) All data continued to be forwarded to the GC&CS for additional work and distribution.[64]

The rising tide of successful Japanese expansionism after Pearl Harbor, however, made it clear that even mighty Singapore was no longer a safe haven for operations. The last FECB personnel were pulled out of Singapore by February 1, 1942. Although a limited number were dispatched to Java (and they, in turn, were ultimately moved to Australia), most found themselves relocated to Colombo on the island of Ceylon.[65]

FECB/Bletchley Park Successes in Breaking Japanese Ciphers

In 1935 British cryptanalysts managed to break the major ciphers of both the Japanese army and navy.[66] Even before this they had enjoyed great success breaking that army's communiqués, which clearly revealed the nature of its intentions in Manchuria.[67] The British did not have the military resources available to do anything to halt the Japanese aggression and there was considerable sentiment among British diplomats that the Chinese government itself bore much of the responsibility for the hostility between the two Asian powers.[68]

Previous successes were undone in 1937 by changes the Japanese introduced in their ciphers.[69] The same year saw an effective division of labor between the homeland GC&CS and the Asian FECB. The England-based analysts targeted the non-naval ciphers while the Far Eastern operatives continued their naval efforts.[70] This situation continued until 1939 when some of the army personnel working at the GC&CS were transferred to work on the naval ciphers.[71] In that same year GC&CS and FECB were able to begin an effective penetration of JN-25.[72]

FECB Data for London: Summaries and Intercepts

FECB regularly provided both summaries and interpretive analysis of data it was receiving as well as forwarding the raw data back to London.

SUMMARIES

FECB prepared summaries of key decrypts as one means of both quickly forwarding the information and making their apparent import clearer. A January 1941 message sent from Tokyo to the consul-general in Singapore was summed up in a report to the director of Naval Intelligence in these words: "Future intelligence and propaganda policy will be 'mainly directed southwards in order to secure supplies of war commodities.' Promotion of agitation, political plots, propaganda and intelligence (particularly naval and military) must be expedited and intensified so that new order in greater East Asia may be expedited."[73]

Another decrypt of late February 1941, this time addressed to the consulate-general stationed in Sydney, Australia, stressed that the Japanese were attempting to avoid war. In the FECB summary sent to the director of Naval Intelligence on March 1 it was summed up, "All talk of impending crisis in Far East is nothing more than British propaganda aimed at winning over American public opinion, checking Japan's southward advance and hindering improvements of her relations with Thailand and Indo China; no action by Japan is indicated."[74]

The practice of sending summaries continued after Pearl Harbor as well.[75]

INTERCEPTS

The intercepts themselves were forwarded from FECB to Navy Huts 8 (codebreaking) and 4 (analysis) at Bletchley Park.[76] Purple material was forwarded in decrypt form to the British Foreign Office.[77]

Naval materials were strictly in-house, for Admiralty use alone. When such materials were decrypted only the Operational Intelligence Centre (OIC) of the Admiralty was provided the data. OIC, in turn, might or might not provide data to rival services or to subordinate command levels of the navy itself.[78]

Messages with decrypts or summaries based upon such sources that were issued from FECB carried the label "Zymotic" to designate both their point of origin and extraordinarily sensitive nature.[79] "Y organization" data referred to information gained from the analysis of Japanese radio traffic but which did not involve actual decryption.[80]

Non-Intercept Methods of Obtaining Japanese Data

Gaining entry into a foreign code or cipher was ordinarily a hard and laborious task. Occasionally a more dramatic method was utilized. Although the following incident happened in North America, it illustrates the British willingness to utilize unconventional means to obtain the desired tools.

In Ian Fleming's first James Bond tale, *Casino Royale*, Fleming tells of Bond beginning his career by assassinating a Japanese consulate official in New York City. Utilizing the consulate office in Rockefeller Center and the assistance of local British intelligence personnel, Bond successfully carried out his assignment of killing a key individual involved in the effort to crack British ciphers.

There are several elements of truth in the tale. As William Stephenson, who headed the British Security Coordination office at Rockefeller Center later explained,

> The truth was, Fleming was always fascinated by gadgets. We were building up our mechanical coding equipment. One floor down was the Japanese Consul-General. We knew he was sending coded messages by short-wave radio to Tokyo. With two of my assistants, I broke into the Japanese consular offices at three in the morning. Fleming came as an onlooker. We cracked the safe and borrowed the code books long enough to microfilm them.[81]

Which ciphers these were, Stephenson did not identify. This type of episode—if successfully carried out—could provide vital assistance on keeping broken these particular ciphers. On the other hand, the action carried the certainty that—if detected—it would alert the opposing side and result in its promptly changing its ciphers and totally eliminating any gain that had been made.

(A joint operation of the Office of Naval Intelligence, Federal Bureau of Investigation, and New York police had carried out a similar break-in at the New York Japanese consulate in the early 1920s. Perhaps because the technology was more primitive at that time, a *series* of break ins were required to completely photograph a copy of the then current Japanese naval code.)[82]

An ongoing source of the undecrypted material was constantly in British hands before Pearl Harbor. Although monitoring stations were vital to the decryption system, a considerable amount of diplomatic traffic —both German and Japanese—went to European locations via the transoceanic cables owned and operated by the Cable and Wireless Company. This was a company not merely influenced but actually controlled by the British government. Anything sent over these wires was routinely copied to Bletchley Park as well as sent along to its intended destination.[83]

Decryption Cooperation in the Pacific

FECB/American Cooperation to Assure No Japanese Messages Were Missed

The Anglo-American collaboration took three forms. First came the need to assure a maximum supply of intercepts. In order to accomplish this goal the two allies shared intercepts (or parts thereof) that one or the other had missed. Second came the provision of any technical assistance that one thought the other could use. Least frequently came the provision of translated texts.

General Sherman Miles encountered considerable congressional skepticism when he kept insisting that he could recall practically nothing at all of how much intercept data had been exchanged with the British. Coming back from the noontime break, he remarked that a subordinate had refreshed his memory on the point and he wished to share it with the committee:

> I am happy to report, sir, that Colonel Bratton has called to my mind a circumstance that enables me to state of my own knowledge that shortly after the British were given the means of deciphering the intercepted Japanese messages the Signal Corps [of the U.S. Army], that is to say, the SIS, arranged with the British a simple code by which we could mutually assure ourselves that both got the same messages. If we failed to get one through that code, the British supplied us with that message, and vice versa.[1]

According to William F. Friedman, who ran the army's part of Magic, the end result of Anglo-American mutual assistance was an essentially identical collection of intercepts:

> General Clarke. To the best of your knowledge and belief then, was all of the traffic which has since become known as the Pearl Harbor traffic in these Pearl Harbor investigations available to the British at the same time as it was available to the American Army and Navy?
>
> Mr. Friedman. I believe that to be a correct statement. The only thing that they might lack would be certain intercepts which they were not in a position to—
>
> General Clarke. You mean by that individual messages?
>
> Mr. Friedman. Yes.[2]

The American army investigator Henry C. Clausen was given the right to examine all the Japanese diplomatic intercepts that he wished at Bletchley Park. He reported in his postwar memoirs that "the British intercepted approximately the same messages as did the Americans before Pearl Harbor."[3] This would point to the British and Commonwealth monitors being approximately as successful as that of the Americans. He acknowledged that there was a free flow of information between the future allies on the matter[4] and he leaves unanswered to what extent the comprehensiveness of the British record grew out of its *independent* work and how much was made possible by the mutual *sharing* of data with its American ally.

It was probably impractical and impossible to attempt to make such a distinction. What was important at the time was that both sides felt they had a thorough record of the available Japanese data. (For the conspiratorially minded, however, it should be noted that Clausen's remarks are only in regard to *Purple*, i.e., diplomatic, intercepts rather than the matter of what JN-25 *navy* communications they may have possessed that the Americans did not have.)

The two future allies were always alert to messages especially relevant to the imminence of war. The emphasis by both the British and the Americans in monitoring for a winds execute is a good example of this. Both Corregidor and Singapore were carefully watching for the issuance of this war-warning.

> Admiral Hewitt. Concerning the "winds" code in the dispatch of 28 November which you recalled having seen, what steps were taken to monitor for the use of this code and what were the results?
>
> Commander Fabian. We assigned one receiver to cover the Tokyo voice broadcasts and each broadcast was listened to by

a linguist. In addition to that, we assigned one receiver on a twenty-four hour basis to the Navy morse press broadcast. The materials therefrom were copied constantly and delivered to the linguists and no indication of any of the phrases set up in the "winds" message appeared.

Captain Mason. The British unit at Singapore was also monitoring the same circuits and it was agreed that anything received by either unit would immediately be exchanged.

Admiral Hewitt. Nothing was received?

Captain Mason. Nothing was received from that.[5]

Comdr. Safford pointed out, to a different investigative tribunal, that the units of three different nations and some 12 different stations were involved in the joint endeavor:

The Director of Naval Intelligence requested that special effort be made to monitor Radio Tokyo to catch the "Winds Message" when it should be sent and this was done. From November 28 until the attack on Pearl Harbor, Tokyo broadcast schedules were monitored by about 12 intercept stations, as follows: N.E.I. [Netherlands East Indies] at Java; British at Singapore; U.S. Army at Hawaii and San Francisco; U.S. Navy at Corregidor, Hawaii, Bremerton, and four or five stations along the Atlantic seaboard. All Navy intercept stations in the continental United States were directed to forward all Tokyo plain-language broadcasts by teletype....[6]

The monitoring actually had even more participants than these. The Australians were also listening,[7] though it is not known whether this was in regard to voice broadcasts or Morse code communications.[8]

Assuring themselves of a more-or-less complete collection of messages represented only half the battle. The other half was to "crack" them on a routine basis. This the two nations proceeded to do. The data-sharing involved the entire spectrum of Nippon's cyphers. As Safford testified, "In all these systems, 'purple,' Jig-19, and the minor systems, we had an exchange between Washington, Singapore, Corregidor, and London. We pooled our efforts on that."[9] But, as we saw in an earlier chapter, this was primarily in regard to technical matters rather than anything more substantive (also see the remarks immediately below).

FECB/Philippines Cooperation
Related to Breaking Japanese Ciphers

WHAT WAS KNOWN AS OF THE
CONGRESSIONAL INVESTIGATION OF 1945

In the period just before the outbreak of hostilities, Corregidor was attempting to get a handle on JN-25 with the help of the British. When asked how successful they were in "breaking the code," Lt. Fabian responded, "We were in the initial stages, sir. We had an established liaison with the British unit at Singapore. We were exchanging values, both code and cipher recoveries, but we had not developed either to the point where we could read enemy intercepts."[10]

Comdr. Safford also referred to the Singapore-Philippines linkage: "Corregidor also had liaison with the British unit at Singapore and anything of interest or importance received from Singapore was forwarded to Washington."[11]

Most of the material shared by the British apparently concerned either the *mechanics* of breaking into the codes or the original language intercepts themselves. In at least some cases, the *translated* text was provided.[12] The most documented example is that of the Winds war-warning message, which was circulated by the Americans in the British translation rather than their own. On November 28, 1941, Washington sent out to Hawaii and the Philippines the following text, along with a candid admission that the wording was that of the British:

> Following Tokyo to net intercept translation received from Singapore X If diplomatic relations are on verge of being severed following words repeated five times at beginning and end of ordinary Tokyo news broadcasts will have significance as follows X Higash Higash Japanese America X Kita Kita Russia X Nishi Nishi England including occupation of Thai or invasion of Malaya and N-e-i [Netherlands East Indies] X on Japanese language foreign news broadcasts the following sentences repeated twice in the middle and twice at the end of broadcasts will be used X America Higashi Higashi No Kaze Kumori x England X Nishi No Kaze Hare X Unquote X British and Comsixteen monitoring above broadcasts.[13]

The reference to "Comsixteen monitoring" indicates that Corregidor was already in possession of this information. Indeed this represented a full cycle of the information since it had been transmitted to Washington via the Philippines.[14]

In Lt. Comdr. Layton's Hawaiian "Intelligence Report" No. 97 of that same date the intercept origin was masked by the accurate but more ambiguous statement, "Absolutely reliable reports from Singapore [note again the reference to the implied British origin of the report] are that the following procedure will be carried out on Japanese news broadcasts in the event that diplomatic relations are on the verge of severance." The code phrases are then typed out in a visually easier to read format. The I.R. ends with the remark that "The British and Com 16 are monitoring the above broadcasts."[15]

Lt. Comdr. Kramer used several justifications for ignoring the American translation and circulating the British rendition in its place. For one thing the United States had intercepted it in a form that "was garbled, appreciably garbled."[16] Work on the American version was incomplete, but the British one was immediately usable.[17] Indeed, if one wished to be contentious, he was convinced that the British translation was not only adequate ("essentially the same as ours")[18] but objectively *better* than the American one. "From current examination, it was in more precise form than the version we had in the Navy Department."[19]

Oddly enough, significantly different English renderings exist in all *three* decryptions—the American, British, and Australian.[20] Indeed, the British had their rendition in circulation among their people on November 25 1941, while the Americans began circulating theirs only on the 28th.[21]

WHAT HAS BECOME KNOWN
IN MORE RECENT DECADES

Although the various military and civilian investigations of the U.S. government clearly revealed that the Japanese ciphers were being successfully tackled by the British, this represented an area of study that did not begin to receive its deserved attention until many years after the war ended. Since then a number of pieces of the cooperative Far East relationship between FECB and the Philippines have become known, of which the following are some of the most significant.

In May 1941 it was agreed that there would be a complete, ongoing exchange of intercept results between the two powers. This would be implemented between the FECB in Singapore and Cast in the Philippines. To begin the execution of the agreement, Cast personnel visited Singapore and vice versa.[22]

On the British side, Comdr. Malcolm Burnett of the Royal Navy was assigned the Philippine visit. So covert was it, that even the army unit engaged in monitoring was not informed of it. Indeed, the story goes, he was smuggled onto Corregidor in a U.S. Navy uniform. The cynical army MP is said to have muttered as he passed him through, "Kind'er old for an Ensign."[23]

During the visit, Comdr. Burnett set up a system whereby Cast and FECB could inquire of each other about whether they had received a missed broadcast or had received, unlike the inquiring location, an apparently uncorrupt one (i.e., undistorted by weather conditions and unclear contents). In such cases, the Pan American clipper was utilized to pass on the missing data via a locked bag.[24]

The British were permitted to place one of their own cryptanalysts — an individual well versed in Japanese — into the Cast operation itself.[25] This was likely "Bouncer" Burnett himself, who received a military award for his liaison work with American Navy units beginning in May 1941.[26] Likewise a liaison officer was placed by the Americans with the FECB in Singapore.[27]

The Conspiratorial Interpretation: Did the British Withhold Essential Data?

Although a very few at least partial decrypts may have been made before the war by the American side of JN-25,[28] these were the exceptions rather than harbingers of ongoing success. Likewise, unless the British were able to impose a successful hidden embargo on their own successes, it is unlikely they were doing substantially better. We refer to a "hidden embargo" because the American participants most intimately involved in breaking JN-25B were fully convinced that the British were falling short of success just as they were.[29] Prohibiting the circulation of vital decryption information, though always possible, would have been extremely hard to accomplish when the two nations were in regular communication with each other and enough data would *have* to be shared to indicate good will, while *crucial elements* were hidden to avoid assisting the Americans to their own ultimate success.

Limiting the circulation of the decrypts themselves would be a different matter. Since both operations were working from the same body of data, there should have been only a matter of days' difference in both countries having the same information available to decision-makers. On those occasions when one or the other might have successfully made a startling and time-precious decrypt, one would naturally expect one's superiors to do the necessary consultation with their opposite numbers. It was, after all, the role of both FECB *and* Cast to monitor and decrypt, *not* to make policy decisions based upon the data.[30]

Indeed, FEBC was under the impression that its superiors *were* forwarding key materials to Pearl Harbor itself. W. W. Mortimer, a cryptologist with the FECB, recalled after the war that all the data he sent to England was marked for relay to CINCPAC—i.e., the commander-in-chief of the Pacific Fleet, Admiral Kimmel at Pearl Harbor.[31] This was the accepted policy at FECB during 1941.[32] Since the director of Naval Intelligence for the Admiralty had approved this data sharing, it had to be an extremely high level decision not to implement it—or to inform subordinates that it was not being carried out.[33] Such is the conspiratorial interpretation.

A non-conspiratorial approach would be that the data *was* being shared with Magic in Washington and it was Magic's responsibility to decide whether it was forwarded to Hawaii. (That would be the "natural" routing of the data.) Alternatively (as anyone acquainted with real life bureaucracies can well imagine) this could have been a case where the designated individuals—pressed with so many other obligations on their time—simply did not execute the policy.

Whatever secrets the suppressed British Japanese archives may eventually reveal, they are extremely unlikely to include any indication of clear foreknowledge that Japanese war plans included a major assault on Pearl Harbor. They may well reveal that key data was mishandled, misinterpreted, or misrouted that *might* have made the picture clearer. (This was certainly true on the American side!) It could even reveal that higher officials *thought* data was being forwarded to Pearl Harbor that was not. (Just as some high ranking Americans were convinced that Pearl Harbor had a Purple machine.)

It might even reveal clear-cut evidence of some military action by the Japanese against the British or Commonwealth navies that would have required a declaration of war if publicly known or admitted: British pride might still have been injured to admit at even this late a date that the nation's resources had been so restricted that they had been forced to swallow such a humiliation without immediate retaliation.

Be that as it may, we have the recorded uncertainties of how, when, and where war would erupt. These go all the way up to the chiefs of staff of the British military and are from men who had access to the decrypts. These records indicate that as late as the day before war broke out they faced the same dilemma as the United States: War was inevitable, but the immediate targets of assault were unclear and uncertain, and Pearl Harbor did not figure in the equation.[34]

In many ways this circumstantial data is the most convincing: Direct lies are easy, destruction or suppression of contradictory evidence not always that hard. To establish a consistent pattern of documentable behavior that would *support* claims of not having prior knowledge would be far, far harder, especially when the materials were never intended for public circulation.

It is extremely hard to prove a negative, that some one did *not* know something. In this case, however, we have the contemporary diary—which the author had absolutely no business having kept due to its inherently constituting a potentially serious (disastrous?) security lapse. It was maintained by Malcolm Kennedy, a Japanese language expert who worked at Bletchley Park during this period.

Less than 24 hours before the attack, Kennedy wrote an entry noting that Churchill "is all over himself at the moment for latest information and indications re. Japan's intentions and rings up at all hours of the day and night, except for the 4 hours in each 24 (2 to 6 am) when he sleeps." After the attack became public he wrote in his diary of his "complete surprise" at the object of the attack.[35] And if as pivotally placed an individual as Kennedy did not recognize the attack was coming at Pearl Harbor, there was no one else who would have either—nor would Churchill have been so persistently inquiring up to the last day before the assault if he were sure what was in the works.

This is not to deny that the British government *wanted* to maneuver the U.S. into any war that erupted against Britain in the Far East. British priorities were Europe centered, and that was the only war they wanted to fight. Resources were already stretched thin and a successful simultaneous war with both Germany and Japan was totally beyond the nation's resources.

Hence the natural preoccupation to assure that any Far Eastern war involved the United States as well. (Their nightmare scenario was an attack strictly on British and, perhaps, Dutch colonies and the United States having to decide whether to enter a war in which its own possessions had not been attacked.) Indeed, the diary kept by General Alan Brooke records how that on both the 6th and 7th of December he had lengthy meetings discussing "all the various alternatives that might lead to war and trying to ensure that in every case the USA would not be left out." Yet his comment upon hearing of Pearl Harbor vividly illustrates that scenario was never all his list, "All of our work of the last 48 hours wasted! The Japs themselves have now ensured that the USA are in the war."[36]

III
Other Covert
Intelligence Sharing

Capital to Capital: The London-Washington Link

The Ultimate American Gift: The Purple Machine

WHAT WAS PUBLICLY AVAILABLE KNOWLEDGE AT THE END OF THE 1945 CONGRESSIONAL INVESTIGATION OF PEARL HARBOR

At this point, it was on the record that the Americans went so far as to share their greatest treasure, their Purple-decryption machine. Adm. Noyes was uncertain as to the source of the Purple machine sent the British and the date it was provided. All he could assert with confidence was that "the Navy did not do that" and that "I didn't have anything to do with it. I did not do it personally." He assumed the army had provided the equipment.[1]

William Friedman, who played the pivotal role in breaking the Purple system, recalled for the Clarke Investigation the circumstances leading to providing the machine to the British: "A joint U.S. Navy-U.S. Army cryptanalytic mission consisting of four officers, two from each service, went to London for the purpose of establishing technical cooperation with the British cryptanalytic service. It was at that time the Army furnished a Purple machine and the technical data to the British."[2] Comdr. Safford recalled it a little differently: He spoke of "how two machines, in fact, [were] sent to London for the use of the British."[3]

General Miles recalled the date as being "sometime in January of 1941 that they were given the means of decoding these messages."[4]

The provision of this equipment overcame a major technological deficiency on the part of the British. Friedman was justifiably proud that his team had been able to accomplish what neither they nor the Germans had been able to do:

> It represents an achievement of the Army cryptanalytic bureau that, so far as I know, has not been duplicated elsewhere, because we definitely know that the British cryptanalytic service and the German cryptanalytic service was baffled in its attempts and they never did solve it. After we solved the Purple system, the technical data necessary to operate the system and a machine constructed by ourselves were turned over to the British so that they were in a position to process Purple messages also. We did the same so far as concerns the [U.S.] Navy. We provided them with a Purple machine or two.[5]

Looking back at this pattern of mutual assistance, the navy commander at Pearl Harbor was understandably disturbed: If the British so freely provided information, why was he denied it when his installation was the largest forward base for the U.S. Navy? "I know of no reason why [the Magics] should not have been supplied to the commander-in-chief of the Pacific Fleet, and I think he was quite as much entitled to them as the British Admiralty was."[6] If he had desired to be harsh, he could have justifiably added, "and more so." The British were, at most, potential allies; in contrast, Admiral Kimmel was in direct command of—and with responsibility over—the Pacific Fleet, on the effective use of which would hinge American success in any war with Japan.

WHAT HAS BECOME KNOWN IN MORE RECENT YEARS

Providing the Magic machines to Britain was another missed opportunity that could have set historians on the track of British decryption efforts long before even European Ultra came to the "official" public eye some two decades later. More of the details can now be sketched in as to how and when the decision was made and how it was implemented.

In Autumn of 1940, the British were informed of the existence of Magic. Whether this was done intentionally or through unauthorized babbling is in dispute; likewise the identity of the party (parties?) who informed them remains in question.[7] Regardless of the method whereby they learned it, the knowledge must have brought with it at least a modest degree of optimism, since the potential allies had proven that cracking the diplomatic ciphers was, indeed, possible.[8]

At some point in the final months of the year, the Americans appear to have first been unofficially informed of the Ultra system. This was part of the British effort to encourage cross-Atlantic scientific cooperation.[9] At this stage there were only the most ginger and cautious efforts on both sides as to sharing even the fact of the existence of these most highly regarded intelligence secrets. Soon, however, a massive step in cooperation was volunteered by the Americans.

Toward the end of January 1941, the *HMS King George V* arrived at Annapolis. Among the Americans to be given tours of the new war vessel was the president himself. Returning with the vessel were four members of the Army SIS (Signal Intelligence Service). Their assignment was to establish cooperation with the Bletchley Park Ultra operation. If their individual cryptographic skills were not sufficient to gain them a warm welcome, it was guaranteed by their carrying two of the very few Purple machines America possessed.[10] These they presented to the British after their arrival in February.

One would have thought that when the American group returned home, reciprocity would have resulted in their bringing an Enigma machine to use against the German ciphers. Whether there was ever an explicit or implicit "understanding" that this would occur, the British were unwilling to part with an Enigma because of reservations about the adequacy of American security precautions.[11] Although there were certainly ways to justify the decision (the British, for example, having far fewer available resources with which to build and provide an Enigma machine due to their limited wartime resources), anyone with Anglophobic sentiments (or merely a suspicious mind) could easily judge it to be a situation in which the British took advantage of American good will.[12]

Even without being provided the machine itself, the Americans received wide access to the various components of the British European-oriented operation. They visited the work sites at Bletchley, communications monitoring locations, and were provided the "keys" that had previously been recovered and made possible decryption of the raw intercepts. The Americans were convinced that the British had been open and fully cooperative. As their report summed it up, "We were invited to ask questions about anything we saw, no doors were closed to us and copies were furnished of any material which we considered of possible assistance to the United States."[13]

The British promptly put their new resource to good use. Within the first few weeks of February they were obtaining their first useful data. Of this period Churchill wrote, "[The Japanese] were evidently in a high state of excitement, and they chattered to one another with much indiscretion."[14]

Exchange of Personnel between Bletchley Park and Hypo

After Pearl Harbor, a modest number of decryption specialists served in the opposite nation's programs targeting the Axis powers. Several Americans, for example, served at Bletchley Park.[15] Just as the United States ultimately provided several individuals to work at Bletchley Park, the British also provided an unknown number of their people to work in Washington later in the war.

Hugh Foss was such a Britisher, and he is of special interest because he had been involved in Pacific Ultra prior to the outbreak of the war. Gordon Welchman played a pivotal part in the breaking of German Engima—both conceptually planning how it could be done, brainstorming the necessary new technology, and organizing the men and women who carried it out. In spite of his understandable preoccupation with German codes, he makes a single mention in his memoirs of the important contribution Foss made in tackling the Japanese intercepts:

> He had returned from Washington, where he had worked with U.S. Navy cryptographers on Japanese ciphers. Before the war he was one of the most brilliant of the professional cryptographers of the Government Code and Cypher School; and during the war he made a considerable contribution. I met him on my first trip [to the United States, in early 1944], and was told that he was highly esteemed by the Americans. I remember him as tall and thin, full of interests, and very friendly. He was certainly one of the GCHQ people to whom I felt strongly drawn, though our separate areas of work did not allow us to develop a close friendship.[16]

Welchman provides no indication of how long he had been aware of the Japanese operation, though his own key position makes it likely that it was from an extremely early date. Nor does he give any indication as to the date or circumstances under which Foss had been dispatched to the United States to assist the Americans.

After the Pacific War had begun, there was cooperation in other places as well. Comdr. Eric Nave, who had done such important work for the FECB and who had created the Australian program, served as part of the on-going Allied effort under MacArthur.[17] Comdr. Macolm Burnett, another of the veteran Japanese cryptographic experts, eventually served as British liaison with the Americans doing similar work in Hawaii.[18]

British Conduits of Intelligence Information to Washington: What the U.S. Investigations Revealed

British sharing of intelligence data (and here we have in mind primarily non-decrypted information) was routed to its future allies by a variety of paths and with a variety of independent recipients. One broad conduit consisted of multi-direct links that existed between London and the United States military and government leaders in Washington. In a far distant part of the world, another conduit involved the communication of information between Singapore and the Philippines, sometimes duplicating and sometimes not what was being provided to Washington via London. The third conduit involved the forwarding of British Far Eastern data via a middle man to the U.S. military authorities in Hawaii. This chapter focuses on the London-Washington channels of communication.

When the matter of intelligence sharing between London and Washington was discussed before the joint congressional committee, generalizations were common. Even some of these, however, provided indications as to the channels through which the information actually moved. In an exchange that could refer to intelligence sharing in either the Pacific or Atlantic theater of war, Sen. Ferguson inquired of General Marshall, "Do you know of any arrangement between the British and America in relation to the giving us other intelligence that they didn't get through Magic?" After a short, "yes, sir," response came the question, "And was that distributed to us?" Again a concise, "yes, sir." The senator did not press for an explanation of the procedure for exchange of information or the mechanism whereby it was carried out.[19]

On the following page, the general explicitly refers to the situation in the Pacific, and that the navy was one intermediary, "I know they [the British] were receiving information, just as we were receiving a certain amount and that a part was coming directly from the Navy."[20] Although he could not recall offhand any specific intelligence report from the British

Admiralty, "My recollection is that we were getting *occasional* information from the Admiralty" (added emphasis). They were handled in a way to prevent confusion with the Magics: "The Admiralty messages would not come across my desk as magic." The expected custom was for them to be "delivered personally" by either Gen. Sherman Miles or Adm. Stark, but in his congressional testimony he could recall none of the specifics of the procedure.[21]

In spite of Gen. Miles's pattern of alleged forgetfulness, he did recall that there was an established policy in dealing with non-Magic British data in the Far East. The issue arose in regard to Britain's preparations for war. He was asked by Sen. Ferguson, "Do you know when the British at Singapore as far as their army was concerned was alerted? Did you get any information on that?" At first Gen. Miles responded, "I do not recall getting that information," but after the question was repeated his memory improved slightly: "I may have [heard], sir. I very probably did because *I was in pretty close communication with the British. I had a special section in my department for interchange of information with the British* but I do not recall [that particular communication]" (added emphasis).[22]

The committee did not pursue the matter of the machinery alluded to, or the amount of data actually forwarded by either side. The statement is of special interest to us, however, because it explicitly reveals that the provision of data was a two-way street rather than a one way transmission.

Concerning the United States being on the receiving end, Layton makes passing allusion to how "British intelligence agencies" provided information indirectly to such places as Pearl Harbor. They did this "through ONI [Office of Naval Intelligence]" in Washington.[23]

Marshall was grilled by the committee about two specific messages, neither of which could Marshall recall having read. The first one was from the First Sea Lord to the Chief of Naval Operations in Washington and expressed confidence that British forces would "acquit themselves" well when war broke out. It was labeled "Personal for C.N.O. [Chief Naval Operations] from First Sea Lord."[24]

The second message was from "the Commander in Chief China" and concerns the sighting of Japanese war vessels . Though it is not explicitly labeled as being provided via London rather than the Far East conduit through Singapore, the reference to it being "an Admiralty message to the Navy here [in Washington]" makes its London origin most probable.[25]

The British conduit to the United States through the American military intelligence agencies was not the only one in use. The British Embassy provided periodic over-all evaluations of the state of the European War through intelligence summaries provided to the president. The congressional hearings reprint several such reports as part of the body of evidence.

The first report is headed "British Embassy, Washington 28th, July 1941." It begins, "Dear Mr. President: I enclose herein two copies of the latest reports received from London on the military situation. They are dated July 25th and July 27th."[26] A British Embassy note dated October 14 enclosed "the latest report received from London," dated October 12.[27] On the 3rd a report dated the 2nd was forwarded.[28] Finally, on December 4, "copies of the two latest reports received from London" were shared.[29] These reports dealt with matters such as recent military activities, including both successes and defeats. German, Italian, and Japanese military movements are discussed and, in some cases, an analysis of apparent intent added.

Since it is inherently improbable that there was a reporting gap between July and October to December—with no reports provided between—it seems certain that these are a very, very limited sample of the type of ongoing information being provided directly by London to the president and, through him, to the State Department and American military.

Some information came from multiple sources, which would tend to reinforce the credibility of the British reports in general and the verified ones in particular. Sen. Ferguson asked Capt. MacCollum whether he recalled "from Great Britain, the message from Winant to the Secretary of State, being, in effect, from Mr. Churchill to the Secretary of State at 10:40 on the morning of the 6th." This summary concerned the citing of ships that "were going into the Kra Peninsula and" were "14 hours" sailing time away at the time of the report.[30]

> Captain McCollum. Yes, sir; I saw that, but we already had it from our own source, sir.
> Senator Ferguson. You already had it from your own source?
> Captain McCollum. Yes, sir. That was merely passing on information along to us that we already had, sir.[31]

What is not stated is whether this information had been forwarded to the secretary of state *through* navy channels, or whether it had been passed to the secretary by the British Embassy and then handed over to the navy because of its informational content. Either way it worked to reaffirm data the United States already possessed.

Finally, there is the odd example of an effort of a British military officer to gain an unscheduled face to face meeting with the secretary of state on the morning of December 7. This illustrates the *personal* element involved in the information exchange and how it was not limited to paper documents or to a rigidly circumscribed number of individuals.

It was "about 9:30 or 10" in the morning on the morning of December 7 when a British officer unexpectedly showed up at the office of Adm. Noyes.[32] As near as Noyes could remember this "was Admiral Little,"[33] who was already an acquaintance of his.[34]

Perhaps concerned that the joint committee would misinterpret Adm. Little's appeal to him to gain quick admission to the secretary of state, Adm. Noyes stressed that this was a very out-of-the-normal request: "Normally a foreigner is supposed to go through the Office of Naval Intelligence, and he wanted to cut a corner and asked me if I would be willing to call the Secretary of State's office. I knew one of the Secretary of State's people and I just called him up."[35] Sen. Ferguson wanted to know why the Britisher made the request. "He didn't tell me, sir. He merely said everybody was busy and would I ring up the State Department and ask if they could see him."[36] Adm. Noyes was fairly confident that the Britisher specifically wished to see the secretary of state, but conceded that it could have been the undersecretary.[37]

Although he was uncertain of what Adm. Little desired to discuss at the State Department, Adm. Noyes did recall what he had been interested in earlier in the day: The two had been discussing the significance of a threatening Japanese fleet movement. "A British officer came to see me with some information that he had on the same [subject], in regard to what information the British received about the movements of the big convoy. I gave him the information we had. He went up to see the Chief of Naval Operations and the Secretary of the Navy" and afterwards asked his assistance in setting up the meeting at the State Department.[38]

Since Noyes had read the dispatch about the sighting of the Japanese Fleet near the Kra Peninsula, the two officers exchanged a few comments on the matter.[39] The American admiral insisted that there was no explicit discussion as to whether war would break out that day.[40] Indeed, he emphasized that the entire conversation was something of a distraction from his own pressing duties:

> You asked me what I was doing, sir. I had a 24-hour a day job. The only thing I remember specifically about that morning was this British officer coming in. In addition I had enough business to do going over my traffic with the Atlantic

where we were in a very serious situation to take the morning without doing anything else. I have no recollection of the British officer except the part that I have explained to you, sir. I had no conversation about Singapore. I had no conversation about political matters. It was purely in regard to the strategic and tactical implications of this convoy movement. Why he came to me, probably was because it was Sunday morning and there probably weren't so many people down there.[41]

As in earlier cases, postwar publications have revealed significant additional data on the various routes through which the data was provided.

British Conduits: Via the U.S. Embassy in London

In a number of cases, data or reports were provided to the U.S. embassy in London for transmission to the United States. The State Department, of course, had its communications with its "Foggy Bottom" superiors in Washington. The army personnel there sent their cables directly to the War Department.[42]

Hence, information might be provided either to the military attachés, naval attachés,[43] commercial attachés,[44] or to members of he diplomatic corps itself—not to mention various special "missions" sent to Britain in 1941 that operated more or less out of the embassy as a base.[45] Ultra type intelligence was not passed on to the diplomats for retransmission not only due to the desire to limit circulation of the material but also because of concerns that the American diplomatic ciphers could be broken.

There were concerns on other grounds as well in the early months of 1941 about the security of *any* information sent via this embassy. As one important Britisher explained to the chief American military attaché, "it went through so many hands in the War Department ... he would not consider having any of it sent through that channel" so long as the German danger was so intense.[46]

Bletchley Park itself was reading the American traffic to European destinations at least by September 1941 and probably much earlier.[47] (A fact not immediately shared with the Americans, but which served as a warning to its own people of American cipher vulnerability). In late February of 1942, Churchill informed Roosevelt that his people had penetrated the ciphers and he had ordered the work stopped since they were allies. The claim about the work stoppage may or may not have been true.[48]

The information from at least one Japanese decrypt (in summary form apparently) *was* sent via the chief army intelligence officer at the embassy. In his diary entry dated May 2, 1941, he writes,

> It is rather interesting to see that our fooling around with the "J" Code had brought some tangible results, because if we had not done that the British would not have had the information which I cabled back to the United States today about the reexports of chrome, copra, hemp and coconut oil from the Philippines to Germany via Japan.[49]

German Ultra data was also passed through the same intermediary. In early September the British passed on to him conclusions based on both Ultra and other sources in regard to battlefield successes in Russia. It expressed serious concern that Kiev might fall to the German juggernaut.[50]

The British gave some information to one official and some to another. As the result, the Americans were upset because no one single source had access to *all* the information being provided.[51] But this was a failure not so much of the British as of the Americans—an organizational failure to assure the adequate distribution to all concerned parties of the data that was being provided.

The British were startled when they discovered that passing data to one of these sources did not automatically mean that others who needed it also received it—either in Washington or among the American military and diplomatic personnel in London itself. Indeed, it was not always shared even with other key people of their *own* particular military service. This problem came to a climax in June 1941 during a dinner between the chief U.S. military intelligence officer in London and a British officer:

> After dinner I talked to Kennedy, who said that he had given Chaney a very complete estimate of the whole Imperial situation as far as the war goes, and hoped that it would produce a profound impression at home. I said that if I were not mistaken Chaney had accepted all this information merely as background for his own plans and that it had probably never gone to Washington, and that if they wanted information to go to Washington, they had better give it to me.[52]

After the British overcame their surprise, they came to an immediate decision: When such data was provided to Gen. Chaney of the Joint

Staff (planning) Mission, the chief American intelligence officer would also be invited to the same meeting.[53] Not a cure of the over-all problem but still a modest step in the right direction.

The American diplomats in London also served as conduit for one-on-one communications between the president and the prime minister. Of 65 documented messages that Churchill sent to President Roosevelt between January 1, 1941, and December 7, 1941, 39 are identified as channeled "via [the] U.S. Embassy" in London. One is referred to as routed "via State Department" and may be a different method of stating the same routing.[54] Of Roosevelt's 38 communications that can be identified as to method of transmission, the bulk (31) came "via [the] U.S. Embassy." Two came "via [the] State Department" and presumably this should be added to the embassy total, as should three more that involved the navy (one of which specifies "via Navy radio to [the U.S.] embassy), for a grand total of 36.[55]

British Conduits:
Via Their Embassy in Washington

The United Kingdom also provided information through its embassy in Washington for forwarding to appropriate American diplomatic or military personnel. Some of this information consisted of routine summaries of the international military situation (including specific details) that were provided for the information of Her Majesty's own representatives and which were forwarded to the president as an act of courtesy. The Pearl Harbor investigation records contain several of these. Two records dated July 25 and 27 1941 were forwarded to Roosevelt by Ambassador Halifax on the 28th.[56] Also included is an update of October 12 (forwarded two days later),[57] one dated December 2 (forwarded the following day),[58] and two undated reports, both presumably received on the 3rd since they were forwarded on the 4th.[59]

The information flowed in both directions. Intelligence estimates based upon the Magic decrypts were forwarded to London via this embassy.[60]

Of Churchill's 65 messages (see above), 18 are referred to as coming "via [the] British embassy." One message is labeled "via Foreign Office," and presumably refers to the same routing. Of 38 messages from Roosevelt (see above), two are recorded as going "via [the] British Embassy.[61]

The embassy was a two way conduit for other sources besides

Roosevelt and Churchill. For example, on July 10, 1941, a top British diplomatic official reported in London that Sumner Welles had shared with Ambassador Halifax "a lot of fairly definite stuff suggesting that the Japs had made up their minds to have a go."[62]

British Conduits: Via British Security Coordination in New York City

A third British conduit was from MI6 (the Secret Intelligence Service) to its Rockefeller Center office in New York, known as British Security Coordination. Because it used the Typex machine (a British evolution of the Enigma approach utilized by the Germans) this was considered extremely secure. Indeed, it appears that the Germans never made a determined effort to crack it, since the underlying theory was so similar to their own "unbreakable" Enigma that they deemed the effort next to hopeless.[63]

In light of its extremely secure communications link, it has been speculated that when pre-Pearl Harbor forwarding of the text of Ultras or Magics were sent that they were likely routed to the two national capitals through New York.[64] In that age of regular, speedy rail transit between the two cities, the use of land lines for retransmission would not even have been necessarily essential; they could have been hand delivered by special courier.

The "complete" (almost so) three volume collection of messages between Churchill and Roosevelt referred to above contains only the most passing references to Magic or Ultra contents. They indicate that at least occasionally the summaries (if not actual decrypts) were shared. The edition of the three volume set argues that if and when these were sent, they were not considered formal president-prime minister exchanges and therefore are not included in the American and British archives as part of these. The editor observes that because of Anglo-American skittishness on the matter there is no way to document how many were transmitted or when they were sent.[65]

Of course non-Magic data (or conclusions based on such) could still be extraordinarily sensitive and could be communicated this way, regardless of how much and whether intercepts were communicated as well. On November 27, 1941, Capt. James Roosevelt, the president's son, appeared at BSC with a message to be relayed to London. As Stephenson reported it to his superiors, "Japanese negotiations off. Services expect action within two weeks."[66] (This incident lends a credence to the assertion made by others that James Roosevelt was regularly used for courier duty between BSC and Washington.[67]) Seeking additional confirmation and additional information, the Foreign Office rushed a message to the American ambassador. He was unavailable. He was out hunting.[68]

Stephenson claimed two thousand highly confidential messages passed between Churchill and Roosevelt via the BSC. This claim has been vigorously denied on the grounds that Stephenson is never mentioned in the known Churchill-Roosevelt exchanges (see below), and one would anticipate in any correspondence that bulky and prolonged at least some passing mention of either him or the BSC. More disturbing is the lack of clear-cut evidence that Stephenson had such a special relationship with Churchill that he would have been entrusted with the responsibility.[69] Furthermore, that Stephenson was not above inflating his own role is clear though the psychology behind it is murky: As Nigel West rightly observes, Stephenson's documentable and genuine role was "quite remarkable enough and never needed any embroidery or exaggeration to enhance it."[70]

None of the exhaustive (literally hundreds of pre-war and wartime) messages between Roosevelt and Churchill in Warren F. Kimball's massive three volume collection[71] explicitly refer to any correspondence transmitted by this source. On the other hand (in behalf of a covert BSC link), the alleged November 27 transmittal about the rupture in negotiations is not mentioned at all by Kimball in his compilation.

Furthermore, at least some communications seem to be missing from the collection. A November 24 Roosevelt memorandum on the American diplomatic stance is present, followed by a message of the 25th concerning the sending of William Bullitt as the president's representative to survey conditions in the Middle East. This is followed by five communications from Churchill. The next message from Roosevelt (actually a telephone conversation with the prime minister) was on December 7, followed on December 8 by a message on the best timing of the British declaration of war on Japan. *One would expect some kind of communication between the 24th message and the war break-out communications of December 7 and 8.* Hence inherent probability backs up the claim that *some kind* of message was sent on war-related subjects during this undocumented interim. In fact, one would expect a number of them.

There is direct evidence of at least some additional communications that have not been released and which passed through somebody's (BSC's?) hands. A late September message of the preceding year (1940) was allegedly passed through BSC and warned the British that the

Japanese invasion of Indo-China was to occur that day, September 22 (British time).[72] This message is preserved in neither the open British nor American archives. Yet two different British leaders who saw the message (or had it summarized for them) mention it. This seems positive proof that Roosevelt had a conduit outside the regular naval and diplomatic channels that he utilized. For want of an alternative, the claim that BSC *was* that alternative is quite credible—which is not quite the same thing as claiming that "Intrepid" of BSC was not above exaggerating his own role in the matter.

What is especially intriguing is that this incident illustrates that even the most "secure" cipher could be jumbled and confused in transmission. Sir Anthony Eden recorded the perplexity the communication had left his government:

> On Sunday, September 22nd, I was working quietly through some papers, when the Prime Minister sent me a message that President Roosevelt had telegraphed saying three o'clock that afternoon was zero hour for the German invasion. If I thought I should come back, he would give me dinner. I replied that it was wet and blowing and I felt quite safe. I went to the top of the hill which overlooked the Channel and afterwards sent a further message, reporting it was so rough that any German who attempted to cross the Channel would be very sea-sick.
>
> The next day the puzzle of Roosevelt's warning was resolved. *The President of the United States used from time to time to send pieces of information which he thought might be useful to us in our embattled island* [added emphasis]. But this time the code had got mixed and the invasion should have read the invasion of Indo-China, which proved true enough, and fateful.[73]

The second source for this otherwise undocumented message is the permanent undersecretary in the Foreign Office, Sir Alexander Cadogan. Sir Cadogan recorded in his diary that he discussed the message with the "Counselor" of the U.S. embassy.[74] This could be read as an indication that it was received via the embassy, but since it is lacking in the available archives this seems unlikely. As diary entries often are when time is short, the entry is so attenuated that all such details are omitted.

British Conduits: BSC and the Office of Strategic Services

Above I have attempted to sketch broadly speculation as to the use of the BSC to provide data to the president. The BSC, unquestionably, attempted to link its services with those of other important American war-related institutions of the period. The Office of Strategic Services (intended to be America's non-military intelligence agency) had the highest priority.

At least in regard to European data, BSC was a backdoor means of providing information to the United States via the OSS. An internal OSS document refers to how during July of 1941 "arrangements were made by Mr. Stephenson [head of B.S.C.] to provide the General [Donovan, head of O.S.S.] with a regular flow of secret information from sources available to his own organization, including highly confidential British censorship material not normally circulated outside British government departments."[75] To facilitate this exchange, Donovan set up a branch office of the OSS (at that early date still known as the coordinator of information) in New York City.[76] This data, in turn, was passed on to the president and the secretary of state and other relevant officials.[77] The claim, in some sources, that Stephenson had regular secret meetings with Roosevelt in 1940 and 1941 is, however, quite questionable.[78]

The BSC conduit was Donovan's main source of foreign intelligence data until months after Pearl Harbor. The British, in fact, took the view that it was "entirely dependent on it" during this period.[79] One example of such information —though not its British source—became public knowledge at the time. This was the (in)famous map of how Germany planned to divide South America if it gained control over that continent. It was disclosed to the public by President Roosevelt in late October 1941. The president had received it from Donovan. Donovan had received it from Stephenson.[80] The disguised origin was particularly desirable since the map was a British made fake.[81]

Indeed, in the kind of conviction they dared not voice aloud to the Americans, the British privately considered that through their information and advisers they were effectively using Donovan as a tool to accomplish their own policy goals.[82] The reality, of course, was a tad more complicated: Much of what the British desired to see done, key American officials were already inclined toward and simply sought an excuse or justification for public consumption. Furthermore, the Americans considered the data being provided as valuable in its own right, to meet needs they could not yet supply on their own. In a very real sense, then, *both* countries were attempting to "use" the other. Of the two, the British were coming out far ahead.[83]

Of course, the OSS was already initiating, within its limited resources, its own intelligence gathering initiatives. (Presumably, most of the results were provided the British in light of their cooperation in establishing the OSS as a functional organization.) For example, in August 1941, Donovan arranged to have Edgar A. Mowrer, a friend of his for over two decades, to use his work for the *Chicago Daily News* as reportorial "cover" for a fact finding mission to the Far East.

Mowrer's wide ranging jaunt included stops in Singapore, Chungking (China), Batavia (Dutch East Indies), and the Philippines. In the Philippines he had an interview with MacArthur, but the general's optimism did not dilute his memories of the fear an American businessman had expressed to him while there: The Japanese would soon be striking toward the Philippines rather than, as often expected, toward Russia. Mowrer shared the information, evaluations, and suspicions of those he met with Adm. Husband Kimmel, the Pacific Fleet commander, and then with an O.S.S.-army conference meeting that Donovan held in his Washington headquarters.[84]

British Conduits: BSC and the Federal Bureau of Investigation

J. Edgar Hoover was as prickly a bureaucrat as ever ran a government agency. Positively, the enhanced honesty and efficiency of the FBI during the 1930s was the direct result of Hoover's overhaul of the agency. Negatively, he was a determined empire builder, dedicated to expanding the FBI's responsibilities against potential foreign enemies working within the country. Ideally, he desired to see those responsibilities expanded outside the nation's boundaries as well. So far as internal subversion went, the FBI was all that was needed—period, and Hoover waged endless bureaucratic war against anyone who infringed upon his agency's prerogatives.

It was essential for the British Security Coordination to gain at least tacit cooperation from Hoover's agency in order to carry out its varied responsibilities of propaganda, undermining pro-German groups, investigating individuals who potentially might act against British interests, and a wide variety of other activities. (Publicly it was the Passport Control Office for Britain; in private it was recognized by the Americans as responsible for the security and safety of all shipments being sent to Britain— a legitimate and significant responsibility in its own right, but only the tip of the iceberg.) Without Hoover's cooperation, many of these wider tasks would have been impractical or impossible; in the worst case scenario, overt FBI action against the BSC could have been possible.

The fact that BSC represented a foreign power—albeit a friendly one—did not endear it to Hoover. Worse yet, BSC's Stephenson was a close friend of the OSS's Donovan—enough to set off every bureaucratic alarm bell in Hoover's brain, especially when data was being provided Donovan that Hoover was convinced should only be provided his own agency.[85]

Two factors overcame Hoover's reluctance. The first was a direct instruction from President Roosevelt to cooperate with the BSC in its various activities.[86] The icing on the cake was the active cooperation of the BSC in investigating potential "fifth column" subversive movements both in the United States and south of the border.[87] The latter was especially important to Hoover's desire to expand the responsibilities and breadth of operations of the FBI. Although only limited intelligence data in the sense of direct war-making information would flow through the BSC/FBI back channel, large amounts of data *did* change hands as to activities that could obstruct American effectiveness and success in any war that might break out. Furthermore, of 42 German spies and agents arrested in 1941 and 1942, 36 identifications had originally been provided by Stephenson's British Security.[88]

Which brings us to one area that was unquestionably within the jurisdiction of Hoover's agency: domestic spying. Cracking spy rings, of course, was easier said than done. BSC, as just noted, was invaluable in providing leads.

One hindrance to effective anti-espionage action was the American veneration for civil liberties in times when the United States was not directly engaged in a fighting war. For example, there was no legal or practical way for American mail to be examined systematically for evidence of spying. On the other hand it was fully within the rights of the British, who *were* at war, to do as they thought best. Hence the American authorities arranged for all outgoing mail to be routed through either Trinidad or Bermuda. Major British operations were created in both locations to covertly examine all mail. Courtesy of an arrangement between the BSC and the FBI, all suspicious correspondence was copied and provided to the FBI.[89]

The Canadian-BSC-FBI link should not be overlooked, either. A number of Canadian decrypts from the German spy networks in South America were passed to the FBI via the BSC.[90] These, at BSC's specific request, were forwarded in the original language and then translated by the BSC staff, resulting in differences of wording between the Canadian translation and that provided to the Americans even though the same intercept was the basis.[91] Until at least the winter of 1941, Hoover's agency shared these with the Office of Strategic Services.[92] (This was another apparent case, like those noted earlier, of some Americans getting data and, unless they consciously shared it with other agencies, the data going no further.)

A South American German spy reported to Berlin from a source it regarded as highly reliable concerning the movement of a massive fleet at sea as of December 3 (translated into English on the 6th).[93] Apparently Hoover immediately shared this with the State Department and the military, since he wrote a letter of inquiry to several such officials on December 9 attempting to discover why the significance of this evidence had been ignored. He received no reply.[94]

Some top-level FBI officials were convinced that this FBI provided data had been overlooked by the other departments and that the evidence of these documents clearly pointed to the imminent outbreak of war.[95] It must be remembered, however, that hindsight is always clearer than foresight, not to mention that Hoover was always determined to enhance the status of his agency at the cost of rivals. Hence the interpretive spin Hoover and his top executives put on the evidence they provided must be taken with a considerable grain of salt.

British Conduits: BSC and American Military Intelligence

An unknown number of contacts occurred between Stephenson and Army Intelligence. General Miles, its assistant chief of staff, sent a memo to Army Intelligence's New York representative about Stephenson: "The subject, who is an Englishman, and whose telephone number is Circle 6-8580, will call you up in the near future. He will tell you who he is, and you will find the contact of interest and value."[96] This was in October 1940, and the wording could reasonably be read as anticipating some type of continuing contact between the two. Some types of at least occasional contacts also occurred with the navy.[97]

The British, of course, appreciated the information that was sent their way as well. But there were times when it totally perplexed them. In the middle of 1941, a high British intelligence official described with a pungent comment certain recent reports funneled through BSC concerning Germany: "The Book of Revelations read backwards would be more helpful."[98]

General Miles spoke of the frequency with which general intelligence data on the Japanese military was shared with the British in his testimony to government investigators: "We exchanged information very freely with the British and, to a certain extent, with the Dutch. They were a little afraid to give us information, as I remember, but we were getting some."[99] He does not state, however, through which of several conduits (such as BSC) that this information came. Since Miles, in the immediately preceding testimony, is discussing data that came to Washington, it is likely that he is speaking of English data that was funneled to U.S. officials in that city rather than that which came from them in outlying sources (via the Philippines and Hawaii, for example).

British Conduits: BSC and the State Department

Beginning in March 1941 the reports received by the U.S. State Department from its consulate located in Vladivostock, USSR, were passed to the BSC for forwarding to London.[100] It is unclear whether this merely involved State Department data, conveyed without the department's awareness, or whether their own personnel were actively involved. Unquestionably the State Department was vigorously pro-British at this stage and it was far more likely done with active involvement on their part.

British Conduit to Hawaii

This is a convenient place to gather several strands of data. One of the most important concerns the establishment of intelligence links between the United States and Britain and their use to provide the Pacific Fleet (and other intelligence related authorities in Hawaii) with data to help them in their contingency planning. Related to this are the intra-Allied discussions of how better to share non-decrypt intelligence from the region and the establishment of a permanent British naval liaison at Hawaii.

Supplementing these matters are two other areas of concern. One revolves around strictly local efforts by the American authorities to gather further intelligence data related to Japanese capabilities and intents. Finally there is the matter of the effort of Australia to assure itself a special niche in the relationship of the United States with the nations of the Pacific.

Non-Decryption Intelligence: The British Secret Intelligence Service Link to Hawaii via the Philippines

As noted in the following chapter Gen. MacArthur's chief of intelligence dismissed the Hawaii link established by Gerald Wilkinson as evidence of a reputation enhancing personal character fault. This evidence is undermined by his own admission that Wilkinson functioned as a faithful agent of British intelligence. Furthermore, Wilkinson's superiors were well aware of what was going on and glad to utilize his availability. This is brought out in a telegram provided Clausen in his efforts to track down the ultimate source of certain information passed to the Americans. A British official (identified simply as "Jones") notes, "Wilkinson was unaware of source." Indeed, the official felt compelled to use Wilkinson because "I possessed no direct communication to Honolulu" and Wilkinson "appreciated that I possessed no direct communications."[1]

On August 22, 1941, the Navy's district intelligence officer, Capt. Irving H. Mayfield, wrote to the head of domestic intelligence (in the Office of Naval Intelligence) concerning Wilkinson's proposition and his personal background. In doing so he referred to the previous exchange with Washington on the subject:

> In reference (a), the District Intelligence Officer outlined the proposal of a Mr. Wilkinson, a British secret agent in the Far East, that an arrangement be effected whereby correspondence between him and his Honolulu agent, Mr. Harry Dawson, be carried in the special locked compartments of Pan American Airways clippers flying between Honolulu and Manila, in return for which accommodation Mr. Wilkinson would furnish the District Intelligence Officer and the Military Intelligence Division with information gathered by himself and his aides in the Far East, and of particular interest to the United States Army and Navy. It was proposed that the District Intelligence offices of the 14th and 16th Naval Districts should make the necessary arrangements with Pan American Airways.
>
> Reference (b) stated that the Department could not authorize the above plan at this time because of the status of the matter and the small amount of information submitted. The District Intelligence Officer informed Mr. Dawson of the Department's decision, and has decided to forwarded any further correspondence from Mr. Dawson to Mr. Wilkinson. However, every clipper from the Orient brings confidential mail from Mr. Wilkinson to Mr. Dawson, forwarded by the District Intelligence Officer, 16th Naval District.
>
> By dispatch from the District Intelligence Officer, 16th Naval District, the Commandant, 14th Naval District was informed that Mr. Wilkinson was thoroughly reliable and trustworthy. Investigation in Honolulu discloses that Mr. Wilkinson is the properly accredited branch manager in Manila for Theo. H. Davies & Co., Ltd., and that his wife is a granddaughter of the original Mr. Theodore H. Davies. This company is one of the five largest corporations in the Territory of Hawaii and, although incorporated as an Hawaiian corporation, the majority of its stock is held by

members of the Davies family who are British subjects and live in England.

Mr. Harry Dawson, above mentioned, is manager of the steamship department of Theodore H. Davies & Company, ltd., a British subject, and British Vice-Consul for Hawaii.

The District Intelligence Officer considers the information received from Mr. Wilkinson to be of value and requests authority by dispatch to effectuate the arrangements proposed by Mr. Wilkinson.

Information so far received by this office from Mr. Wilkinson has been furnished the Director of Naval Intelligence on 14th Naval District dissemination cards....[2]

An apparently later communication from Mayfield to the director of Naval Intelligence in Washington passes over the fact that the Clipper was being used to carry information on to Dawson and stresses, alone, the fact that the American side was receiving it: "British Agent in Manila continues to forward information via lock box in Pan American clipper planes to the District Intelligence Officer, 14th Naval District. *Much of this information is of value* to the Military Intelligence in Hawaii, and to this office as well as to the Office of the Federal Bureau of Investigation." Mayfield refers to specific reports, reaffirms their value, and notes that authority had been requested to approve officially the British utilization of the airplane lock box.[3]

On October 14, the Navy finally officially approved its use. In doing so, any quid pro quo (lock box for data) was explicitly rejected on the grounds that this method of providing the information was an inadequate one. The key sections follow:

> 1. In paragraph 1 of reference (a) the District Intelligence Officer stated that a British secret agent in the Far East suggested that an arrangement be effected whereby correspondence between him and his Honolulu agent could be carried in special locked compartment of the Pan-American Airways clipper between Honolulu and Manila, in return for which accommodation, the British agent in the Far East would furnish the District Intelligence Officer and the Military intelligence Division with information of particular interest to the United States Army and Navy as gathered by him or his agents in the Far East.
>
> 2. In reference (b), the Commander in Chief, Asiatic Fleet and the Commandant, Fourteenth naval District, were authorized to arrange for the transmission of correspondence between accredited British intelligence officers in the Far East and in the Fourteenth Naval District by locked com-

partments or locked boxes in the Pan-American Airways service between Honolulu and Manila wherever space and other considerations within the discretion of the Commander in Chief, Asiatic Fleet and of the Commandant, Fourteenth Naval District, render such service practicable.

3. It is to be understood that this service is not to be considered in exchange for information gathered by the British intelligence in the Far East and sent to the Fourteenth Naval District via clipper for transmission to the District Intelligence Officer. Such transmission is decidedly cumbersome, slow and impractical. Any such information should be transmitted by the British representatives to representatives of the Commander in Chief, Asiatic Fleet, for his information and further transmission at his discretion. The proper British authorities in Washington have been informed of the foregoing and requested to make arrangements accordingly.

4. As a matter of interest to the Commandant, Fourteenth Naval District, he is advised that information contained in enclosure (A) with reference (a) was not of importance or particular interest to the Division of Naval Intelligence, because it was too detailed in its nature, too local in its application and too late in its reception.

5. It is to be noted that reference (b) cancels reference (c).[4]

(Signed) A. G. Kirk

However true Washington's criticisms may have been in the abstract, Pearl Harbor conspicuously did not decline future offers of information, and the provision of British data continued down to the Pearl Harbor attack itself. The procedure violated the "best" and bureaucratically "most appropriate" chain-of-command in which the highest levels decided what was disseminated horizontally and downward. On the other hand the British intelligence provided an additional source of information free and independent of this preliminary screening, permitting the Hawaiian military authorities to supplement what they were receiving from mainland American sources. This and the possibility that they might catch something of significance missed by those higher up provided more than adequate reason to continue the arrangement.

The center of interest in the correspondence examined here has been the military and naval relevance of Wilkinson's data. Wilkinson was politically astute enough, however, to recognize that the passive cooperation of the FBI was desirable as well. At the least Hawaii was a very "American" piece of property (a territory decades from becoming a state), where the roots were long and deep and, unlike the Philippines, the linkage was regarded as permanent and irrevocable.

The intelligence activities of a foreign power—even a friendly one—would thus be far more likely to be scrutinized with care than when conducted farther abroad. In addition, the politically perceptive knew that FBI Director J. Edgar Hoover passionately wanted to expand the agency's role in espionage and intelligence operations. Providing his agency with intelligence data would be a means of buying his neutrality and, quite probably, make him more acquiescent to British activities on the American mainland as well.

In light of this political context it comes as little surprise that Wilkinson wanted to give the FBI the information that would be provided to Hawaii. The FBI agent in charge in Honolulu provided a statement in April 1945 concerning how his office became a party involved in the arrangements:

> Gerald Wilkinson, the manager for the Theo. H. Davies Co., Manila, P.I. [Philippine Islands] called on me about July 1941 and stated he was the representative in the Pacific area for the Special Intelligence Service of the British government, reporting direct to the British Foreign Office at London; that he had established Mr. Harry Dawson, an English citizen and British Vice Consul for the Hawaiian Islands, as the operative representative of the said SIS in the Hawaiian Islands; that Mr. Dawson would be concerned with no internal matters of the Hawaiian Islands, but would be concerned with developing foreign intelligence information pertaining to Japan, which information Dawson would get from persons returning to Hawaii from Japan; that Wilkinson proposed to furnish the FBI, ONI and G-2 at Honolulu, information, thru Dawson, of information received from other SIS operatives in the Pacific area, concerning conditions and intelligence affecting Japan; that pursuant to consent of higher authority, arrangements were made for the receipt of such information by the FBI, ONI and G-2 at Honolulu, and such information was furnished as proposed during the period from July to and including December, 1941....[5]

The handling of the information passed on to Hawaii is discussed in the government investigations from the standpoint of both the army and naval use of the information. First let us examine what the Army did with it. The contact there was with Lt. Col. Bicknell, who held the position of Assistant G-2 in the Hawaiian Department, from October 1940 through April 1943. His specific responsibility was counter-intelligence and his superior was Col. Kendall J. Fielder.[6]

Although a subsidiary of G-2 (whose primary emphasis was "to safe-

guard against internal disorders and sabotage"),[7] Bicknell's unit constituted the numerical bulk of the section. As Col. Fielder summarized the
organizational arrangement,

> The organization of the Section just prior to and on
> December 7, 1941, was as follows:
> a small administrative section of one officer, two clerks;
> a public relations section of two officers and three clerks;
> a combat intelligence section of two officers and several
> clerks organized to expand rapidly in an emergency;
> a counter-intelligence section of approximately twelve
> officers and thirty agents, known at that time as the "Contact
> Office," in charge of Lt. Col. George Bicknell and located in
> the City of Honolulu. Other than the "Contact Office," the
> G-2 section was at Fort Shafter, and most of the personnel
> had dual responsibility since the section was small and the
> duties varied.[8]

Bicknell himself confirmed that various British Secret Intelligence
Service reports introduced before the joint congressional committee had
been provided him and "received by me on or about the dates set forth on
the documents." This information was provided "to General Short promptly,
in one form or another."[9] This was done through both personal contact and
the regularly scheduled weekly staff meeting. Both the elements of personal
contact and the weekly meetings were described in the Fielder affidavit:

> It was customary prior to December 7, 1941, to hold weekly
> staff meetings, usually on Saturday morning; at that time the
> Contact Officer [Bicknell] presented a brief summary of the
> international situation while the undersigned [Fielder] usu-
> ally presented the European War situation. The Contact
> Officer then reported items of information to me or the Chief
> of Staff, or the Commanding General, prior to 7 December,
> 1941. I informed both the CG [commanding general] and
> C/S [chief of staff] of everything that came to my attention
> regardless of its source. The three of us were in adjoining
> rooms at headquarters and were in contact many times each
> [day?].[10]

The data provided by Wilkinson in the Philippines to the vice coun-
sel and, thereby, to the army,[11] was also distributed to a wider audience.
To accomplish this Bicknell issued "signed weekly estimates which were
mimeographed and distributed to the chief of staff; G-2, Hawaiian
Department; G-2, Hawaiian Air Force; G-2, Schofield Barracks; G-3,
Hawaiian Department; FBI, Honolulu, and ONI [Office of Naval
Intelligence], Honolulu...."[12]

These written summaries were important because not all of the British documents were shared with all three parties involved in the arrangement. If information went to only one party, Clausen implied that it was most likely to be Captain Mayfield of the Navy:

> Now, this Exhibit 6 [of the Clausen Report] are the British Secret Intelligence Service dispatches from Manila to Hawaii and what I did was to speak in Hawaii to the three sources or three recipients. They were not always the same. In some cases you will see marked on these in my exhibit that the copies went to, perhaps, maybe in some cases just to Captain Mayfield. Now, Captain Mayfield was the District Intelligence Officer. In some cases they went to the three of them.[13]

Although Clausen does not speculate as to what percentage went to only one source, one can perceive the rationale behind it. The army, navy, and FBI would be especially interested in information that had the most important impact upon their own functions, though they would have at least broad interest in other reports as well.

The navy was the other military recipient of Wilkinson's information. The most important user of it was Comdr. Edwin Layton, the Pacific Fleet's chief intelligence officer. These reports were one of a number of sources he weaved together in preparing his estimates of current Japanese military activity and potential future actions. In his most complete description of the types of data he had available, he told the Navy Court of Inquiry,

> The main sources of information were from Chief of Naval Operations, Office of Naval Intelligence, who forwarded us reports from naval observers, naval attaches, other competent observers, State Department, consular agents. Also from Chief of Naval Operations via Office of Naval Communications certain highly secret information under the classification of communication intelligence.
>
> Also local reports from the local district intelligence office here regarding local security conditions; *through liaison with British intelligence of the Secret Intelligence Service, intelligence as to Japan's activities in the Far East* [emphasis added]. Also from the commandants of the Twelfth and Sixteenth Naval Districts and Panama Sea Frontier regarding movements of Japanese merchant vessels; reports also from the Commandant of the Third Naval District regarding movements of Japanese merchant vessels. I think that is all.[14]

Omitted from his list was the U.S. Army, which routed its information through the ONI.[15] Layton supplements his list of sources in a later affidavit. There he refers to how "by mid-November 1941 a series of intelligence reports from various sources, including Dutch, British, Chinese, and American, collectively indicated that Japan was on the move in a southerly direction. These consisted of Consular Reports, Attaché and Agent Reports, [ship] Master's Reports, and reports from other Intelligence Agencies...."[16]

When Layton referred to the matter at all, it was common for him to refer to the *fact* of receiving British data but without any detailed discussion of its amount or significance. Before the Roberts Commission he simply referred vaguely to "reports ... from British intelligence...."[17] To the Hewitt Inquiry he referred to "information passed to me from British intelligence sources in the Far East...."[18] He informed the Army Board, "There was also information of the highest secrecy from the British sources and other sources which indicated invasion of the Kra Isthmus was impending" as of middle and late November 1941.[19]

An interesting side issue is the question of who provided Layton his copies of the British material. It was certainly not the FBI's Shivers, for he makes clear that "my direct liaison on Naval matters with other Government Agencies in the Fourteenth Naval District" was through Mayfield.[20] Nor was it the Army's Bicknell since he had met him only once.[21] The most natural source would be via his fellow officer, Mayfield.

Layton's testimony, however, indicates that at least some of it may have been provided directly by Dawson at the consulate. In at least one place he refers to information "received by the British Consul," as if he had provided it directly.[22] Before the Hart Inquiry he remarked that he received information "via liaison with British intelligence, *both* through ONI *and* direct through a representative attached to the British Consulate in Honolulu."[23] If such a dual channel existed it was presumably established in the hope of cementing friendly relations with a more importantly placed American officer than even Mayfield. It is interesting that in his postwar memoir, neither Wilkinson, Dawson, nor the British-Hawaii linkage is mentioned at all by Layton.[24]

However it reached Layton, the information itself was also forwarded to Washington. Hawaii was naturally happy to receive any information it could. In contrast, the attitude of the Office of Naval Intelligence in Washington toward the material was far more cynical. Adm. A. G. Kirk described the materials sent from June through October as "not of importance or of particular interest to the Division of Naval Intelligence, because it was too detailed in its nature, too local in its application, and too late in its reception."[25]

One of the British-provided documents is of interest not only for the information it provided but also because of what it reveals concerning the British conception of the proper use of intelligence information. This was a report that resulted in Wilkinson's own company using the information as well, in order to cancel shipments and avoid financial loss. In this case the message was one received by "cable," indicating that the Hawaiian consulate *did* have its own codes that could be used to receive information from the Philippines and that the lock box method was not an essential of communication. Even so the British shared it with the local American authorities. The joint congressional committee was read the document, which illustrates the type of report shared with the United States:

> Urgent Cable received from Manila night of December 3, 1941.
>
> We have received considerable intelligence confirming following developments in Indochina.
>
> A-1. Accelerated Japanese preparation of airfields and railways.
>
> 2. Arrival since November 10 of additional 100,000 repeat 100,000 troops and considerable quantities fighters medium bombers tanks and guns (75 millimeter).
>
> B. Estimate of specific quantities have already been telegraphed Washington November 21 by American military intelligence here.
>
> Our considered opinion concludes that Japan envisages early hostilities with Britain and the United States. Japan does not repeat not intend to attack Russia at present but will act in South.
>
> You may inform Chiefs of American Military and Naval Intelligence Honolulu.
>
> Carbon copy: Colonel Bicknell, Mr. Shivers, Captain Mayfield.[26]

Since this information is referred to as having already been provided Washington via the American intelligence establishment in the Philippines, why was the need felt to share it with Hawaii as well? Was there the fear that the significance of the information might not have been adequately relayed down the administrative totem pole?

Be that as it may, in his congressional testimony, Col. Clausen noted that this report was shared with a British businessman and cites this as an example of British willingness to utilize secret data to protect the business interests of its citizens:

Colonel Clausen.... I have a statement from the man who got it. That was received by [the] Theodore F. Davies [firm], on the strength of which they canceled some shipments from the Philippines. *The British always tied in their magic to the commercial interests of their country* [emphasis added].

Senator Ferguson. Colonel, when you say the British always tied it in, you mean that the British used the messages to take care of and protect her commercial shipments?

Colonel Clausen. Yes, sir. There, you see, this message that I have just read for the Vice President, was one of many sent by a man named Wilkinson, who was in Manila. Wilkinson was in the commercial business.[27]

To be even more exact than Clausen was, both Wilkinson and the Hawaiian Vice Counsel Dawson were employed by that firm. On the other hand there is nothing in the government investigations to support an accusation that such information sharing with private concerns was ongoing, either with British run businesses in general or with Wilkinson's firm in particular. On a sporadic and occasional basis there is nothing to argue against it, either. It would certainly have been felt justified by the participants as rudimentary common sense and nothing more than unofficially confirming the usual press reports of the danger of imminent war. (Should their own businesses be financially scorched when they had knowledge to prevent it?)

The president of the company provided this 1945 account of how he came to have the report:

> You asked me to recall the circumstances surrounding my receipt of confidential information before December 7, 1941, which was so indicative of coming trouble in the Philippine area that I had acted immediately to cancel orders for shipment to that Territory.
>
> My records indicate that on December 4th, I telephoned to Mr. C. V. Bennett, Manager of our San Francisco office, and asked him to take steps to cancel all out-standing orders for shipment to the Philippine Islands and to endeavor to stop shipments that were en route there.
>
> I personally received no message on this subject from the Philippines, but I saw a copy of a message dispatched by Col. G. H. Wilkinson (then working secretly for the British Government) addressed to his agent in Honolulu, and he had requested the agent to show me the message. Mr. Harry L. Dawson, the agent in question, is sitting beside me while I dictate this memorandum, and states that after showing this message to me a copy of it was left with Col. Bicknell, Capt.

Mayfield and Mr. Robert Shivers, then with the FBI. Mr. Dawson finds that all his records of this incident were destroyed immediately after December 7, 1941.

On December 15th I wrote to Mr. Bennett as follows: "Thank you for your letter of December 5th about Philippine indent orders. It is certainly interesting to say the least that we should have taken steps on December 4th to stop this type of business. I took some similar precautions here at the same time, but cannot give any logical explanation as to why I had taken such steps. it just looks like one of those lucky hunches that one gets at times."

I do not recall, exactly, what was in the message that was shown to me, but believe it indicated some Japanese troop dispositions which were very illuminating in the light of diplomatic exchanges then taking place. I do not believe that the message said that trouble would begin on December 7th; but as I told you today the general tone of the message was sufficiently alarming to cause a reaction in the mind of a businessman, strong enough to warrant the cancellation of a considerable volume of orders for delivery in the Philippines.

I am sorry that I have no other data that might throw light on this subject; and in the light of what I have said above in connection with Mr. Dawson's files, he is not submitting a memorandum on this subject; but I can say that his recollection of the incident is substantially in agreement with what I have given you herein.

jer-m

John E. Russell,
President, Theo. H. Davies & Co., Ltd.
April 10, 1945
At Honolulu.[28]

The burning by Dawson of his records might be read in a conspiratorial sense: Burnt documents (today, shredded ones!) always tend to be read in such a fashion. One should remember, however, that Hawaii was swept by a tidal wave of fear and insecurity as the result of the destruction inflicted upon the Pacific Fleet. Invasion seemed a real possibility. Destruction of unneeded files was a natural and understandable reaction.

Resident British Naval Liaison with the American Pacific Fleet

In November 1940 Comdr. C. R. L. Parry traveled to the United States as one of three "observers" assigned by Britain to American duties.

Officially Parry was assigned to observer status on the battleship *West Virginia*. His real function, however, was to serve the broader purpose of emergency conduit to the British military. Indeed, he carried with him to Hawaii highly secure ciphers for emergency communication—a clear preparation for whatever contingencies lay ahead.[29]

In May 1941 the ranking officer of the New Zealand navy wrote Parry raising the issue of a more active exchange of data. "We have a good deal of information both from the Naval and Air aspect about our area, but naturally I do not know whether the United States authorities are more or less up to date than we are. It is obvious that we could each learn a good deal from the other."[30]

During the summer Parry's status was upgraded from "observer" to that of a formal "liaison officer."[31] As part of his new responsibilities, he traveled to the capitals of Australia and New Zealand as well as the FECB in Singapore. He carried with him a request from the Pacific Fleet for data on Japanese held islands in the South Pacific and as up-to-date as possible naval charts depicting them. He was able to gain a good supply of both for the Americans.[32]

Proposals for More Comprehensive Anglo-American Sharing of Pacific Intelligence Data

On May 31, 1941, the army's military attaché in London presented a War Department proposal for a full sharing of intelligence data in the Orient. On June 11, the British instructed their Far Eastern personnel to share all information except the highly sensitive Secret Intelligence Service and Special Operations Executive material—these represented a major potential loophole, depending upon how the directive was interpreted upon the local basis.[33]

The British at least did not think the Americans were being adequately cooperative in the matter. In July 1941 to the British War Council (an interservice conclave that charted war policy) passed on a request to the American naval attaché urging greater exchange of reports. It stressed more than six priority sites in Asia that particularly concerned them.[34] The U.S. Navy Department discussed the matter with the army and both services pledged to have their attachés in the specified cities begin a regular exchange of data with the British.[35]

The British quickly responded that they had issued orders for their own attachés to begin implementation of the proposal as well. The Admiralty recommended that, in addition, regular contact should be maintained with the FECB in order for the Americans to obtain data from Britain's Secret Intelligence Service operatives in the region.[36]

Since neither New Zealand nor Australia was aware of the agreement, the British informed them of it in September. It urged similar complete interchange of data—with the sole exception of decrypt material which needed to be solely sent to the FECB rather than the different countries independently.[37]

Australian Efforts to Reach an Accommodation with the United States

The Australian-American effort to build up a closer bilateral relationship was not related to the narrow area of intelligence data. It embraced the broader scope of the relationship of the two powers and ultimately involved Washington, Hawaii, and the Philippines in the effort.

In November 1940, Australia dispatched Comdr. H. M. Burrell to the United States in civilian guise with a two-fold agenda. Publicly, he attempted to speed up the purchase of material for the Australian navy. In private, he briefed key intelligence offices in Army G2, the ONI, and the State Department with a considerable amount of regional intelligence data. In Hawaii, he stopped to similarly brief Pacific Fleet intelligence personnel. Soon after arriving at home, he was returned to Washington as the country's naval attaché.[38]

The following November, Gen. MacArthur sent Maj.-Gen. Lewis H. Breton on a mission to Australia to discuss the building and preparation of the air transport bases that had been agreed to during discussions between the two nations. A secondary goal was to arrange contingency operating guidelines for the American forces that would pass through the country in wartime and to assure that they could adequately carry out further training. With war palpably imminent, the Australian government greeted Breton with great enthusiasm.[39]

Independent or semi-independent action by the Australians grew from their exposed position as a geographically large but population-limited nation far from the British homeland. The two perspectives inevitably produced points of tension, disagreement, and even suspicion.

Even with the best of good will on the part of Britain, Australia's first security interest had to be in the region nearest to it rather than

Europe. The regional source for Commonwealth military intelligence data in general was the FECB. The suspicion that it was not adequately alert to Australia's interests and need for intelligence and naval cooperation with the Dutch in Java led Australia to establish its own direct ties independent of the Singapore operation. The conduit was the naval liaison officer assigned by the Netherlands to Melbourne. In April of 1941 New Zealand also started utilizing his services to provide information that might be of use to the Dutch and, in turn, to seek data that might be of value in its own defense efforts.[40] In September Australia assigned its own naval officer to Batavia, Dutch East Indies, to further implement the exchange of data. The same month found him gaining responsibility for providing information to and from New Zealand as well.[41]

In spite of this additional conduit for information, there remained the lingering suspicion that potentially important data was being denied by the home country of Great Britain. A superior wrote to the Australian liaison officer in Batavia in October of 1941, "I have an uneasy feeling that we, here in Australia, do not receive all the information that Singapore has to give us, and that Singapore does not provide all the information they should to [the Dutch naval forces in the East Indies]."[42]

Locally Gained Non-Decrypt Intelligence Sources Utilized by the United States

The emphasis on Anglo-American cooperation should not blot out the fact that the Americans developed their own *local* sources of intelligence data as well. These imitated the types of techniques the British used independently in other locations.

Bugging of telephone lines had proved itself a British intelligence asset, for example. The pre-war Japanese embassies of both Thailand and Japan had taps placed on their telephone wires. In February 1941 the results were considered sufficiently important that a summary of the conversations were provided to President Roosevelt by Great Britain.[43]

The United States tapped the telephone lines of the Honolulu consulate for a lengthy period in 1941 as well. This was blatantly illegal—an explicit violation of the 1934 Federal Communications Act, which (Section 605) forbade any interception of either incoming or outgoing foreign communications.[44] When his superiors refused to defy the prohibition the 14th Naval District chief intelligence officer implemented taps on his own initiative.[45] Up to 60 messages a day were intercepted.[46]

In spite of the significant number of messages involved during the time the wiretaps were in place, nothing useful was discovered that materially assisted war planning.[47] Common prudence would have led to a reluctance to be very explicit on the telephone;[48] on the other hand, with whom the consulate spoke, about what, and how long would provide at least some broad guidance of potential security concerns if war broke out.

When David Sarnoff, president of RCA, visited Hawaii, he met with the commandant of the local naval district, Adm. Claude C. Bloch. Bloch convinced him that it would be highly useful to obtain copies of all Japanese consulate telegraphic communications, and it was agreed that RCA would pass these to the district's intelligence officer, Capt. Mayfield.[49] These began to be passed along in December, just before overt warfare broke out.[50] It could not begin sooner because the consulate divided its outgoing traffic between two companies, and it was not RCA's turn until December 1st.[51]

The communications were in the J-19 diplomatic code, which was far less secure than Purple. Furthermore, the solution could be in the hands of Pearl Harbor within 12 hours of being received in Washington.[52] It could be, not necessarily was. The process of J-19 decryption and translation there could lag as much as two weeks behind the date of initial interception.[53]

The new system provided Pearl with its own source of messages to decrypt on a local basis. Unfortunately, Pearl's new source of data was too little, too late. Indeed, the original "bomb plot" message (as it is commonly called) that divided the harbor into zones for reporting purposes was sent back on September 24, 1941. Like so much else it had not been passed on from Washington, either.[54]

Much of the diplomatic correspondence was only indirectly relevant to the military—by revealing attitudes, inclinations, and policy shifts—and, on that grounds its not being conveyed can be defended . In contrast, the "bomb plot" message was *directly* and militarily relevant to the Pearl Harbor command. Its not being forwarded represented a major blunder. Whether it would have done anything more than heighten the already high "war nerves" in Hawaii is one of the unanswerable questions of the period. In retrospect one would think so—but until the actual attack would it have been regarded as all that conclusive?

British Conduit to the Philippines

Gerald Wilkinson: The British SIS Link for Intelligence Data

The non-decrypt connection between British Intelligence in the Far East and both the Philippines and Hawaii was through Mr. Gerald Wilkinson. As a British business executive in Hawaii who was acquainted with Wilkinson's pre-war status later recalled, Wilkinson was "then working secretly for the British Government...."[1] Wilkinson's public position was that of manager for the Manila branch of Theodore H. Davies & Company.[2]

The longest single discussion of the Britisher in the government investigations comes in the form of a lengthy and vitriolic discussion by the officer who had been head of Gen. MacArthur's intelligence operations in the Philippines just before war broke out:

> 8 May 1945
> The British SIA messages, their purport and evolution and the curious role played by Mr. Gerald Wilkinson, in Manila and Hawaii are an integral part of this investigation, in my opinion.
>
> The whole story is one of duplicity, evasion, bargaining, horse-trading of information and a sort of E. Phillips Oppenheim international intrigue.
>
> Wilkinson married into the Davies family and represented his father-in-law, in Manila, as a sugar broker, for many years;

hence, the casual reference to a "Colonel Wilkinson", that appears in the affidavits of Mr. Russell and Dawson, suggesting a perfect stranger are obviously intended to be misleading. Wilkinson combined the convenient status of a respected local business man, with that of a secret agent, reporting to the British Ministry of Information; contrary to U.S. Law, he never registered as a foreign agent. He apparently came out of hiding in Manila, and contacted or obtained tolerance by then G-2's Philippine Department, Colonels O'Rear, retired, and J. K. Evans, MID. When I took over he approached me, quoting Evans, etc.

I was not impressed with the intelligence material he desired to file with me; they contained mimeo reprints of old Jap military data and some sprinkling of China-based reports. It became apparent to me, though, that Wilkinson had dealings with Hawaii and the local Navy, that he possessed his own cryptographic systems and decoding clerks, etc. I became convinced that his main purpose was to ingratiate himself into some official Army-Navy recognition, that he was willing to trade information for that recognition but that he was and still is an agent of British authorities, reporting thereto and executing orders therefrom. This net of potential spies is world wide; it is still in operation; I employ both SIA and SOE, British, and find them loyal to no one but themselves and the Empire.

My intelligence evaluation of his messages to Hawaii is not high—a horse-trading proposition, pure and simple; I am convinced that this bundle represents not all of the messages sent; the commercial deductions are obvious; Davies canceled sugar shipments in the nick of time.

Wilkinson is a completely untrained civilian. His Government gave him a military status to protect him, in case of capture. He attached himself to us at the outbreak of the War, leaving his wife and children to fend for themselves, in the Japanese-occupied city; they were promptly interned, in Sto Tomas, for the duration.

We made use of him and his cypher system, to send an occasional message to Wavell and Singapore; he continued to report "home" though his stuff was severely edited by me; the General finally sent him to Wavell's Headquarters, as a liaison, utilizing his cypher system; he then made his way deviously to Washington and London, where he capitalized heavily on this "status" with GHQ, USAFFE; he was "promoted" to Colonel and attempted to return to our Headquarters, as a "liaison"; he even had the support of the Prime Minister; with a complete lack of military knowledge, such a position had its ludicrous side, except for local espionage, and we declined to have him. He was promptly demoted and attached to duty with the British Office of Information at Washington-New York.

> C. A. Willoughy, [signature]
> C. A. Willoughby,
> Major General, G.S.C.,
> Asst. Chief of Staff, G-2
> General Headquarters, SWPA.[3]

Although the bias is vehement, Gen. Willoughby still provides a great deal of concise information: the pre-existing close connection with American army and naval intelligence, the source of the information in Singapore, and the maintenance of Wilkinson's own communications system with both Singapore and Australia. Much of the vitriol must be dismissed: How many secret agents have *ever* registered as the agent of a foreign power—local law or not? If Wilkinson had his own decrypting facilities, why was Willoughby so naive as to believe that he could make him send back *edited* reports to Singapore?

As to Wilkinson's lack of "loyalty" that is hardly surprising— Wilkinson was a *British* national, not an American. He was loyal where he was supposed to be loyal—to Great Britain. (Note Willoughby's indignation that *all* British intelligence operatives he had met shared that priority.) Or could it be that Willoughby's real problem was lack of partisan loyalty to the MacArthur command? As to "deserting" his wife, that was indeed a startling act. On the other hand, if Wilkinson had remained behind and the Japanese had learned of his intelligence status would the life of either have been safe?

Willoughby's extremely negative evaluation of the intelligence information passed on by the British also deserves considerable skepticism. Although he may well have begun the relationship by providing "mimeo reprints of old Jap military data" in order to illustrate the material already provided, the information passed on to Hawaii (previous chapter) was ongoing and far more recent. It seems inherently improbable that he was not providing the same material to the Philippines. Like all intelligence data it was of varying qualities and reliability and a broad dismissal of it all suggests bias rather than conviction, an evaluation buttressed by the bitter tone of Willoughby's entire affidavit.

In one case, the information was deemed sufficiently credible to alter the sailing plans of an outward bound convoy from the Philippines. This information comes from no less than Joseph K. Evans, who himself was head of G-2 in the Philippine Department [army] prior to his departure:

I left the Philippine Islands on 27 November 1941 enroute to the United States by Army Transport "H. L. Scott." About two days before I left I received information, *which to the best of my recollection came from the British Secret Intelligence Service at Singapore* [emphasis added], to the effect that hostilities between the United States and Japan were imminent and that large Japanese Naval forces were concentrating in the vicinity of the Marshall Islands. For these reasons, the convoy of which the "H. L. Scott" was a part did not proceed in the usual direct route from Manila to Pearl Harbor, but went by a circuitous route south through the Torres Strait which separates Australia and New Guinea.

On my arrival in Pearl Harbor on or about 15 December 1941, I for several hours discussed G-2 matters with Colonel Bicknell, Assistant G-2, Hawaiian Department, and Mr. Shivers, F.B.I. Agent in Charge. During the course of these discussions I told Colonel Bicknell and Mr. Shivers of the information I had received and was in turn told by Colonel Bicknell that he also had received this information at the same time.[4]

Since the "British Secret Intelligence Service in Singapore" had been the ultimate source of the information, and since Wilkinson functioned as its Philippine contact man, he is virtually certain to have been utilized in this case as well. This is reinforced by the fact that both Bicknell and Shivers also had the information, in Hawaii, and that it is well documented that Wilkinson was the source of their British Far Eastern originated data (see previous chapter).

During his own approximately two year sojourn as G-2 for the Philippine Department "there was ... close liaison with the British S.I.S. at Manila." That Wilkinson was the go-between is indicated by Evans's suggestion that to obtain further information on the matter one could consult "Lieutenant Colonel Gerald H. Wilkinson" whose then-current address was "International Building, Room 3501, 630 Fifth Avenue, Rockfeller Center."[5]

It is uncertain how much of Willoughby's low opinion of Wilkinson was contemporary with the outbreak of the war and how much grew out of suspicion (or knowledge) of Wilkinson's low opinion of Gen. MacArthur himself. Late in 1943, Wilkinson provided his S.I.S. superiors this vigorous critique of Gen. MacArthur's limitations:

> He is shrewd, selfish, proud, remote, highly-strung and vastly vain. He has imagination, self-confidence, physical courage and charm, but no humour about himself, no regard for truth, and is unaware of these defects. He mistakes his emotions

and ambitions for principles. With moral depth he would be a great man: as it is he is a near-miss, which may be worse than a mile ... his main ambition would be to end the war as pan-American hero in the form of generalissimo of all Pacific Theatres.[6]

Henry C. Clausen was a special investigator for the secretary of war in regard to the availability and handling of decrypt-related data. Three and a half decades later Clausen could still vividly recall Willoughby's gut resentment of Wilkinson. "By the way Willoughby said the name, I knew he disliked Wilkinson intensely...."[7] Clausen had his own opportunity to interview the Britisher. He conceded that it was "difficult to judge," but so far as he could tell, even though Wilkinson was "something of a maverick," that he was still an effective intelligence operative and one who "could be relied on."[8]

The British government and military certainly maintained its trust in Wilkinson, the slurs of Willoughby notwithstanding. Even before the war Wilkinson was on a close enough basis to Churchill to share lunch with him upon occasion.[9] (This may be, in part, because of the political connections of relatives.)[10] Indeed, the instruction to set up a direct Far Eastern link to the Americans in the Philippines and Hawaii was a policy decision determined by the head of the SIS himself, Sir Stewart Graham Menzies.[11] Menzies referred to his knowledge and use of the man in explaining why one particular message was sent through him: "Wilkinson was unaware of source [i.e., that it was a deduction based upon a decryption] and passed information to Honolulu as he appreciated that I possessed no direct communications."[12]

Furthermore, when Wilkinson was assigned to British Security Coordination it was far from the disgrace that Willoughby pictured it to be—and perhaps even genuinely *thought* (hoped?) it to be. Wilkinson was assigned there to head up the China section and he was given the assignment of setting up a spy system in China. Wilkinson successfully persuaded Donovan to agree to a joint SIS-OSS operation with that goal in mind. Indeed, Donovan came through with the initial financing for it and agreed that Wilkinson would be in charge.[13]

Efforts to Establish a More Formal Arrangement for Intelligence Sharing

In October 1941 the commander in chief of all British military activities in the region, Air Chief Marshal Sir Robert Brooke-Popham, visited

Gen. MacArthur in the Philippines. As he soon wrote to him, he considered such personal contacts the best and most effective means of securing understanding—far better than relying on the written word alone.[14]

An October 25, 1941, message from the army observer at Singapore informed Gen. MacArthur that he had received instructions from the War Department to begin data sharing. The same limitation that the British had placed was to be adhered to by the Americans as well: The observer had been instructed that "there will be free exchange of information *except cryptography* between intelligence agencies of [the] British and United States."[15] As near as he could tell, he reported, the "British are complying fully."[16]

Gen. MacArthur's own reservations about data sharing are revealed by two requests for specific information his command received. In late October he declined to provide anything and made a vague response claiming loyalty to the concept of data sharing but concern as to how it would be carried out. On November 18 the general responded to a request for information concerning the Japanese navy's activities at Camranh Bay with an evasive denial that his command had any data the British did not already possess.[17]

The navy moved slower in setting up top level cooperation. On December 2, 1941, Adm. Harold R. Stark, the American chief of Naval Operations, urged the prompt establishment of an exchange of data with Adm. Thomas C. Hart's equivalents in the British and Dutch navies in the region. Just as the British had exempted Ultra decrypts, the commander of the Asiatic Fleet was urged to provide data "except in cases where you consider it definitely inadvisable."[18] (Which would actually authorize a *broader* denial, if he so chose.) The medium of exchange would be the naval observers the United States had in Singapore and Batavia, Dutch East Indies.[19]

On December 5 secret meetings were held in Manila among Adm. Hart, Gen. MacArthur, and the newly arrived Vice Adm. Sir Tom Phillips, who was to command Britain's strengthened Far Eastern fleet. Although Adm. Hart found himself in vehement disagreement on some points (Phillips had more than a few contentious disagreements with Churchill as well), Hart was impressed by Vice Adm. Phillips's abilities. He also agreed to share four of his precious (and very limited) U.S. destroyers to help the British defend Singapore.[20] On the following day word that a major Japanese naval movement had entered the Gulf of Siam resulted in Vice Adm. Phillips cutting short his stay and returning to his command. This British data was forwarded to Washington by several circuits (indicating the diverse ways the goal could be accomplished): directly by Adm. Hart, through American personnel at Singapore, and from London via the U.S. embassy in that city.[21]

Joint Intelligence Sharing from Reconnaissance Flights

The implication of at least a limited ongoing exchange of non-decrypt information can also be deduced from the sharing of results of reconnaissance flights in the region. Speaking from the perspective of the Philippines, one U.S. officer first mentioned the American activities and then similar ones by the friendly powers

> We flew such aerial reconnaissance so as to insure that no surface force could approach Luzon from any of what might be termed the expected directions and escape detection. Chiefly, as I recall it now, we put most stress on the lines from slightly eastward of the east coast of Formosa down through Bako, where they had a naval base, and also towards Camranh Bay in the later days after the sighting of these various units moving south.
>
> We also had in the late days *some sort of an agreement with the Dutch about reconnaissance* [emphasis added] toward Palau, thinking that perhaps an attack on the Mindanao and Davao area would come from that direction. I am not prepared to try to give exact details of that because I can't recall that, sir. The Dutch were flying, I am certain, something up from the general Halmahera area towards Palau and, I think, we were flying something along the general Davao-Palau line.
>
> And *the British, too,* [emphasis added] in the final days were flying reconnaissance *out of Singapore* [emphasis added] towards Camranh Bay and over the Gulf of Siam. I think that is about all I can really recall about the reconnaissance.[22]

The existence of such broadly "coordinated" efforts (explicitly stated as to the Dutch and implied by the actions of the British since it would be inherently foolish to coordinate with the lesser power and ignore the more important one) required some means of exchange of information. The natural response to Mason's testimony was to ask whether he could "recall any [specific] information from the British and Dutch sources?" Mason could only remember receiving data from the former, "From the British, yes, sir. I have mentioned it previously. They sighted the task force that was to eventually invade Malaya somewhere in the general Poulo Condore area."[23] Since this was non-decrypt data, presumably Wilkinson functioned as the conduit.

The American reconnaissance program was instituted on a local basis. Acting on his own initiative (so the higher command could blame him if anything negative grew out of it), Adm. Hart had his planes begin scouting out Indochina harbors in late November 1941. This brought the first confirmation that a major Japanese fleet was gathering at Camranh Bay.[24]

The chance of a reconnaissance plane actually observing the Japanese fleet on its way to Pearl Harbor was minimal. If, by remote chance, one had accidentally done so—and the course had been carefully plotted to minimize the danger of anyone detecting the fleet—it is likely that the plane would have promptly been shot down. It might or might not have gotten off a message beforehand, but one could be sure that it would *not* have escaped safely.

Yet a report circulated in both the United States and Australia in the last years of the war that a reconnaissance plane of the Australians had detected the attack fleet three days before the attack. Three warnings, it was said, were provided to the Americans, but for unknown reasons these were not forwarded to Hawaii. In a September 17, 1944, cable to Secretary of State Hull, Prime Minister Curtin bluntly labeled this a "pure invention. Our cables had no data concerning the Japanese fleet."[25] Even if one were to dismiss this as a falsehood, one would still be faced with the improbability that such Australian aircraft would either stumble across the fleet or have successfully issued a radio warning if it had.

How European Ultra Was Revealed Before Congress— And No One Paid Attention

So far as public perception went, the "Ultra secret" (the breaking of the German codes) was not public knowledge until the 1970s. This was only because no one paid adequate attention to what was revealed in the joint congressional investigation of the attack on Pearl Harbor. In more than one way, the existence of this successful decryption program was explicitly referred to. The amount of detail requires quotation of material at greater length than in previous chapters, but the very volume of the evidence increases the wonder that the quite visible clues—no, not "clues," but *direct assertions*—could have been so easily missed.

General Marshall's Plea to Governor Dewey for Maintaining Decryption Secrecy

General George Mashall implied the existence of the Ultra secret to candidate Thomas Dewey in his successful effort to persuade the Republican not to make the Japanese code breaking a public political issue. With the 1944 presidential campaign well under way, Republican candidate Dewey was well aware of reports that the United States had been reading the Japanese ciphers prior to Pearl Harbor. There was a great chance that Dewey would make this a public issue and challenge the Roosevelt Administration on how the Japanese attack could have been so successful when the American side had such comprehensive access to the Japanese diplomatic exchanges. At the minimum this would imply near-criminal incompetence upon the part of the administration; at the most it would imply acquiescence in "allowing" the attack to occur. The issue would have revived prewar suspicions of Roosevelt, embittered a massive part of the public against Roosevelt, and probably given Dewey the edge in the presidential race.

Laying aside the political issues, Secretary of War George Marshall was far more concerned with the military repercussions of the exposure of the secret. He sent a letter dated September 25, 1944, to the candidate with the introductory capitalized words, "FOR MR. DEWEY'S EYES ONLY." Although the British role was not referred to in this initial correspondence, note the references (here italicized) to the fact that the *German* codes were being read as well:

> My Dear Governor:
> I am writing you without the knowledge of any other person except Admiral King (who concurs) because we are approaching a grave dilemma in the political reactions of Congress regarding Pearl Harbor.
> What I have to tell you below is of such a highly secret nature that I feel compelled to ask you whether to accept it on the basis of your not communicating its contents to any other person and returning this letter or not reading any further and returning the letter to the bearer.
> I should have preferred to talk to you in person but I could not devise a method that would not be subject to press and radio reactions as to why the Chief of Staff of the Army would be seeking an interview with you at this particular moment. Therefore I have turned to the method of this letter, to be delivered by hand to you by Colonel Carter Clarke who has charge of the most secret documents of the War and Navy Departments.
> In brief, the military dilemma resulting from Congressional political battles of the presidential campaign is this:
> The most vital evidence in the Pearl Harbor matter consists of our intercepts of the Japanese diplomatic communications. Over a period of years our cryptograph people analyzed the character of the machine the Japanese were using for encoding their diplomatic messages. Based on this a corresponding machine was built by us which deciphers their messages. Therefore, we possessed a wealth of information regarding their moves in the Pacific, which in turn was furnished the State Department—rather than as is popularly supposed, the State Department providing us with the information—but which unfortunately made no reference

whatever to intentions towards Hawaii until the last message before December 7th, which did not reach our hands until the following day, December 8th. [1]

Now the point to the present dilemma is that we have gone ahead with this business of deciphering their codes until *we possess other codes, German as well as Japanese*, but our main basis of information regarding Hitler's intentions in Europe is obtained from Baron Oshima's messages from Berlin reporting his interviews with Hitler and other officials to the Japanese Government. These are still in the codes involved in the Pearl Harbor events.

To explain further the critical nature of this set-up, which would be wiped out almost in an instant if the least suspicion were aroused regarding it, the battle of the Coral Sea was based on deciphered messages and therefore our few ships were in the right place at the right time. Further, we were able to concentrate our limited forces to meet their naval advance on Midway when otherwise we almost certainly would have been some 3,000 miles out of place. We had full information of the strength of their forces in that advance and also of the smaller force directed against the Aleutians which finally landed troops on Attu and Kiska.

Operations in the Pacific are largely guided by the information we obtain of Japanese deployments. We know their strength in various garrisons, the rations and other stores continuing available to them, and what is of vast importance, we check their fleet movements and the movements of their convoys. The heavy losses reported from time to time which they sustain by reason of our submarine action, largely result from the fact that we know the sailing dates and routes of their convoys and can notify our submarines to lie in wait at the proper points.

The current raids by Admiral Halsey's carrier forces on Japanese shipping in Manila Bay and elsewhere were largely based in timing on the known movements of Japanese convoys, two of which were caught, as anticipated, in his destructive attacks.

You will understand from the foregoing the utterly tragic consequences if the political debates regarding Pearl Harbor disclose to the enemy, *German or Jap*, any suspicion of the vital sources of information we now possess.

The Roberts' Report on Pearl Harbor had to have withdrawn from it all reference to this highly secret matter, therefore in portions it necessarily appeared incomplete. The same reason which dictated that course is even more important today because our sources have been greatly elaborated.

As a further example of the delicacy of the situation, some

of Donovan's people (the OSS) without telling us, instituted a secret search of the Japanese Embassy offices in Portugal. As a result the entire military attaché Japanese code all over the world was changed, and though this occurred over a year ago, we have not yet been able to break the new code and have thus lost this invaluable source of information, particularly regarding the European situation.

A recent speech in Congress by Representative Harness would clearly suggest to the Japanese that we have been reading their codes, though Mr. Harness and the American public would probably not draw any such conclusion.

The conduct of General Eisenhower's campaign and of all operations in the Pacific are *closely related in conception and timing to the information we secretly obtain through these intercepted codes.* They contribute greatly to the victory and tremendously to the saving in American lives, both in the conduct of current operations and in looking towards the early termination of the war.

I am presenting this matter to you, for your secret information, in the hope that you will see your way clear to avoid the tragic results with which we are now threatened in the present political campaign. I might add that the recent action of Congress in requiring Army and Navy investigations for action before certain dates has compelled me to bring back the Corps commander, General Gerow, whose troops are fighting at Trier, to testify here while the Germans are counter-attacking his forces there. This, however, is a very minor matter compared to the loss of our code information.

Please return this letter by bearer. I will hold it in my secret file subject to your reference should you so desire.

Faithfully yours,

(Sgd.) G. C. Marshall[2]

Although primarily concerned with the security of the Japanese decryption program, the intriguing brief glimpses into the anti-German effort not only verify its existence but also its importance. The British, however, have been left out of the decryption picture—so far.

Dewey declined to read any further than the letter's request for a commitment not to reveal its contents. A loud alarm would go off in the mind of any seasoned politician when receiving such a communication: Marshall was a top official of the administration and could easily be regarded as writing out of self-preservative interests. Furthermore the subject concerned Pearl Harbor and it could easily be read as a clear attempt to remove at least a large part of a potentially embarrassing issue that could be used against the incumbent.

Desperately seeking Gov. Dewey's cooperation, Gen. Marshall wrote a second letter to provide the same information, but avoided any commitment to absolute silence concerning matters he already knew. He noted to the joint committee that, "The second letter is dated the 27th of September, 1944, and is headed 'top Secret,' and 'FOR MR. DEWEY'S EYES ONLY.'" He then proceeded to read the first part into the record:

> My Dear Governor:
> Colonel Clarke, my messenger to you of yesterday, September 26th, has reported the result of his delivery of my letter dated September 25th. As I understand him you (a) were unwilling to commit yourself to any agreement regarding "not communicating its contents to any other person" in view of the fact that you felt you already knew certain of the things probably referred to in the letter, as suggested to you by seeing the word "cryptograph" and (b) you could not feel that such a letter as this to a presidential candidate could have been addressed to you by an officer in my position without the knowledge of the President.
> As to (a) above I am quite willing to have you read what comes hereafter with the understanding that you are bound not to communicate to any other person any portions on which you do not now have or later receive factual knowledge from some other source than myself. As to (b) above you have my word that neither the Secretary of War nor the President has any intimation whatsoever that such a letter has been addressed to you or that the preparation or sending of such a communication was being considered. I assure you that the only persons who saw or know of the existence of either this letter or my letter to you dated September 25th are Admiral King, seven key officers responsible for security of military communications, and my secretary who typed these letters. I am trying my best to make plain to you that this letter is being addressed to you solely on my initiative, Admiral King having been consulted only after the letter was drafted, and I am persisting in the matter because the military hazards involved are so serious that I feel some action is necessary to protect the interests of our armed forces.
> I should very much preferred to talk to you in person but I could not devise a method that would not be subject to press and radio reactions as to why the Chief of Staff of the Army would be seeking an interview with you at this particular moment. Therefore I have turned to the method of this letter, with which Admiral King concurs, to be delivered by hand to you by Colonel Clark who, incidentally, has charge of the most secret documents of the War and Navy Departments.[3]

At this point the general stopped reading and said, "Mr. Chairman, the remainder of the letter is a repetition of what I read in the first letter. Do you want me to read it?" The chairman responded, "No. I suppose it will be published in full as it is without the necessity of reading it. *Is it exactly the same?*" Came the reply, "*It is exactly the same*" (emphasis added in both cases).[4]

It is *essentially* the same but certainly not "exactly" the same. Why then the desire to avoid reading the entire letter? Perhaps it was the desire not to go through the same message a second time. On the other hand, the British desired to keep their program out of the hearings, and it is tempting to believe that the general was cooperating with them in their effort. Weighed against this is the major objection that Gen. Marshall made too many other references to the British program for this to have been his intention. Hence his own reluctance to reread what had already been (mostly) covered may have just happened to go hand-in-hand with the British preference.

Regardless of our conclusion on motivation, between the letter's reference to the OSS break-in at the Japanese embassy in Portugal and Representative Harness's allusion to Magic data comes this new statement (emphasis added), "*A further most serious embarrassment is the fact that the British government is involved concerning its most secret sources of information, regarding which only the Prime Minister, the Chiefs of Staff and a very limited number of other officials have knowledge.*"[5]

Although done in a manner that did not explicitly state that the British were successfully involved in code breaking, the context required that such be under consideration. Could it be that the anti-Japanese (rather than anti-German) efforts are in mind? This would fit in well with the Japanese embassy being the target in the preceding paragraph and the congressional reference in the following one being to the reading of the Japanese codes. The emphasis in the previous paragraph on the denial of information "regarding the European situation," however, makes a German allusion possible.

Senator Ferguson pressed Gen. Marshall about what information the British had shared before Pearl Harbor. The general called the summaries and interpretation "evaluations" and the senator wished to know whether the joint committee had been provided these. "I am quite certain that would not be in your records, sir, *because we have been trying to keep that quiet as much as we could*" (emphasis added). A disturbed Sen. Ferguson took this to mean that information was being suppressed, which Gen. Marshall denied. Then what did he mean? "My last answer was that we did not wish to disclose the fact that the British had a capacity and a method of obtaining information *which I referred to in that letter of Governor Dewey's* (emphasis added) which has now become public, not that they did not give us information."[6]

Other Testimony by Marshall Concerning the Existence and Operation of British Ultra

When asked by the joint congressional committee what he recalled of the arrangements for obtaining British Ultra intercepts of German communications, Gen. Marshall made clear that he did not recall the details. Two points, however, he remembered quite clearly. The first concerned why the United States did not choose to go it alone rather than secure British cooperation: "I believe, Senator, what we were more concerned about was obtaining from the British the information they had, *which was more extensive than ours*" (added emphasis).[7]

The second thing he recalled quite firmly was the British reluctance to share the raw intercepts with their American ally:

> ... [F]or quite a long time we only received the British estimates. We did not receive the direct intelligence on which the evaluation was made, as the basis for the estimates. It was a long period before they gave us the direct material, because they were very fearful of our letting them get out of the basis of secrecy. Finally, and I think we were well into the war, a long ways into the war, before they were willing to take the hazard of giving us the direct information, which involved, of course, a knowledge of how they acquired it.[8]

In order to obtain a steady supply of raw intercepts it was necessary to agree to strict secrecy guidelines to protect the source and guide the usage of the information. Gen. Marshall outlined some of these in his testimony before the Army Board. In parts below to which emphasis has been added, the general makes plain that these guidelines also covered the use of British decrypts of the German communications as well:

> ... I have here the headings for the secret, ultrasecret information for the Far East, *for Europe*, and for the diplomatic summary. They all have this general reading "Top Secret," which means the extreme of secrecy observed by the War and Navy Departments, and so understood by the *British*.
> They have, under the heading, "Note:" four paragraphs

alternating red and black. The first one reads: "No one, without express permission from the proper authorities, may disseminate the information reported in this Summary or communicate it to any other person."

Now, in black is another paragraph: "Those authorized to disseminate such information must employ only the most secure means, must take every precaution to avoid compromising the source, and must limit dissemination to the minimum number of secure and responsible persons who need the information in order to discharge their duties."

The next is in red: "No action is to be taken on information herein reported, regardless of temporary advantage, if such action might have the effect of revealing the existence of the source to the enemy."

I might state, in connection with that paragraph, that there have been cases where convoys have been permitted to go into the most serious situations rather than diverting them from the assemblage of the so-called wolf packs because of the fear that would convey to the Germans that we had some means of knowing just how this was managed. Here at the present time, the German submarine activity in the Atlantic being on the decided decrease, we have a series of sinkings going on in the Philippines and elsewhere in that general region which are timed entirely on this particular information. The hazard is to what extent we can continue uninterruptedly proceeding on that basis without conveying to the Japanese the fact that we have some means of reading the schedule for the convoy.

We are continuing to use it for the reason that from this secret information, secret source of information, we learn of the Japanese thought as to how we are obtaining knowledge of these convoy movements. They think it is done by spies and by observation posts in the Philippines and along those other coasts, of which we had a great deal in the Solomons, and Australian lookout posts, and in New Britain, new Ireland, and New Guinea. So long as they show they think that it is some such methods as that, we feel free to go ahead; but if there is any danger of our giving away our sources, then we would have to hold off somewhat on seizing each opportunity, for fear we would lose tremendous long-term advantages. That is what is meant in these instructions when it says, "No action is to be taken on information herein reported, regardless of temporary advantage."[9]

When questioned as to the source of these data-usage restrictions, Gen. Marshall made plain (though one might note that he does not over-emphasize it) that the German decrypts (especially in the early part of the war) were courtesy of the British and that, therefore, the rules protecting the security of decrypted information had to be drawn up so that the British would be confident of ongoing security:

> [These are the] agreed instructions between ourselves in the War Department and the Navy Department *and the British.* It was necessary for us to show them, in the most positive manner, how we would guard *their information, which they were very reluctant to give to us* [emphasis is added]. They would give us the results, just as we gave it to General Short and Admiral Kimmel, without giving us their source on which these statements were based; and we were, oh, I guess a year and a half or two years breaking down their reluctance to tell us that.[10]

Although the British were sharing a sanitized, summary version of the intercept data, the Americans were still in the dark about how quickly the code-breaking was being accomplished. Although some of the information obviously implied a relative dating, other documents were not as clear-cut. This was brought out in an exchange between Sen. Brewster and the general concerning whose intelligence was more up to date, prior to Pearl Harbor, about conditions on the German-Russian front:

> Senator Brewster. What I am concerned with is how far you had gone in developing the interchange of the military information regarding enemy movements.
> General Marshall. At that time, I am quite certain that the facts of the British source of information was not known to us—I am quite certain of that, naturally, it was not known to us—but in addition they were not giving us the facts. They were not jeopardizing the source.
> Senator Brewster. Yes, and they would probably—
> General Marshall. It was quite some time after that, quite a long time after that before they took the risk of telling us exactly what they had. They gave us the sense of the reports, but the actual authoritative statements of what it was, and who said it, we did not know.
> Senator Brewster. Would it be a fair inference that prior to December 7, the British were in all probability far better informed regarding events around Moscow, in the month of November than was our own Intelligence?
> General Marshall. I couldn't give an opinion on that, Senator Brewster, for the reason that I don't know just when the British accomplished the break-down of the German codes. It was not only a question of breaking it down, but the rapidity with which you could pick up the changes. All of

which was a tremendous development. I don't know what
that was at that time. They may have been 3 or 4 weeks
behind the events.[11]

Uncertainty of how well the Russians would adequately protect the
secrecy of the program played a pivotal role in the decision not to share
the German intercepts with the Russians:

I might say, we have had a continuing very delicate situation
with the Russians where we have told them we had good reason—not good reason—we had the best evidence that certain
actions were going to be taken by the Germans against them,
but we couldn't tell them why, and there was quite a long
debate as to whether we should not go into the whole thing,
but that was felt most dangerous from two points of view.
One was, we were spreading the thing out, and we didn't
know who all would become involved in it; and more particularly, they would probably get infuriated because they had-
n't had it from the start. So it has been a matter all the time
of guarding this thing so that we have it tomorrow and do
not expand it today and lose tomorrow.[12]

Doubtless there were other factors as well: How good were the
Russian ciphers? Even relatively sanitized versions could give the game
away if the Russian codes were breached sufficiently often. Furthermore,
Stalin had slaughtered his millions before the Nazis even began their own
butchery. The British (being more pragmatists than the war-idealistic
Americans) may well have feared that too great an insight into the intri-
cacies of Ultra might greatly strengthen the Russian hand in the postwar
world, where such brutalities might easily be continued. (For almost a
decade after, they *were* continued, the worst only being brought to an end
by Stalin's death.)

A hidden "joker" in the entire matter was the extensive Russian espionage system operating in Britain: How much did Russia already know
and on how consistently were they receiving it? These were the kinds of
questions neither side could openly discuss while allies due to the exi-
gencies of the war, nor when competition was open and visible in the
postwar world.

More surprising than any of this information (at least to the current
author) was the willingness of Gen. Marshall to estimate the relative
resources devoted by both the Americans and the British to their intercept programs. One of the biggest American problems at the beginning
of the war was limited manpower to tackle code-breaking. Gen. Marshall
noted to the Army Pearl Harbor Board that there was simply no com-

paring the resources then available for decryption (presumably for use in *both* theaters of war) with those on hand when the conflict began:

> Our facilities, of course, at that time were not vaguely to be compared to our facilities and organization today, in the matter of this secret material. We can get a mass of that culled through in a few hours by these thousands of people we have employed: some 10,000 by us [in the Army] and 6,000 by the Navy and *30-odd thousand by the British* [emphasis added]. No such forces as that were available in those days, and no machinery of the nature they have now. In some respects the remarkable part about this procedure was that the critical messages were absorbed so quickly.[13]

Before the joint congressional committee Gen. Marshall gave an even more vivid picture of the growth of American Magic while again alluding to the British program as being approximately twice as large:

> ... I was aware of the fact that they were short-handed and it was very difficult to obtain people that we could trust and that had the necessary qualities. I looked up several days ago what the status of that was and, as I recall, on December 7, 1941, there were some 44 officers and about 180 men, women, civilians and soldiers, in Washington in the Army engaged in this work and some 150 out in the field at what they call the monitoring stations, that is, merely intercepting the material.
>
> Now, I compared that with the situation at the end of the war and there were in Washington some 666 officers and a total of 10,000 individuals here in Washington at this work. *The British had 30,000* [emphasis added]. The Navy of ours here I think had 6,000.[14]

In the earlier testimony, Gen. Marshall had spoken as if the *total* manpower commitment to Ultra was double that provided Magic. Before the congressional investigators he spoke as if the comparison were more narrowly drawn, strictly with the Washington-based aspects of the U.S. effort. Assuming that this was not an accidental misstatement, the relative size of the two programs remains intriguing. Assuming that about half of the Americans involved in Magic were based in Washington, the total army-navy personnel comes to approximately 32,000, roughly comparable to that of the British. The greater the proportion one assumes was based in Washington, the more impressive is the figure, since even an *equality* in numbers represented a far larger commitment of resources in relation to the total available to Britain.

Gen. Marshall was not the only individual who dealt with the personnel aspects of the subject. Even the normally oblivious Gen. Miles recalled at least a little of substance when dealing with this aspect of the matter. Although speaking, in context, of British intercept work in the Pacific, Sen. Ferguson posed a broader-worded question about the comparative size of the two nations' intelligence activities. "Now you told us yesterday that Congress would not give to the Army enough money for intelligence work, and you told us about the money, as I recall, that England was spending, that it had a much bigger staff, and so forth. That is true, isn't it?" Miles answered in a similar generalization, "On the secret service; yes, sir."[15] In other words, regardless of the respective size of the two nations' decryption programs at the end of the war, the *overall* intelligence effort had been much larger on the British side when the war began.

Cumulatively, this constitutes a surprising amount of detail. What was most important to the British was to keep European Ultra as much out of the picture as possible. In this American interests worked in their behalf: The Americans were preoccupied with Pearl Harbor. The war with Germany had been a success and the possibility of political contamination of the handling of intelligence data with Germany had not been an issue. Hence these revealing pieces of information went unnoticed by the American public at large. Even historians and political scientists would be equally startled by the revelation of the "Ultra Secret" a quarter century later. Yet the evidence had been lying in plain sight—in plain sight but unnoticed because it wasn't the source where one would expect to find such information.

IV
Suppression and Revelation of the British Role

Attempted Suppression of European and Pacific Ultra at the Congressional Investigation of Pearl Harbor

The congressional hearings on Pearl Harbor gingerly approached the topic of the British role in decryption. In part the investigators probably feared that any public avowal of the U.S. role in the Pacific would deeply embroil them in the bitter controversies of who knew what and when. The investigation was a potential quagmire that Great Britain fervently desired to avoid. It could easily have led to embarrassing questions concerning the nature and extent of pre-war "understandings" and "commitments" between the two powers that would revive the popular suspicions that Britain had been determined to drag the United States into the world war by hook or crook.

For that matter, once the question was brought to the forefront: How much *did* the two powers cooperate? Was it a free exchange or one-sided? Did the British government perhaps hold back key intercepts or other materials that could have made a difference? Worse yet, could that government through embarrassing inefficiency or blundering, have botched the transmission of key data that would have alerted the Americans? If so, many Americans were so willing to believe the worst of their own government, it took no genius to recognize the potential field day if the British role were seriously examined. So even assuming the purest of intentions, the British government understandably brought to bear all the pressure it could to assure that its role would be minimized.

Efforts to Limit the Introduction of Information at the Congressional Investigations Relating to Intelligence Information Exchanges

The general counsel for the joint committee, Seth M. Richardson, either on his own initiative or at the encouragement of the British or the U.S. State Department, attempted to keep out of the public record a considerable part of the documentation that involved the activities of other powers. In defense of this approach he stressed their alleged minimal value: "Now, I say just for what it may be worth, which is probably nothing, as we go through the documents there are only one or two that we can, by any particular stretch of the imagination, feel are germane."[1]

Certain members of the joint committee had been encouraging Richardson to obtain blanket permission to print the entire bundle of documents.[2] He countered this behind-the-scenes initiative by a public request of his own, that the committee members examine the files outside the hearings so that the volume of material could be reduced to the much smaller number directly relevant to their investigation.[3]

The vice chairman of the committee, Congressman Cooper emphatically backed the proposal to reduce the included documents to the minimum. "It would look to me like the committee would want very carefully to consider [whether they are really relevant] before we go to all the trouble of *having the State Department get the clearances of the foreign governments* on something that may not be even material or relevant to this inquiry."[4] Essentially the vice chairman's proposal (effectively adopted by acquiescence rather than formal action) was that only a limited number of documents would be introduced unless specifically demanded by a member of the committee and the committee supported the member's request.[5]

This dramatic pruning of the data was really for the public benefit, insisted the vice chairman: "I might say personally what I am afraid of is that we are getting such a mass of material in here, much of it that is so remotely, if at all, related to the subject under consideration, we are going to get our record so terribly large that it will be difficult for people interested in the matter to find the things that are really material and important."[6]

One of the only two additional participants in the exchange of comments asked what this information was. General counsel for the committee responded, "Senator, it is a series of documents that have to do with the troubled relations existing between the United States and Japan and England and China."[7] The final participant in the exchange effectively conceded the question by noting that there were only three such messages that concerned him.[8]

The counsel's description of the nature of the documents under consideration dramatically underplayed their true significance and the underlying reason foreign governments were so concerned. As Richardson had said almost at the beginning of his plea, "Mr. Chairman, some time ago we compiled a group of documents which relate to *certain transfers of information and inquiry* between the United States and other Governments."[9] At the minimum this implies the exchange of intelligence between the two governments. The *degree* of hyper-sensitivity would imply the kind of decryption successes that Great Britain kept from general public notice until the 1970s. That the latter is in mind is confirmed by the two other major documented examples of British concern printed in the hearings (see below).

Efforts to Suppress the Reference to British Code Breaking in General Marshall's Letter to Candidate Dewey

Although Gen. Marshall's letters to Thomas Dewey during the 1944 presidential campaign deserve attention in their own right due to their explicit mention of British Ultra (see the previous chapter), it is of interest in the present context that there was an effort to suppress the embarrassing disclosure. The joint committee met in secret session and an effort was made to present all testimony concerning the matter behind closed doors and to edit out certain information that would be embarrassing to the British. Returning to a public format, committee members aimed barbs at each other, and in the parts of the following extract with added emphasis, the members make plain that the silencing effort had been made to please a U.S. ally and that it would have been successful except for the refusal of two committee members to cooperate.

In defense of what had been attempted it was stressed that:

> The object of the executive session was to discuss the very question involved here because it was thought it could be more freely discussed in executive session than here in an

open session, as to whether *the entire letter should go into the record or as to whether there should be eliminated the sentence or two to which I have referred to and to which General Marshall called our attention.*

Now, the Senator from Illinois may amplify that statement in any way that he may see fit.

Senator Lucas. Mr. Chairman, the position taken by the Senator from Michigan is not the same position that the Senator from Illinois takes. The Senator from Michigan absented himself from the committee meeting and refused to participate in executive session and hear General Marshall's statement upon this question.

The Senator from Illinois also absented himself from the session. I know nothing about the contents of the letter. The Senator from Illinois was not willing for one member of the committee to absent himself from the meeting without himself going out with Gen. Marshall [see below].

Mr. Murphy. Mr. Chairman.

The Chairman. The Congressman from Pennsylvania.

Mr. Murphy. I would like to say, Mr. Chairman, in my opinion it was a question whether or not the rules of this committee, or the feelings of any individual on this committee should come before the security of the Nation.

Senator Brewster. Mr. Chairman.

The Chairman. The Senator from Maine.

Senator Brewster. I think in order to complete the record, it ought to appear that the members of the committee who remained excused General Marshall at the same time that we excused the Senator from Michigan or the Senator from Illinois, so no information of any character was received from General Marshall aside from that given in the letter, *with the underlining of the passages which he previously stated he thought perhaps might be left out.*

The Chairman. That statement is correct. The committee excused General Marshall simultaneously with the excusing of the two Senators, who had excused themselves. The Chairman might suggest if we had excused anybody else we might not have had a quorum present.

The upshot of the whole thing is the entire letter will be read into the record and made public. I might say that the committee accepts responsibility for that procedure.

I might also say it was the viewpoint of the Chairman that notwithstanding *any possible embarrassment that might accrue between our Government and an allied nation over the publication of confidential information contained in General Marshall's letter,* that in the long run, it would be less embarrassing to publish the whole letter than to be required later to explain

why we left any of it out, and for that reason the Chair felt, and now feels that the entire letter should be made part of the record, and made public.
Mr. Clark. Mr. Chairman.
The Chairman. Congressman Clark.
Mr. Clark. I, of course, accept my part of the responsibility to which the Chairman has just referred, but I regret exceedingly that some sensible and perfectly simple plan could not have been adopted, as I thought it could, to the satisfaction of everybody who is reasonable about it, rather than to put up against *exposing a matter here that is wholly irrelevant to Pearl Harbor, that may have consequences that we cannot foresee....*[10]

Those opposing the suppression did so on the grounds that all testimony should be in public rather than in executive session. Sen. Ferguson argued,

I want to make it clear that my only reason this morning, as I stated, was not that General Marshall was a witness—I have the highest respect for General Marshall—but it is the fact that I was unwilling to take any testimony in executive session, no matter what it was about or who was the witness.... It was not the question that General Marshall was the witness, it was merely that all meetings, in my opinion, should be open meetings, no matter what is to be discussed with the witness. They should be here and be sworn as witnesses. We should get our testimony from the witnesses in sworn statements, in an opening hearing.[11]

British Fears that Clausen's Investigations Would Disclose the Secret of Their Code Breaking

Since Col. Clausen had investigated in depth a number of aspects of intelligence gathering (which itself forms a volume of the joint committee's published record), it was natural that he be called before the congressional investigation. As he recalled the situation for the committee, he had been very concerned that an early December British intelligence communiqué indicating imminent war *might have been based upon British interception of a winds execute message* (which implies that the British were also reading the Japanese codes):

Now, when I was in London, I talked with the British party in charge of all this magic stuff, and he couldn't find, he said, any connection between what I have just stated and an implement message to the winds code, but after I got back here, I gave more thought to it, and I went to see Colonel Wilkinson who was then working in New York.

I showed him this portion and I said … I would like to know if you know the source of that. He said he didn't know. And since it was British, I said, "Will you find out for me?"[12]

Clausen was also concerned with a late November telegram predicting a Japanese military move on December 1. Had this prediction been based upon intercepts?[13]

Wilkinson personally conveyed Clausen's queries to the appropriate authorities in the United Kingdom. They responded with the following message emphasizing both the Ultra-basis of the two assertions and the fear that this might be made public:

TOP SECRET ULTRA

From London, 31st August 1945
IMPORTANT
ULTRA
GOR 682 from GCCS 11279

Following from C.S.S. for Jones.

A. Colonel Wilkinson who was stationed at Manila and is now with 48000 and temporarily in U.K. was recently approached by Lieutenant Colonel H. C. Clausen, of Judge Advocate General's Department U.S. Army, in connection with investigation of General Short and Admiral Kimmel for Pearl Harbour disaster. He carried credentials from Secretary of War.

B. He brought copies of 2 telegrams from Manila to Honololou, of November 26th and December 2nd, which were as follows:

1. "November 26th, 1941. Most Immediate. Secret Source (usually reliable) reports:

(a) Japanese will attack Krakow Isthmus from sea on December 1st without any ultimatum or declaration of break with a view getting between Bangkok and Singapore.

(b) Attacking forces will proceed direct from Hainan and Formosa. Main landing point to be in Songkhia area valuation for above is number 3 repeat 3 (i.e., only about 55 to 60 percent probable accuracy). American military and naval intelligence Manila informed."

2. "December 3rd, 1941. Most Immediate.

(a) We have received considerable intelligence confirming following developments in Indo-China:
(I) Accelerated Japanese preparation of airfields and railways.
(II) Arrival since November 10th of additional 100,000 repeat 100,000 troops and considerable quantities fighters medium bombers tanks and guns (75 pmm).
(b) Estimates of specific quantities have already been telegraphed to Washington November 21st by American military Intelligence here.
(c) Our considered opinion concludes that Japan envisages early hostilities with Britain and United States. Japan does not repeat not intend attack Russia at present but will act in south. You may inform Chiefs of American Military and Naval Intelligence Honolulu."

C. Colonel C. anxious to know basic source of para. C. of telegram of December 2nd, and in particular, whether this was in "special" category. In point of fact, para C. was based on a B.J. [i.e., a Japanese intercept]. Wilkinson was unaware of source and passed information to Honolulu as he appreciated that I possessed no direct communications.

D. As far as can be judged, the earlier information was based on agent's reports, but Clausen only pressing for origin of para C.

E. *You should consult with G-2, as security Ultra at stake if this evidence made public* [emphasis added].[14]

Two key phrases are of importance. The first is the reference to the December message as being based on information "in [the] 'special' category." As Clausen explained to the congressional committee, "They mean that it was magic."[15] Then there is the reference to "B.J." As Clausen also pointed out to the committee, "B.J. is magic. If you want to prove that, you can call General Carter Clarke."[16]

The concluding words of the telegram to "consult with G-2, as security Ultra at stake if this evidence made public" indicates the British desire to suppress any effort to reveal the existence of their success in reading the Japanese ciphers. This cannot be dismissed as a security consideration, which had been the case when Gen. Marshall contacted Thomas Dewey. Then the lives of soldiers and sailors might have been sacrificed as the result of a Japanese wholesale revocation of their codes and substitution of new ones. (Assuming, of course, that at that late stage of the war such would have been practical.)

This concern was now past. On August 15 the emperor effectively offered surrender in his message to the nation. On the 28th Gen.

MacArthur and a small first wave of occupation forces entered the country. On August 31 the British message was sent. On September 2, the formal surrender was signed in Tokyo Bay. All that was left was secrecy for secrecy's sake.

In all candor, the American side wasn't thrilled about a public discussion of the subject either. If the fact of successful code-breaking had not already been widely known among political leaders, the entire subject might well have been suppressed in an act of alleged national interest. Even the knowledge of the code-making might not have been sufficient to provoke a public examination if pre-war suspicions of President Roosevelt's interventionist policies had not combined with the humiliating tragedy of Pearl Harbor to demand a public accounting of responsibility. Within that framework, a consideration of at least American decryption was inescapable, since any advance warnings received by the administration would most likely have been by that source.

On the other hand, those who had suspicions were primarily concerned with Roosevelt and the foreknowledge he and others of the top echelon might or might not have possessed. Although those most inclined to such doubts were from the pre-war isolationist current of thought (a world-view with deeply entrenched suspicions of British actions and motives), the successful joint effort against Nazi and Japanese militarism had made the voicing of such attitudes very much less respectable. Indeed, this feeling had been further diluted by what the two nations had gone through together, and there would have been the tendency to give a faithful ally the benefit of the doubt. Being so generous to the *domestic* foe (as embodied in the Roosevelt administration) was something else again.

Hence there was no passionate determination to present information embarrassing to the British, in vivid contrast to the enthusiasm to investigate every possible indication of Rooseveltian malfeasance. By and large the British effort to minimize its decryption role was successful. The potentially incendiary accusations that could flow from full disclosure were avoided. Most Americans were so preoccupied by their own government's failures that they paid minimal attention to what *was* said on the subject.

The Americans who testified repeatedly refer to the British activities, though in passing and rarely at any great length. Whether they had been "encouraged" to downplay the British role is unknown, but since the congressional investigators were willing to go along with minimizing the public record as to the British role, there certainly was no incentive to go into great detail.

A few (to use the terminology of a later generation) engaged in "stone walling." Gen. Miles repeatedly pled his lack of memory concerning such matters: "I imagine they did, sir." "I can't answer that question, Senator, offhand." "I know nothing now. I might have at the time, but I know nothing now about the details of where the British intercepting stations were, sir."[17] Perhaps he was being candid but the incredible degree of forgetfulness (as to broad facts and not just technical details) is startling from a man in his position.

Yet as the earlier chapters in this book exhibit, a surprising amount *did* seep out from behind the veil of secrecy—even some from the very unwilling Gen. Miles. Sometimes information came in the form of tidbits; other times in substantial amounts. In short, the British were flat lucky: Americans' interests lay elsewhere. They didn't pay attention to it.

Reasons the British Were Able to Maintain Secrecy on German and Japanese Ultra Long after the War Ended

A number of factors worked together to keep both the British European Ultra and Pacific Ultra from becoming public knowledge. One pivotal factor lay in the proportion of involvement of British and American personnel. So far as Pacific Ultra went, the U.S. Magic program was well known and Americans centered their attention on it and any possible relationship it might have to the unpreparedness for the Pearl Harbor attack. The British did the best they could to allow the Americans to take full credit (or blame) for the handling of Japanese language diplomatic intercepts.

With the British unwilling to make their role any better publicly known than they could avoid and in light of the United States being the senior partner in Japanese language work, the role of its European ally was easily ignored.[18] This was true even of those who had served at Pearl Harbor. Even several years after the outing of European Ultra, W. J. Holmes (an administrator for Magic in Hawaii) wrote an entire volume on intelligence work in the Pacific without mentioning the pre-war intelligence and decryption sharing with the British.[19]

In regard to European Ultra the situation was reverse: Although Americans became significantly involved, the senior partner in that effort was recognized to be Great Britain. Respect for that country's major role in helping produce the European victory meant acquiescence in its desire to avoid telling the dramatic story of the breaking—and repeated breaking—of the German Enigma system. Since Americans had their attention on the Pacific and since there were fewer Americans potentially to leak their personal knowledge of the European Ultra, the major danger of its being revealed came from the British side, but the British were well equipped to protect against leakage. The British government was effectively able to discourage its nationals from discussing either effort through the Official Secrets Act, which could put any would-be revealer in jail for many years.

Finally, there was the sense of moral obligation to adhere to one's sworn word to keep the decryption work secret. To cynics of the early 21st century that may sound incredible, but the fact remains that thousands of British participants *did* keep it concealed for decades, at least until the "official" outing of it in the mid–1970s.

Even lower echelon participants felt a similar sense of obligation. Gordon Welchman, a participant in the breaking of Enigma, tells the story of a wartime member of the Womens Royal Naval Service (the "Wrens") who was involved in a support role in the project. After the war, she married an officer who, about 1956, was moved to Singapore to serve as an intelligence officer for the British army. Throughout the intervening decade she carefully avoided telling her spouse what she had done during the war.

A major participant in the decryption program had given a wartime series of lectures to support personnel such as this woman. At a cocktail party in 1956 she, her husband, and the lecturer happened to meet. She went up to him and mentioned that their paths had briefly converged during the conflict: "I was with the Wrens during the war and went to hear your lectures." Her husband, knowing what the guest had been involved in, overheard the conversation, grinned broadly, and proclaimed, "So *that's* what you did in the war!"[20]

Thousands of others shared this woman's commitment to the wartime oath of secrecy; their silence was eloquent tribute to what a sense of duty and obligation can produce.

Possible Reasons for the Obsession with Secrecy

A major factor behind the British screen of silence was cultural, the long entrenched mind-frame of its bureaucrats: The British government had a tradition of suppressing data even when it seemed to have only the most speculative possibility of providing harmful insights into contemporary intelligence work. It appears to have been a case of what one historian describes as "the congenital paranoia of British officials" who needlessly postpone the release of data. "Papers infuriatingly locked up for as long as seventy-five years," he groans from personal experience, are "then released [and] have turned out to be inexplicably, even boringly, harmless."[21] This does not rule out the possibility of there being something embarrassing in the material; merely that it makes it improbable that some vast conspiracy is being shushed up as the new millennium begins.

Of Japanese data in particular, when Alan Stripp wrote a book in the 1980s on his wartime work for Pacific Ultra, he desired to include an estimate of how many Japanese intercepts were received and broken on a typical day in 1944. Since this was more than three decades after than the events, one is hard pressed to see what this would reveal about contemporary British intelligence capacity. Yet the government was so convinced that *somehow* "it might still be a relevant clue ... to our present cryptanalytical abilities" that they demanded it be removed—and he did so.[22]

If the British government had this paranoid a reaction to such historically interesting but otherwise useless information, it takes little imagination to see why such a government would desire to totally suppress all data from the immediate pre-Pearl Harbor period concerning the Far East. Americans *still* have passionate reactions to that disaster, and more than a few heated controversies as to real and imagined causes persist. Hence, even in the most optimistic scenario, the provision of data would, at the minimum, encourage speculation and fuel yet additional questions.

Another reason was pragmatic and quite practical: During the war, some 100,000 Enigma machines were distributed among the German military and government.[23] At the end of the conflict, Great Britain seized an unknown (but large) number of these machines from the defeated enemy. As a moneymaking method, the British sold these to newly independent countries throughout the world so that they could have a "secure" means of diplomatic communication. For the next 25 years, these remained in service, thereby assuring that Her Majesty's Government could have access to whichever of these communications it desired.[24] The United States resold its own seized Enigmas under the same pretense.[25]

Two Slowly Evaporating Secrets:
European and Japanese Ultra

If these factors worked together to suppress both the European and Far Eastern programs of British decryption, Her Majesty's Government was able to suppress knowledge of the anti-Japanese program even longer than the European One. The "first" and "official" unveiling of European Ultra was in F. W. Winterbotham's *The Ultra Secret* in 1974. This was recognized even by participants in the decryption program as the first time it had been revealed to the public.[26]

Yet the secrecy had previously begun to slip. Malcolm Muggeridge's autobiography *The Infernal Grove* (1973) discussed the effort, as had the earlier French language work, *Enigma*, by Gustave Bertrand.[27] The editor's commentary on Sir Alexander Cadogan's wartime diaries (1971) refer to how at least certain German "machine cyphers" had been broken as of 1942. Passing mention is also made of the ability to read the Japanese diplomatic communications, though credit is given to the Purple machine provided by the Americans.[28]

Winterbotham's work created the equation in the public mind of "Germany" and "Ultra." This was a quite natural misinterpretation due to the fact that 21 of the book's 22 chapters focus on Europe or North Africa. Only one paragraph is devoted to the Pacific War in 1941.[29] The one chapter discussing the Pacific War in general primarily narrates the story of Winterbotham's visit to the Pacific in order to assure that necessary secrecy measures were preserved.

His scattered references to "ultra" later in the war[30] can be read as allusions to the American's decryption program, since they had adopted the British terminology for such data. *If* they are intended to be, in part, an allusion to the British work, these scattered remarks blend in so well with the text, that unless one is consciously thinking of the British involvement one is unlikely to recognize their significance, since the vast bulk of the volume is on the anti-Nazi effort.

Even as Britain's Far Eastern decryption program became more widely known, the British government continued a policy of information limitation alarmingly similar to that which they had once pursued during their breaking of the German Enigma. The refusal of Britain to fully release its Japanese intercepts and its decision to obstruct the release of data related to them had provided grounds for speculation.

Of those Japanese diplomatic decrypts that have been released from Bletchley Park's records, the earliest are from August of 1941, although there is good evidence that usable material was being provided as early as February of that year.[31] What has *not* been released have been penetrations of the JN-25B intercepts (the variant in effect throughout 1941).[32] Operational orders would have been issued in this system to the fleet.

The original version had been successfully penetrated by the British and the Americans, but when "B" went into effect in December 1940, the entire effort had to be started all over again.[33] Three individuals intimately connected with the BP, FECB, or the Australian programs were convinced that JN-25B continued to be at least partially read and clearly pointed to either the outbreak of war in early December or to an attack on Pearl Harbor in particular.[34]

Some penetration seems certain, but how much and how consistently is impossible to resolve without the availability of the full BP Far East archives. John Costello, for example,[35] quotes from an "early postwar" hitherto secret volume, *Special Intelligence in the Far East and Pacific*, that admits to such successes and explains how it was possible. On the other hand when it lists the two most important successes, they were "ample warning that Japan was going to war in 1941," and evidence from "Japanese signals [that] had been decoded" that the *Repulse* and *Prince of Wales* would be attacked by the Japanese. Conspicuously missing—and virtually certain to be not in a volume never intended for publication consumption—is any mention of foreknowledge of the *site* of the initial attack, if it had been known.

Those suspecting the worst maximize the success rate on cracking JN-25B. The common view is that it was a far more modest 10 percent—which, in all but the most exceptional case, meant that little could be read.[36]

My own judgment has been suggested, in passing, earlier in this book. *If* the British knew anything particularly incriminating which they are trying to suppress, it probably relates to something embarrassing about their own policy failures or military weakness in the region. Permitting a known attack force to assault Pearl Harbor and not provide warning would have been reckless. If the least serious hint of such conduct had gained root in the American consciousness, it could have shattered the Western Alliance. It is a quite reasonable scenario that American arms and supplies would have been cut off as the result of public outrage and the Germans would have ruled triumphant. The United States did not need Britain to win the Pacific War. Britain *did* need the Americans to win the European one. At the very least there would have been a continued alliance that was but an empty shell, and even that would have splintered as soon as the war was ended.

Notes

Introduction

1. Bicknell, Joint Committee, PHA, 10/5090. (= Joint Committee on the Investigation of the Pearl Harbor Attack. *Pearl Harbor Attack: Hearings before the Joint Committee on the Investigation of the Pearl Harbor Attack.* Washington, DC: U.S. Government Printing Office, 1946.) Future references to the various investigations will follow the format followed in this note: the witness's name, the investigation involved, PHA as a contraction for the collection of all the investigations together in printed form by the Congress, and the volume number followed by a slash and the page number.

2. As quoted by Gerald M. VanDyke, who was in charge of preparing the reports, in his "Military Intelligence," in *Eyewitness to Infamy: An Oral History of Pearl Harbor,* edited by Paul J. Traveers (Lanham, MD: Madison Books, 1991), 29. A half century later VanDyke was still angry with the intelligence officers directly reporting to Admiral Kimmel and General Short for not heeding the admonition.

3. In his memoir of the attack, Edwin Layton, chief intelligence officer of the fleet at Pearl Harbor, discusses the usefulness and limitations of traffic analysis with specific reference to the December 7th assault. See his work co-authored with Roger Pineau and John Costello, *"And I Was There:" Pearl Harbor and Midway—Breaking the Secrets* (New York: William Morrow and Company, 1985), 185.

4. Layton, *"And I Was There,"* 81.

5. Layton, *"And I Was There,"* 77–78.

6. To provide an example from the newspaper world as to how this perception is still with us: As I returned to this subject after a lapse of several years, I happened to be reading the *Jerusalem Post* when I came across a three page (tabloid-size) article entitled "The Code Breakers," in which the overwhelming emphasis is on how "[t]he massive operation carried out at Bletchley Park was devoted to breaking German military codes" (Abraham Rabinovich, "The Code Breakers," *Jerusalem Post,* International Edition [February 12, 1999, 20]). Yet buried in this lengthy recounting is a short section on Japanese code breaking, but this is included only because Rabinovich became an immigrant to Israel and because it concerned information obtained on Germany through the intercepts of the Japanese embassy located in Berlin (21).

Chapter 1

1. Safford, Hart Inquiry, PHA, 26/388.

2. Rochefort, Hewitt Inquiry, PHA, 36/31.

3. Rochefort, Hewitt Inquiry, PHA, 36/31.

4. McCollum, Joint Committee, PHA, 8/3395.

5. The Navy ("Cavite") part of the operation was based at Corregidor; the Army's at Manila and only, much later, moved to Corregidor.

6. Gordon W. Prange, in collaboration with Donald M. Goldstein and Katherine V. Dillon, *At Dawn We Slept: The Untold Story of Pearl Harbor* (New York: McGraw-Hill, 1981), 82.

7. Ronald Clark, *The Man Who Broke Purple: The Life of Colonel William F. Friedman, Who Deciphered the Japanese Code in World War II* (Boston: Little, Brown, 1977), 145.

8. Herbert O. Yardley. *The American Black Chamber* (Indianapolis: Bobbs-Merrill, 1931), 262, 318.

9. For a detailed account of how his team accomplished it, see Yardley, *Black Chamber*, 283–317.

10. Edward van Der Rhoer, *Deadly Magic: A Personal Account of Communications Intelligence in World War II in the Pacific* (New York: Charles Scribner's Sons, 1978), 75.

11. Robert Guillain, *I Saw Tokyo Burning: An Eyewitness Narrative from Pearl Harbor to Hiroshima*, translated by William Byron (Garden City, New York: Doubleday, 1981), 53.

12. As quoted by Edward J. Drea, *MacArthur's Ultra: Code-Breaking and the War against Japan, 1942–1945* ([N.p.]: University Press of Kansas, 1992), 11.

13. This is used as an illustration in Drea, 7.

14. Friedman, Clarke Investigation, PHA, 34/84–85.

15. Laurance F. Safford, "A Brief History of Communications Intelligence in the United States" (written March 1952), as reprinted in *A Subject and Name Index to the MAGIC Documents: Summaries and Transcripts of the Top-Secret Diplomatic Communications of Japan, 1938–1945*, edited by Paul Kesaris (Frederick, MD: University Publications of America, 1982), 13.

16. Clark, 144–145.

17. Michael Slackman, *Target: Pearl Harbor* (Honolulu: University of Hawaii Press and Arizona Memorial Museum Association, 1990), 26.

18. James Rusbridger and Eric Nave, *Betrayal at Pearl Harbor: How Churchill Lured Roosevelt into World War II* (New York: Summit Books, 1991), 78.

19. Bratton, Army Board, PHA, 29/2345.

20. The Signal Intelligence of the Signal corps did the decryption for the army while "the code encipher section of naval communications" handled that function for the navy. Bratton, Army Board, PHA, 29/2336.

21. Safford, Army Board, PHA, 29/2366–2367.

22. Safford, "Brief History," 7–8.

23. Ibid., 8.

24. Ibid.

25. Ibid.

26. Ibid., 7.

27. Safford, Hewitt Inquiry, PHA, 36/72.

28. Alfred McCormack, "Origin, Functions and Problems of the Special Branch, M.I.S," in *A Subject and Name Index to the MAGIC Documents: Summaries and Transcripts of the Top-Secret Diplomatic Communications of Japan, 1938–1945*, edited by Paul Kesaris (Frederick, MD: University Publications of America, 1982), 34.

29. Prange, *At Dawn We Slept*, 81.

30. As quoted by Slackman, 32.
31. Ibid., 31–32.
32. Ibid., 32.
33. Safford, Army Board, PHA, 29/2367.
34. Safford, Joint Committee, PHA, 8/3774.
35. Ibid.
36. Ibid.
37. Ibid.
38. Safford, Hewitt Inquiry, PHA, 36/64–65. Ranks in the extracted testimony are as of the time of the particular investigation. In the text, we have retained that of the individual at the time of the Pearl Harbor attack.
39. Rusbridger and Nave, 80–81.
40. Louis Morton, *Strategy and Command: The First Two Years,* in the *United States Army in World War II: The War in the Pacific* series (Washington, D.C.: Office of the Chief of Military History, Department of the Army, 1962), 117.
41. Rusbridger and Nave, 119.
42. Slackman, 27.
43. As quoted by R. J. C. Butow, *The John Doe Associates: Backdoor Diplomacy for Peace, 1941* (Stanford: Stanford University Press, 1974), 393.
44. As quoted by Butow, 394.
45. Rusbridger and Nave, 119.
46. Ibid., 119–120.
47. As quoted by Warren F. Kimball, editor, *Churchill & Roosevelt: The Complete Correspondence*; Volume One: *Alliance Emerging, October 1933–November 1942* (Princeton: Princeton University Press, 1984), 215.
48. Slackman, 26.

CHAPTER 2

1. John Prados, *Combined Fleet Decoded: The Secret History of American Intelligence and the Japanese Navy in World War II* (New York: Random House, 1995), 174.
2. Rusbridger and Nave, 78.
3. Prados, 174.
4. Layton, *"And I Was There,"* 93, notes that the original name was Communications Intelligence and that Rochefort insisted that the name be changed to Combat Intelligence to provide greater security.
5. Bloch, Hart Inquiry, PHA, 26/21.
6. Prados, 174-175.
7. Ibid., 175.
8. Ibid., 176.
9. Rochefort, Army Board, PHA, 28/862.
10. Safford, Hart Inquiry, PHA, 26/388.
11. Safford, Hewitt Inquiry, PHA, 36/61.
12. Lieutenant Rudolph J. Fabian, who headed the Navy Magic work in the Philippines, explained the quite logical reason behind this decision: "To the best of my knowledge, they weren't performing any cryptanalysis or reading of diplomatic system[s]." Hewitt Inquiry, PHA, 34/46.
13. Wilkinson, Joint Committee, PHA, 4/1741.
14. Safford, Hewitt Inquiry, PHA, 36/61-62.
15. Layton, *"And I Was There,"* 339.

16. Ibid., 174.

17. Ibid., 534. An anonymous memorandum of war-time origin put the figure at 50 percent, but Layton's co-authors discredit it by an appeal to these postwar remembrances.

18. Safford, Hart Inquiry, PHA, 26/388.

19. Rochefort, Army Board, PHA, 28/862.

20. Rochefort, Hewitt Inquiry, PHA, 36/32. These subsidiary intercept stations are also named in "Appendix to Narrative Statement of Evidence at Navy Pearl Harbor Investigations," as reprinted as an exhibit in Joint Committee, PHA, 16/2294. Safford provides the same list, but substitutes "Oahu" for Pearl Harbor. Safford, Hart Inquiry, PHA, 26/387.

21. Rochefort, Army Board, PHA, 28/863.

22. Layton, "*And I Was There,*" 93.

23. Ibid., 93.

24. Ibid., 423.

25. John Costello, *Days of Infamy: MacArthur, Roosevelt, Churchill: The Shocking Truth Revealed—How Their Secret Deals and Strategic Blunders Caused Disasters at Pearl Harbor and the Philippines* (New York: Pocket Books, 1994), 298.

26. Layton, "*And I Was There,*" 422. The IBM cards were made of thick manila paper, three by seven inches, and could individually hold eighty columns (422). "IBM machines" were data processing machines, the precursors to computers.

27. Ibid., 423.

28. As quoted in ibid., 423-424.

29. For a concise description of how the JN system worked see Rusbridger and Nave, 86-87.

30. Ibid., 87.

31. On the use of the additive table see ibid.

32. Ibid., 86.

33. Costello, 299.

34. Ibid., 298.

35. Ibid., 299.

36. Ibid., 298-299.

37. Ibid., 299.

38. Eric Larrabee, *Commander in Chief: Franklin Delano Roosevelt, His Lieutenants, and Their War* (New York: Harper & Row, 1987), 360.

39. Costello, 298.

40. Dan van der Vat, *The Pacific Campaign: World War II—The U.S.-Japanese Naval War, 1941-1945* (New York: Simon & Schuster, 1991), 94.

41. Prange, *At Dawn We Slept*, 82.

42. Edwin T. Layton, "Admiral Kimmel Deserved a Better Fate," in *Air Raid: Pearl Harbor: Recollections of a Day of Infamy*, edited by Paul Stillwell (Annapolis, MD: Naval Institute Press, 1981), 281.

43. Slackman, 27.

44. Ibid., 31-32.

45. As quoted by Prange, *At Dawn We Slept*, 488.

46. Ibid., 488-489.

47. Ibid., 449.

48. Rochefort, Army Board, PHA, 28/863.

49. Ibid., 863.

50. Prados, 82.

51. Layton, Army Board, PHA, 28/1591.

52. Rochefort, Army Board, PHA, 28/863.
53. Ibid., 863-864.
54. Ibid., 864.
55. Ibid., 864.
56. Noyes, Joint Committee, PHA, 10/4714.
57. Layton, Roberts Commission, PHA, 23/659.
58. As quoted by Stanley Weintraub, *Long Day's Journey into War: December 7, 1941* (New York: Dutton/Truman Talley Books, 1991), 74.
59. Ibid., 102.
60. Wyman H. Packard, *A Century of U.S. Naval Intelligence*, a joint publication of the Office of Naval Intelligence and the Naval Historical Center (Washington: Department of the Navy, 1996), 397.
61. Hewitt question to Rochefort, Hewitt Inquiry, PHA, 36/32.
62. Rochefort, Hewitt Inquity, PHA, 36/32.
63. For the early history of the program see Packard, 367.
64. Ibid.
65. For a list of all trainees and the military positions they served in see ibid., 367-371.
66. Wilkinson, Joint Committee, PHA, 4/1741.

CHAPTER 3

1. As quoted by Michael Schaller, "General Douglas MacArthur and the Politics of the Pacific War," in *The Pacific War Revisited*, edited by Gunter Bischof and Robert L. Dupont (Baton Rouge: Louisiana State University Press, 1997), 18.
2. Kemp Tolley, "Army Snubs Navy in the Philippines," in *The Pacific War Remembered: An Oral History Collection*, edited by John T. Mason, Jr. (Annapolis, Maryland: Naval Institute Press, 1986), 27, 29.
3. As quoted by William H. Bartsch, *Doomed at the Start: American Pursuit Pilots in the Philippines, 1941–1942* (College Station, [Texas]: Texas A & M University Press, 1992), 5.
4. Schaller, 19.
5. As quoted by Schaller, 24. For other similar remarks by Roosevelt, see pages 24–25.
6. Drea, 11.
7. Howard W. Brown, "Reminiscences of Lieutenant Colonel Howard W. Brown," Document SRH-045; dated July 1945; as reprinted in *Listening to the Enemy: Key Documents on the Role of Communications Intelligence in the War with Japan*, edited by Ronald H. Spector (Wilmington, Delaware: Scholarly Resources, Inc., 1987), 49.
8. Drea, 15.
9. Ibid. For a detailed account of what happened to one such individual, both before the American surrender and during imprisonment by the Japanese conquerors, see Lyn Crost, *Honor by Fire: Japanese Americans at War in Europe and the Pacific* (Novato, California: Presidio, 1994). 25–30.
10. Prados, 211.
11. This interchangeability is especially noticeable in the testimony of Noyes, Joint Committee, PHA, 10/4713–4715. Since the locations are so geographically close this is quite understandable.
12. Fabian, Hewitt Inquiry, PHA, 36/45.
13. Noyes, Joint Committee, PHA, 10/4715.
14. Noyes, Joint Committee, PHA, 10/4715.

15. Safford, Hart Inquiry, PHA, 26/388.
16. Fabian, Hewitt Inquiry, PHA, 36/48.
17. Mason, Hewitt Inquiry, PHA, 36/46.
18. Safford, Hewitt Inquiry, PHA, 36/64.
19. Drea, 11.
20. Prados, 213.
21. As quoted by Prados,
22. Ibid.
23. Ibid.
24. Ibid.
25. Fabian, Hewitt Inquiry, PHA, 36/45.
26. Safford, Hart Inquiry, PHA, 26/388.
27. Wilkinson, Joint Committee, PHA, 4/1741.
28. Safford, Hewitt Inquiry, PHA, 36/61.
29. Noyles, Joint Committee, PHA, 10/4715. Memory is never a foolproof thing: Joseph K. Evans, G-2 for the American Army's Philippine Department during October and November, 1941, was convinced that *both* the army and a navy had their own Purple machines in the Philippines. See affidavit of Colonel Joseph K. Evans, Clausen Investigation, PHA, 35/41.
30. Noyes, Joint Committee, PHA, 10/4714.
31. Ibid., 4773.
32. Ibid., 4714.
33. Ibid., 4773.
34. Kramer, Joint Committee, PHA, 9/4176.
35. Noyes, Joint Committee, PHA, 10/4715.
36. Ibid.
37. Ibid.
38. Safford, Hewitt Inquiry, PHA, 36/61.
39. Ibid., 61.
40. Mason, Hewitt Inquiry, PHA, 36/47.
41. Ibid.
42. Fabian, Hewitt Inquiry, PHA, 36/45.
43. Ibid., 46.
44. Ibid., 45.
45. Safford, Hart Inquiry, PHA, 26/387.
46. Ibid.
47. Rochefort, Army Board, PHA, 28/863.
48. Ibid., 864.
49. Prados, 215.
50. Ibid.
51. Ibid.
52. For an in-depth analyses of the relationship by the office manager for MacArthur throughout World War II, see Paul P. Rogers, *The Good Years: MacArthur and Sutherland* (New York: Praeger, 1990), 71–76. For a navy viewpoint which paints in detail MacArthur's perceived stubbornness and uncooperativeness, see Tolley, 30.
53. For an account of the officer who had the unfortunate duty to convey word to the admiral, see Robert L. Dennison, "The Philippines: Prelude to Departure," in *The Pacific War Remembered: An Oral History Collection*, edited by John T. Mason, Jr. (Annapolis, MD: Naval Institute Press, 1986), 32–33.
54. Slackman, 54.
55. Noyes, Joint Committee, PHA, 10/4722.

56. Ibid.

57. For extracts of the dispatch see Noyes testimony, Joint Committee, PHA, 10/4721.

58. Mason, Hewitt Inquiry, PHA, 36/46.

59. Drea, 11.

60. On the built in delays caused by the divided locations and the typical length of time required to overcome the built-in difficulty, see Drea, 11.

61. As quoted by Ronald Lewin, *The American Magic: Codes, Ciphers and the Defeat of Japan* (New York: Farrar, Straus, Grioux, 1982), 130.

62. Drea, 11.

63. Layton, *"And I Was There,"* 379.

64. Alan H. Bath, *Tracking the Axis Enemy: The Triumph of Anglo-American Naval Intelligence* (Lawrence, KS: University Press of Kansas, 1998), 170.

65. For memories of the trip from Corregidor to Java see Prados, 246.

66. Bath, 170.

67. Layton, *"And I Was There,"* 379

68. Ibid.

69. Bath, 170.

70. Drea, 16.

CHAPTER 4

1. McCollum, Joint Committee, PHA, 8/3422.

2. Ibid.

3. Noyes, Joint Committee, PHA, 10/4717.

4. Ibid.

5. Ibid.

6. Ibid., 4720.

7. Ibid., 4717.

8. Ibid., 4721.

9. Safford, Hewitt Inquiry, PHA, 36/61.

10. Ibid., 62.

11. Noyes, Joint Committee, PHA, 10/4720.

12. Layton, Joint Committee, PHA, 10/4878.

13. Safford, Hewitt Inquiry, PHA, 36/62.

14. Safford, Hart Inquiry, PHA, 26/392–393.

15. Ibid., 388.

16. Rochefort, Hewitt Inquiry, PHA, 36/33.

17. Safford, Hewitt Inquiry, PHA, 36/62.

18. Layton, Hart Inquiry, PHA, 26/226.

19. Ibid., 227.

20. Bloch, Hart Inquiry, PHA, 26/21.

21. Layton, *"And I Was There,"* 119–120.

22. Layton, Joint Committee, PHA, 10/4878.

23. Ibid., 4879.

24. Rochefort, Hewitt Inquiry, PHA, 36/33.

CHAPTER 5

1. Alan Stripp, *Codebreaker in the Far East* (London: Frank Cass, 1989), 65.

2. Ibid., 65.

3. McCollum, Joint Committee, PHA 8/3394.
4. Safford, Joint Committee, PHA, 8/3797.
5. Memorandum by Safford, cited by himself before the Joint Committee, PHA, 8/3615.
6. Safford, Joint Committee, PHA, 8/3798.
7. Ibid.
8. McCollum, Joint Committee, PHA, 8/3422.
9. Safford, Joint Committee, PHA, 8/3798.
10. Marshall, Joint Committee, PHA, 3/1200.
11. Memorandum by Safford, cited by himself before Joint Committee, PHA, 8/3615.
12. Ibid.
13. Ibid.
14. Safford, Hewitt Inquiry, PHA, 36/64.
15. David Dilks, editor, *The Diaries of Sir Alexander Cadogan, 1938–1945* (New York: G. P. Putnam's Sons, 1971; first U.S. edition, 1972), 427. For a concise summary of German success against various types of British ciphers, see F. H. Hinsley, et al. *British Intelligence in the Second World War: Its Influence on Strategy and Operations* (volume 2) (New York: Cambridge University Press, 1981), 634–642.
16. William F. Friedman, "Expansion of the Signal Intelligence Service from 1930–7 December 1941" (dated December 4, 1945), in *A Subject and Name Index to the MAGIC Documents: Summaries and Transcripts of the Top-Secret Diplomatic Communications of Japan, 1938–1945*, edited by Paul Kesaris (Frederick MD: University Publications of America, 1982), 30.
17. Drea, 5.
18. Ibid., 6–7.
19. Prados, 81.
20. Rusbridger and Nave, n. 57 (276).
21. Safford, "Brief History," 12.
22. Ibid., 13.
23. Ibid., 4.
24. Ibid., 12.
25. Ibid., 13.
26. Prados, 83.
27. Ibid., 173. For the memories of another individual assigned there, see p. 83 in the same source.
28. For example, Capt. Mitsuo Fuchida, who led the aerial assault, noted the prohibition under which the fleet was operating. See Mitsuo Fuchida, "I Led the Air Attack on Pearl Harbor," in *Air Raid: Pearl Harbor: Recollections of a Day of Infamy*, edited by Paul Stillwell, 1–17 (Annapolis, MD: Naval Institute Press, 1981), 4.
29. Prados, 173. For comments on other alleged radio transmissions by the Japanese fleet—which was under the strictest orders to observe radio silence—see 172–173.
30. Bath, 160.
31. Ibid.
32. Ibid.
33. Prados, 210, who mentions the withdrawal, refers to it as "Station A." On 52, he three times calls it "Station E." In the index to the book (828), *both* listings are given. For a history of the station—it had the distinction of being set up twice and deactivated twice—see "Radio Security Station, Fourth Marine Regiment, Shanghia, China" (Document SRH-179), as reprinted in *Listening to the Enemy: Key*

Documents on the Role of Communications Intelligence in the War with Japan, edited by Ronald H. Spector (Wilmington, DE: Scholarly Resources, 1987), 28–39.

34. As quoted in Prados, 52.

35. Kramer, Joint Committee, PHA, 9/4176.

36. Safford, Hart Inquiry, PHA, 26/387.

CHAPTER 6

1. James Bamford, "Introduction" to Herbert O. Yardley, *The Chinese Black Chamber: An Adventure in Espionage* (Boston: Houghton Mifflin, 1983), xxiii.

2. For a tracing of the repeated pressures in this direction and the Canadian reluctance to yield, see John Bryden, *Best-Kept Secret: Canadian Secret Intelligence in the Second World War* (Toronto: Ontario Lester Publishing, 1993), 77–89.

3. Ibid., 89.

4. Ibid., 14.

5. Ibid., 12, 45.

6. Ibid., 16, 45.

7. Ibid., 16.

8. Ibid.

9. Safford, Joint Committee, PHA, 8/3708.

10. Ibid., /3709. Again, on the same page of testimony, Safford repeats that he had no idea what the British qualifications were on this score.

11. Ibid., 3633.

12. Bryden, 53–55.

13. Ibid., 84.

14. Ibid., 14–15.

15. Ibid., 15.

16. Ibid., 8–9.

17. Ibid., 10.

18. As quoted in ibid., 52.

19. Miles, Joint Committee, PHA, 2/947.

20. Ibid.

21. Bryden, 53.

22. Ibid., 85.

23. Ibid., 85, 88, 91.

24. Ibid., 91.

25. Ibid.

26. Ibid.

27. Ibid., 91–92.

28. For the text, see ibid., 93–94. For the American Office of Naval Intelligence reaction to this report when it was provided to them after the attack, see 95–96.

29. Ibid., 94.

30. Ibid.

31. Ibid., 95.

32. Safford, quoting a memorandum he himself had written, Joint Committee, PHA, 8/3614.

33. Stripp, 94.

34. For Nave's background and how he came to be available, see the concise summary in D. M. Horner, *High Command: Australia and Allied Strategy, 1939–1945* (Canberra, Australia: Australian War Memorial, 1982), 224–225.

35. Ibid., 225.

36. Stripp, 94–95.

37. Horner, 224.

38. Ibid., 225.

39. Ibid.

40. Ibid.

41. Ibid.

42. Stripp, 94–95.

43. As quoted by Horner, 225.

44. Citing his own earlier memorandum, Safford, Joint Committee, PHA, 8/3614.

45. Ibid.

46. Marsten, Joint Committee, PHA, 6/3323.

47. Safford, Joint Committee, PHA, 8/3710.

48. Although the joint plan of action had been tacitly accepted by all parties, it was unquestionably not revealed to the general public and even among professional American military men its exact legal and official status was ambiguous. Bratton, for example, doubted that the proposal had "ever [been explicitly] approved by the President." Bratton, Joint Committee, PHA, 9/4569. The ambiguity permitted the United States to enter into semi-official arrangements with probable future military allies without being irrevocably locked into having to implement them.

49. Quoted by Senator Ferguson in the interrogation of Bratton, Joint Committee, PHA, 9/4568. For the source of this quote see O'Dell's testimony before the Clarke Investigation, PHA, 34/59–60.

50. Bratton, Joint Committee, PHA, 9/4566.

51. O'Dell, Clarke Investigation, PHA, 34/60, 64–65.

52. Reprinted as part of Bratton testimony, Joint Committee, PHA, 9/4566.

53. O'Dell, Clarke Investigation, PHA, 34/64.

54. Ibid., 60.

55. Noted at beginning of reprint of text f message, Joint Committee, PHA, 9/4566.

CHAPTER 7

1. Stripp, 96.

2. Prados, 247.

3. Stripp, 96.

4. Antony Best, *Britain, Japan and Pearl Harbor: Avoiding War in East Asia, 1936–1941* (London: Routledge and London School of Economics, 1995), 140.

5. Prados, 247.

6. Ibid.

7. Kramer, Joint Committee, PHA, 9/3984.

8. Safford memorandum, as quoted by him before Joint Committee, PHA, 8/3614.

9. Prados, 247.

10. Ibid., 248.

11. Ibid.

12. Ibid.

13. Stripp, 96.

14. Prados, 247.

15. Bath, 167.

16. Ibid.

17. Safford, Joint Committee, PHA, 8/3622.
18. Krammer, Joint Committee, PHA, 9/3952–3953.
19. Ibid., 4064.
20. Friedman, Clarke Investigation, PHA, 34/85.
21. Quoted by Senator Ferguson in connection with testimony of Kramer, Joint Committee, PHA, 9/4067. The navy had received the Dutch translation at 1:21 A.M. the previous day and, hence, was also aware of its contexts: Joint Committee, PHA, 9/4066.
22. Kramer, Joint Committee, PHA, 9/4067.
23. Elliott R. Thorpe, *East Wind, Rain: A Chief of Counter-Intelligence Remembers Peace and War in the Pacific, 1939–1949* (Boston: Gambit, 1969), 51.
24. Ibid., 51–52.
25. Ibid., 53.
26. Ibid.
27. Ibid., 54.
28. Ibid., 51.
29. John E. Marsten speaking to Joint Committee, PHA, 6/3323.
30. Safford, Joint Committee, PHA, 8/3710.
31. Ibid., 3620.
32. Ibid., 3621.
33. For a concise summary of the arguments pro and con see Slackman, 29. At greater length, see Clark, 172–177.
34. Slackman, 27.
35. Costello, 316.
36. Ibid.
37. Ibid.
38. The report is photographically reprinted in Joint Committee, PHA, 17/2648, with the reliability evaluation referred to in the following paragraph.
39. Photographically reprinted in Joint Committee, PHA, 17/2650.
40. Photographically reported in Joint Committee, PHA, 17/2651.
41. Layton, Army Board, PHA, 28/1592–1593.
42. Thorpe, 51.
43. Bamford, xvii–xviii.
44. Ibid., xviii.
45. Ibid., xix.
46. Ibid., xx.
47. Ibid., xx–xxi.
48. Ibid., xxi.
49. Ibid., xxi–xxii.
50. Ibid., xxii.
51. Ibid.
52. Ibid., xxii–xxiii.
53. Ibid., xxiii.
54. Kimmel, Joint Committee, PHA 6/2512.
55. Miles, Army Board via Clarke Investigation, PHA 34/149.
56. Prados, 55.
57. Ibid.
58. Ibid.

CHAPTER 8

1. Miles, Joint Committee, PHA, 2/947.
2. Clausen, Joint Committee, PHA, 9/4334.
3. Ibid.,4340.
4. Clausen, Joint Committee, PHA, 9/4334.
5. Safford, Hewitt Inquiry, PHA, 36/73.
6. Ibid.
7. Safford, Joint Committee, PHA, 8/3629.
8. Ibid., 3708–3709.
9. Paraphrasing of Incoming Telegram," Joint Committee, PHA, 18/3312.
10. Safford, Joint Committee, PHA, 8/3629.
11. Ibid., 3710.
12. Reasons for the location of GC&CS at Bletchley Park are discussed by Stripp, 13–14.
13. R. V. Jones, *The Wizard War: British Scientific Intelligence, 1939–1945* (New York: Coward, McCann & Geoghegan, 1978), 58.
14. For various names that were utilized, see Stripp, 146.
15. Gordon Welchman, *The Hut Six Story: Breaking the Enigma Codes* ([Harmondsworth]: Penguin Books, 1982), 145.
16. Peter Calvocoressi, *Top Secret Ultra* (New York: Pantheon Books, 1980), 13.
17. Stripp, 15.
18. Ibid.
19. Ibid.; Calvocoressi, 72; Patrick Beesly, *Very Special Intelligence: The Story of the Admiralty's Operational Intelligence Centre, 1939–1945* (Garden City, New York: Doubleday 1978 45; Brian Johnson, *The Secret War* (New York: Methuen, 1978), 305; and David Kahn, *Kahn on Codes: Secrets of the New Cryptology* (New York: Macmillan, 1983), 118.
20. F. H. Hinsley and Alan Stripp, "Preface," in *Codebreakers: The Inside Story of Bletchley Park*, edited by F. H. Hinsley and Alan Stripp (New York: Oxford University Press, 1993), v.
21. Lewin, *Magic*, 19, implies this figure by stating that the British program was approximately a fourth the size of the 50,000 person American Magic.
22. Ibid.
23. Calvocoressi, 63–64.
24. Stripp, 22.
25. Ibid.
26. Prados, 170.
27. Ibid.
28. Ibid.
29. Ronald Lewin, *Ultra Goes to War* (London: Hutchinson & Company, 1978; paperback edition, New York: Pocket Books, 1980), 141–142.
30. For example, Rebecca R. Raines, *Getting the Message Through: A Branch History of the U.S. Army Signal Corps* (Washington D.C.: Center of Military History, United States Army, 1996), 432.
31. For reasons for the change see Rusbridger and Nave, 113.
32. Ibid., 112, "Appendix 3" introduction (193).
33. F. H. Hinsley, 2:70, speaks of how the diplomatic "reports from Berlin were especially valuable on German intentions."
34. Ibid.
35. For the usefulness of Ambassador Oshima's reports from Berlin in helping

the Allies better understand what they were up against in invading the Continent, see Anthony C. Brown, *Bodyguard of Lies* (New York: Harper & Row, 1975), 356–358.

36. As quoted by Carl Boyd, *Hitler's Japanese Confidant: General Oshima Hiroshi and Magic Intelligence, 1941–1945* (Lawrence, KS: University Press of Kansas, 1993), 1. For other assessments in a similar vein see 1–2.

37. Jones, 491. Although Jones never explicitly says that Bletchley was reading the Japanese "traffic," the fact that these reports were from *Japanese* and they were reporting to their homeland carries with it the implication of British success at breaking the Japanese ciphers.

38. Ibid.

39. Ibid.

40. Ibid.

41. Horner, 225.

42. Michael Lowe, "Japanese Naval Codes," in *Codebreakers: The Inside Story of Bletchley Park*, edited by F. H. Hinsley and Alan Stripp (New York: Oxford University Press, 1993), 263.

43. Hugh Denham, "Bedford—Bletchley—Kilindini—Colombo," in *Codebreakers*, edited by Hinsley and Stripp, 267.

44. Ibid. No identification is provided as to the first name of the "Mr. Nichols" referred to in the text.

45. Hinsley and Stripp, v. They place the number of Japanese and Italian documents at only "slightly smaller" than the 4,000 German ones, which would indicate in the 3,000 range. One wonders whether the total figure might be including those being produced in the field.

46. Ibid., v. (The reference to "Washington" is presumably to the American Magic program.)

47. Bath, 139.

48. Quoted during the Safford Testimony, Joint Committee, PHA, 8/3625.

49. Safford, Joint Committee, PHA, 8/3625.

50. Bradley F. Smith, *Sharing Secrets with Stalin: How the Allies Traded Intelligence, 1941–1945* (Lawrence, KS: University Press of Kansas, 1996), 11.

51. Ibid., 11–12.

52. On the tendency of the British to over-estimate the significance and amount of the Ultra material they provided in this period see B. F. Smith, 81–82.

53. Richard Overy, *Why the Allies Won* (New York: W. W. Norton edition, 1996), 88.

54. Hinsley 2:40.

55. Ibid.

56. Ibid.

57. Bath, 140.

58. Ibid.

59. On contemporary disgruntlement with the SIS in the Far East, see ibid.

60. Rusbridger and Nave, 75.

61. Ibid., 87.

62. Ibid., 91.

63. Hinsley, 2:40.

64. Ibid.

65. Bath, 170.

66. Hinsley, 2:52.

67. Christopher Andrew, *Her Majesty's Secret Service: The Making of the British Intelligence Community* (1985; New York: Viking/Elisabeth Sitton Books, 1986), 353.

68. Ibid.
69. Hinsley, 2:53.
70. Ibid., 2:24
71. Ibid.
72. Rusbridger and Nave, 88.
73. As quoted by Best, 140.
74. As quoted by Ibid., 143.
75. For examples from 1942, see Rusbridger and Nave, 187–192.
76. Ibid., 92.
77. Ibid.
78. Ibid.
79. Ibid., 161.
80. Ibid., 161.
81. As quoted by William Stevenson (no relationship to Stephenson of the BSC), *A Man Called Intrepid: The Secret War* (New York: Harcourt Brace Jovanovich, 1976), 270, who also discusses Fleming's highly fictionalized account of the incident.
82. Safford, "Brief History," 4, 7.
83. Costello, n. 19 (412).

CHAPTER 9

1. Miles, Joint committee, PHA, 2/951.
2. Friedman, Clarke Investigation, PHA, 34/85.
3. Henry C. Clausen and Bruce Lee, *Pearl Harbor: Final Judgment* (New York: Crown, 1992), 44.
4. Ibid.
5. Fabian and Mason (joint) testimony, Hewitt Inquiry, PHA, 36/50.
6. Safford, Hart Inquiry, PHA, 26/393.
7. According to John E. Marsten, one of the legal counsels for the joint committee, the committee had "communications from … the Australians" stating or indicating this. PHA, 6/3323.
8. Safford, Joint Committee, PHA, 8/3710.
9. Safford, Hewitt Inquiry, PHA, 36/64.
10. Fabian (Fabian and Mason testified together), Hewitt Inquiry, PHA, 36/48.
11. Safford, Hewitt Inquiry, PHA, 36/61.
12. Safford spoke as if this were a common phenomenon between Singapore and the Philippines and that the British almost certainly followed the same policy in regard to their Australian compatriots: "The Australian C.I. Unit had liaison with the Singapore C.I. Unit, including exchange of translation and keys except for the purple and red machines. The winds 'set-up' message … were in J-19. Singapore sent translations to Corregidor … and undoubtedly sent these same translations to Australia." Safford, quoting his own earlier written memorandum, Joint Committee, PHA, 8/3614.
13. Document quoted in Joint Committee, PHA, 6/2702.
14. We received a tip-off from the British in Singapore in late November 1941, which was immediately forwarded to the Navy Department by the Commander-in-Chief, Pacific Fleet" (Safford, Hart Inquiry, PHA, 26/393; cf. Kramer, Joint Committee, PHA, 9/3934).
15. Intelligence Report 97, photographically reproduced, Joint Committee, PHA, 17/2660.
16. Kramer, Joint Committee, PHA, 9/3933.

17. Ibid., 3934. At one point he dates the receipt of the British translation as on the same day that the U.S. Navy worked up its own translation (Joint Committee, PHA, 9/3934), which strengthens the justification for substitution. Later he is a little vaguer, speaking of how "about the same date" as the navy did its translation, the British one was received (Joint Committee, PHA, 9/3951), which makes the case for substitution a bit weaker.

18. Ibid., 3951.

19. Ibid., 3934.

20. Costello, 309. For the text of the Australian rendition (far less often seen than that of the two major powers), as well as of the United States and Great Britain, see n. 29 (414–415).

21. Ibid., 310. For an interesting argument that this message resulted in Churchill coming down against the American desire for a modus vivendi with Japan to indefinitely postpone the danger of war, see 310–311.

22. Ibid., 323.

23. Bath, 161.

24. Ibid.

25. Lewin, *Magic*, 46; Prados, 170–171.

26. Rusbridger and Nave, n. 14 (260).

27. Prados, 171. Best, 146, reports that there were two.

28. For evidence see John Costello, 323.

29. For the views of Duane L. Whitlock, who was a Cast participant, see Ibid.

30. For additional criticisms of the theory of British foreknowledge coming through their reading of JN-25B, see Prados, 171.

31. Rusbridger and Nave, 94.

32. Rusbridger and Nave, n. 20 (263), discuss the fervent search of Singapore records immediately after Pearl Harbor to assure that their material had, indeed, been sent per procedure.

33. Ibid., 94. Nave is convinced that his superiors withheld information that clearly pointed to Pearl Harbor. Although he was certainly in an ideal position to know what was available and what was forwarded to Bletchley Park, the other data discussed here argue strongly that the available decrypts did not point conclusively to one attack point, as Nave asserts they did. If this were not true the ignorance of the other individuals cited is utterly incomprehensible.

34. For a discussion of this evidence see Costello, 326–330.

35. As quoted by David Stafford, *Churchill and Secret Service* (Woodstock, New York: Overlook Press, 1997, 235. Cited but not quoted in Best, 190–191.

36. As quoted by Best, 191.

CHAPTER 10

1. Noyes, Joint Committee, PHA, 10/4773.

2. William F. Friedman, Clarke Investigation, PHA, 34/85.

3. Safford, Hewitt Inquiry, PHA, 36/64.

4. Miles, Joint Committee, PHA, 2/947.

5. Friedman, Clarke Investigation, PHA, 34/85.

6. Kimmel, Joint Committee, PHA, 6/2835. On the security of the courier method of providing the messages see 6/2834.

7. Thomas Parrish, *The Ultra Americans: The U.S. Role in Breaking the Nazi Codes* (New York: Stein and Day, 1986), 61.

8. Ibid., 60–61.

9. Ibid., 58–59, conjectures that Sir Henry Tizard's mission to the United States for the Air Ministry may have been the means of doing so.

10. Ibid., 65.

11. Ibid.

12. Cf. the remarks in ibid., 65–66.

13. As quoted by David Kahn, *Seizing the Enigma: The Race to Break the German U-Boat Codes, 1939–1945* (Boston: Houghton Mifflin, 1991), 237. For an assessment of the visit by American specialists that minimizes the element of British cooperativeness, see Stafford, 201–202.

14. As quoted by Joseph P. Lash, *Roosevelt and Churchill, 1939–1941: The Partnership that Saved the West* (New York: W. W. Norton, 1976), 295. For evidence of the British reading the Japanese ciphers in early July 1941 see Waldo Heinrichs, *Threshold of War: Franklin D. Roosevelt & American Entry into World War II* (New York: Oxford University Press, 1988), 122 and n. 4 (243).

15. Recounting their work was one of the purposes of Parrish's book. For a short summary by one of the participants see Robert M. Slusser, "An American at Bletchley Park," in *Codebreakers*, edited by Hinsley and Stripp, 74–76.

16. Welchman, 179.

17. Bath, 151.

18. Ibid., 161.

19. Marshall, Joint Committee, PHA, 3/1197. In the immediate context, this seems more likely to refer to cooperation in the Atlantic, a subject which (as noted earlier) he had a desire not to elaborate on any more than the minimum. On the other hand the explicit topic a half page earlier and beginning at least by the middle of the following page, is *Pacific* data.

20. Marshall, Joint Committee, PHA, 3/1198.

21. Ibid., 1337.

22. Miles, Joint Committee, PHA, 3/1548.

23. Layton, Hart Inquiry, PHA, 26/226.

24. Quoted in paragraphed form in Joint Committee, PHA, 3/1341.

25. For the quote and accompanying paraphrase of the communication see Joint Committee, PHA, 3/1341.

26. For entire text see Joint Committee, PHA, 20/4545–4546.

27. For entire text see Joint Committee, PHA, 20/4546–4547.

28. For entire text see Joint Committee, PHA, 20/4547–4548.

29. For entire text see Joint Committee, PHA, 20/4548–4550.

30. McCollum interrogation, Joint Committee, PHA, 8/3439.

31. Ibid., 3439.

32. Noyes, Joint Committee, PHA, 10/4764.

33. Ibid., 4790. Cf. similar remark on 10/4789.

34. Ibid., 4790.

35. Ibid., 4790.

36. Ibid., 4765.

37. Ibid., 4765.

38. Ibid., 4764.

39. Ibid., 4764.

40. Ibid., 4765.

41. Ibid., 4765.

42. James Leutze, *The London Journal of General Raymond E. Lee, 1940–1941* (Boston: Little, Brown, 1971), 303–304.

43. For an example see Leutze, 277.

44. For an example, see Leutze, 337.
45. For an example concerning Maj. Gen. James E. Chaney and his Joint Staff Mission see Leutze, 296; cf. 236]
46. Ibid., 203.
47. For examples see Costello, 307–308.
48. For an examination of the evidence that the work continued see Costello, 308, and Stafford, 235.
49. Leutze, 264. Leutze, n. 3 (264), was intrigued by this passing reference because, as he observes, "it is generally assumed that this was purely an American breakthrough."
50. Heinrichs, 170.
51. Leutze, 296–297.
52. Ibid., 318.
53. Ibid., 318–319.
54. A very few additional messages are recorded as hand delivered or via the U.S. Navy during an at-sea meeting between the two leaders. For our purposes these numbers have not been included, nor rough drafts that were never sent. Of Church's messages, 24 additional ones are not identified as to means of transmission.
55. The numbers were compiled by this author from the exchanges in Kimball.
56. For text see Congressional Committee, PHA, 20/4545–4546.
57. For text see Congressional Committee, PHA, 20/4546–4547.
58. For text see Congressional Committee, PHA, 20/4547–4548.
59. For text see Congressional Committee, PHA, 20/4548–4550.
60. Lewin, *Magic,* 47.
61. The numbers were compiled by this author from the exchanges in Kimball.
62. As quoted by Lash, 379.
63. On the nature and evolution of the Typex see Costello, n. 19 (412).
64. See the discussion in Costello, 307. Stevenson, 86, 102, 152, repeatedly implies that FDR received Ultras via BSC.
65. See the discussion of Kimball, xxi–xxii.
66. As quoted by Lash, 473. Also quoted by Anthony C. Brown, *"C": The Secret Life of Sir Stewart Graham Menzies—Spymaster to Winston Churchill* (New York: Macmillan, 1987), 376.
67. Rusbridger and Nave, n. 44 (274).
68. Lash, 473.
69. For an analysis of the Stephenson-Churchill relationship that concedes the ambiguity of the evidence, but considers that, on balance, it indeed was likely a close one, see William Troy, *Wild Bill and Intrepid: Donovan, Stephenson, and the Origin of CIA* (New Haven, Connecticut: Yale University Press, 1996), 178–190. Page 188 and n. 35 (238), cite the limited contemporary evidence that some type of confidential data was being forwarded through BSC on behalf of the president.
70. Nigel West, *A Thread of Deceit: Espionage Myths of World War II* (New York: Random House, 1985), 138. For a critique of a number of inaccuracies in the popular biography of Stephenson, *A Man Called Intrepid,* see 127–138.
71. Based on an examination of the entirety of Kimball's work.
72. Kimball, 69–70.
73. As quoted by Kimball, 70.
74. Ibid.
75. As quoted by Richard Dunlop, *Donovan: America's Master Spy* (Chicago: Rand McNally,1982), 316–317.
76. Ibid., 317.

77. Ibid.

78. For comments on the exaggeration of Stephenson's importance in *A Man Called Intrepid*, see Thomas F. Troy, *Donovan and the CIA: A History of the Establishment of the Central Intelligence Agency* ([N.p.]: Central Intelligence Agency, 1975; declassified and slightly rewritten version, Frederick, MD: Aletheia Books/University Publications of America, 1981), vi. In more detail see his *Intrepid*, 40–45. On the other hand (178–201), he believes that the anti-Stephenson naysaying has itself become excessive and exaggerated.

79. The claim was that of William Stephenson, of B.S.C., as quoted by Richard Dunlop, 318.

80. Troy, *Donovan*, 83. For a discussion of the great impact of BSC on the OSS in the first part of its existence see pages 80–83.

81. Andrew, 467.

82. For expressions of this attitude see Anthony C. Brown, *The Last Hero: Wild Bill Donovan* (New York: New York Times Books, 1982), 166, and Nigel West, *MI6: British Secret Intelligence Service Operations, 1909–1945* (New York: Random House, 1983), 208. For examples of the British advisers who helped him organize the emerging O.S.S., see Anthony C. Brown, *Donovan*, 174.

83. Roosevelt was aware of the close relationship between Donovan and the British and, at times, it caused him concern. For an example from 1942 see Maochun Yu, *OSS in China: Prelude to Cold War* (New Haven: Yale University Press, 1996), 19.

84. Dunlop, 302–303.

85. R. Harris Smith, *OSS: The Secret History of America's First Central Intelligence Agency* (Berkeley, California: University of California Press, 1972), 20.

86. For the text of Stephenson's report on this see Lash, 140.

87. Bradley F. Smith, *The Shadow Warriors* (New York: Basic Books, 1983), 29.

88. West, *MI6*, 209.

89. Bryden, 57.

90. Ibid., 84.

91. Ibid., n. 45 (349).

92. Ibid., 84–85.

93. For the case that Hoover's source had to have been the Canadians rather than an American intercept, see the reasoning in Bryden, n. 45 (349).

94. Bryden, 97.

95. For an example, see ibid.

96. As quoted by Troy, *Wild Bill*, 71.

97. For a March 1941 report indicating this, see ibid., 72.

98. As quoted by Andrew, 467.

99. Army Pearl Harbor Board via Clarke Investigation, PHA 34/150.

100. Best, 146.

CHAPTER 11

1. From British telegram dated August 31, 1945, reprinted in entirety in Clausen Investigation, PHA, 35/203–204.

2. Quoted by Clausen, Joint Committee, PHA, 9/4402.

3. Text quoted in full by Clausen, Joint Committee, PHA, 9/4401–4402.

4. As reprinted in Clausen Investigation, PHA, 35/577.

5. Amendment to Affidavit" of FBI agent in charge, dated April 20, 1945, as printed in the Clausen Investigation, PHA, 35/44. It is also quoted in full by Clausen

before the Joint Committee (PHA, 9/4361). In that context, however, a verbal lapse transforms "Gerald Wilkinson" into "General Wilkinson."

6. Affidavit of Bucknell, quoted by Clausen, Joint Committee, PHA,9/4346.

7. Affidavit of Kendall J. Fielder, as quoted by Clausen, Joint Committee, PHA, 9/4355.

8. Affidavit of Kendall J. Fielder, as quoted by Clausen, Joint Committee, PHA, 9/4355.

9. Affidavit of Bicknell, quoted by Clausen, Joint Committee, PHA, 9/4348.

10. Affidavit of Fielder, quoted by Clausen, Joint Committee, PHA, 9/4355.

11. In his affidavit, Bicknell referred to "the reports which Gerald Wilkinson of the British Secret Intelligence Service sent to Mr. Harry Dawson" and which were then conveyed to him. Affidavit as quoted by Clausen, Joint Committee, PHA, 9/4348.

12. Affidavit of Bucknell, quoted by Claussen, Joint Committee, PHA, 9/4347.

13. Clausen, Joint Committee, PHA, 9/4345.

14. Layton, Navy Court of Inquiry, PHA, 33/832.

15. Layton (Army Board, PHA, 28/1578–1579): "... I presume the military attache at Chungking [China], if he received some information, he would pass it in turn to G-2, who in turn would pass it to O.N.I., who in turn would pass it to us. Most of our dispatches coming from China direct or from Japan direct or from the Philippines or from French Indo-China or from the Singapore area would be passed through the naval observers there, but it wasn't necessarily their original information; it may have come from some other source."

16. Affidavit of Layton, Clausen Investigation, PHA, 35/49. The affidavit is also quoted by Clausen before the Joint Committee, PHA, 9/4370.

17. Layton, Roberts Commission, PHA, 23/658.

18. Layton, Hewitt Inquiry, PHA, 36/112.

19. Layton, Army Board, PHA, 28/1578.

20. Affidavit of Layton, Clausen Investigation, PHA, 35/49. It is also quoted by Clausen before the Joint Committee, PHA, 9/4370.

21. Affidavit of Layton, Clausen Investigation, PHA, 35/51. Clausen quotes this particular evidence before the Joint Committee, PHA, 9/4371.

22. Layton, Hart Inquiry, PHA, 26/232.

23. Ibid., 226.

24. Neither in the index nor text of his *"And I Was There"* (1985).

25. As quoted by Anthony C. Brown, *Secret Life*, 375.

26. Clausen quotes this document in segments in his testimony and we have run it together for convenience of presentation. Clausen, Joint Committee, PHA, 9/4335–4336. Cf. Clausen Investigation, PHA, 35/42 and 35/203.

27. Clausen, Joint Committee, PHA, 9/4336.

28. Memorandum of John E. Russell as printed in the Clausen Investigation, PHA, 35/42.

29. Bath, 161–162.

30. As quoted by Bath, 162.

31. Ibid.

32. Ibid., 163.

33. Best, 146–147.

34. Bath, 163.

35. Ibid.

36. Ibid., 163.

37. Ibid., 164.

38. Ibid., 162.

39. John Robertson, *Australia at War: 1939–1945* (Melbourne, Australia: William Heinemann, 1981), 106–107.

40. Bath, 151.

41. Ibid., 152.

42. As quoted by Bath, 139.

43. Best, 145.

44. Prange, *At Dawn We Slept,* 79.

45. Ibid.

46. Ibid.

47. Packard, 297.

48. Prange, *At Dawn We Slept,* 79.

49. Packard, 297.

50. Ibid.

51. Prange, *At Dawn We Slept,* 357.

52. Ibid.

53. Nathan Miller, *Spying for America: The Hidden History of U.S. Intelligence* (New York: Paragon House, 1989), 253.

54. Ibid.

CHAPTER 12

1. Affidavit of John E. Russell, dated April 10, 1945, as printed in Clausen Investigation, PHA, 35/42.

2. Amendment to Affidavit of Robert L. Shivers, March 16, 1945, as quoted in full by Clausen, Joint Committee, PHA, 9/4361. Text is also reproduced in full in Clausen Investigation, PHA, 35/44.

3. Appendix A to Affidavit of C. A. Willoughby, as printed in Clausen Investigation, PHA, 35/86–87.

4. Affidavit of Joseph K. Evans, as quoted in full by Clausen, Joint Committee, PHA, 9/4358. Also printed in full in Clausen Investigation, PHA, 35/41. Shivers was convinced in a March 1945 affidavit that the three had *not* discussed the matter though he conceded that he could "not recall the details of our conversation." See "Amendment to Affidavit," quoted by Clausen, Joint Committee, PHA, 9/4361; text is also found in the Clausen Investigation, PHA, 35/44.

5. Affidavit of Joseph K. Evans, dated March 22, 1945, as quoted in full by Clausen, Joint Committee, PHA, 9/4358.

6. As quoted by Lewin, *Magic,* 178.

7. Clausen, *Pearl Harbor* 146.

8. Ibid.

9. Anthony C. Brown, *Secret Life,* 374.

10. Ibid.

11. Ibid.

12. As quoted by Anthony C. Brown, 379.

13. Ibid., 484–485. For the text of Wilkinson's SIS orders (one of the rare cases that such orders ever became publicly available), see the unnumbered footnote on 485.

14. Bath, 164.

15. Ibid.

16. Ibid.

17. Ibid.

18. Ibid.

19. Ibid.
20. Bath, 165.
21. Ibid.
22. Mason, Hewitt Inquiry, PHA, 36/49–50.
23. Ibid., 50.
24. For Adm. Hart's explanation of why he acted this way, see Thomas C. Hart, "War on the Horizon," in *The Pacific War Remembered: An Oral History Collection*, edited by John T. Mason, Jr. (Annapolis, MD: Naval Institute Press, 1986), 20–21. Hart was convinced that Roosevelt's reaction to the report—send several naval vessels into the area—was designed as an excuse to get into the Pacific War (21–22). Acting on this assumption, critics have sometimes called Roosevelt's proposal the "fishbait mission," bait to provoke a hostile military reaction and justifying intervention.
25. As quoted by Norman Harper in *A Great and Powerful Friend: A Study of Australian American Relations between 1900 and 1975* (St. Lucia, Qld., Australia: University of Queensland Press, 1987), 03. For date of cable see n. 3, 368.

CHAPTER 13

1. One wonders what message he has in mind. The last section of the final Japanese diplomatic message (breaking off negotiations) was in the hands of the secretary of state before its delivery by the Japanese diplomats themselves on December 7. What message was it, then, that reached American hands only on the 8th and what did it say? Further complicating the question is that none of the diplomatic intercepts (the subject under discussion) explicitly or implicitly mention Pearl Harbor as the object of attack.

The closest is the Foreign Ministry message to Honolulu instructing its personnel to divide the harbor into sections and provide a regular update as to which vessels were in port and moored in each section—but this was available long before the 7th. Since this was the only harbor singled out for such treatment it, arguably, should have set off loud alarm bells. One wonders what type of message seemed to point to a Hawaiian attack and from what source it was obtained.
2. Quoted by George Marshall in Joint Committee, PHA, 3/1128–1129.
3. Quoted by George Marshall, in Joint Committee, PHA, 3/1129–1130.
4. George Marshall, Joint Committee, PHA, 3/1130.
5. As reprinted in Joint Committee, PHA, 3/1133.
6. Exchange between Ferguson and Marshall, Joint Committee, PHA, 3/1198.
7. Marshall, Joint Committee, PHA, 3/1197.
8. Ibid., 1197–1198.
9. Marshall, Army Board, PHA, 29/2403.
10. Ibid., 2404.
11. Marshall, Joint Committee, PHA, 11/5178.
12. Marshall, Army Board, PHA, 29/2404.
13. Ibid., 2407–2408.
14. Marshall, Joint Committee, PHA, 3/1146–1147. Late on 1147 Marshall again repeats the 10,000, 6,000, and 30,000 figures.
15. Miles, Joint Committee, PHA, 2/948.

CHAPTER 14

1. Richardson, Joint Committee, PHA, 6/3321.
2. Ibid.

3. Ibid., 3321-3322.

4. Cooper, Joint Committee, PHA, 6/3322.

5. Ibid.

6. Ibid.

7. Ibid.

8. Ibid., 3322–3323.

9. Richardson, Joint Committee, PHA, 6/3321.

10. Joint Committee, PHA, 3/1126–1127.

11. Joint Committee, PHA, 3/1127.

12. Clausen, Joint Committee, PHA, 9/4336–4337. "I would like to know if you know the source of that" is printed in different point size, as if Clausen is quoting from the text of the telegram sent back by the British. In context, this seems unlikely. He is simply saying he asked the question that the British later responded to in their telegram.

13. Ibid., 4337.

14. As reprinted in the Clausen Investigation, PHA, 35/203-204.

15. Clausen, Joint Committee, PHA, 9/4337.

16. Ibid.

17. Miles, Joint Committee, PHA, 2/947.

18. In May 1943, a formal agreement between the two nations explicitly recognized the differing leading roles the powers would play in decryption in Europe versus Asia (Parrish, 98).

19. W.J. Holmes, *Double-edged Secrets: U.S. Naval Intelligence Operations in the Pacific During World War II* (Annapolis, MD: Naval Institute Press, 1979). The only time the subject of decrypt sharing is mentioned concerns American data going to the British in 1945 (204).

20. As quoted by Welchman, 146.

21. van der Vat, 98.

22. Stripp, 66.

23. Lewin, *Ultra*, xviii.

24. On the sale of these machines as a reason for secrecy see Kahn, *Codes*, 213.

25. Rusbridger and Nave, n. 33 (279).

26. Welchman, 2.

27. Parrish, 286-287.

28. Dilks, 427.

29. Winterbotham, *The Ultra Secret* (New York: Harper & Row, 1974), 168-169.

30. The successes at the Battle of the Coral Sea, the Battle of Midway, and the shooting down of Admiral Yamamoto are attributed to "ultra" (ibid., 175-176). Winterbotham makes the broad remark that "Ultra was being particularly useful" at one point in the Pacific (161) and that it played a role in "the naval battles of World War II, both in the Atlantic and the Pacific" (86). He goes so far as to "suggest that Ultra played a leading role in the strategy of MacArthur and Nimitz" (191).

31. For a discussion see Costello, 306.

32. Ibid., 318.

33. Ibid., 319.

34. For a summary of their views see Costello, 319–321.

35. Ibid., 323.

36. For example, Stafford, 233.

Bibliography

PRIMARY SOURCES

Bartsch, William H. *Doomed at the Start: American Pursuit Pilots in the Philippines, 1941–1942.* College Station, [TX]: Texas A & M University Press, 1992.

Brown, Howard W. "Reminiscences of Lieutenant Colonel Howard W. Brown." Document SRH–045; dated July 1945. As reprinted in *Listening to the Enemy: Key Documents on the Role of Communications Intelligence in the War with Japan,* edited by Ronald H. Spector, 43–76. Wilmington, DE: Scholarly Resources, 1987.

Bryden, John. *Best-Kept Secret: Canadian Secret Intelligence in the Second World War.* Toronto: OntarioLester Publishing, 1993.

Calvocoressi, Peter. *Top Secret Ultra.* New York: Pantheon Books, 1980.

Clausen, Henry C., and Bruce Lee. *Pearl Harbor: Final Judgement.* New York: Crown, 1992.

Denham, Hugh. "Bedford—Bletchley—Kilindini—Colombo." In *Codebreakers: The Inside Story of Bletchley Park,* edited by F. H. Hinsley and Alan Stripp, 264–281. New York: Oxford University Press, 1993.

Dennison, Robert L. (Admiral) "The Philippines: Prelude to Departure." In *The Pacific War Remembered: An Oral History Collection,* edited by John T. Mason, Jr., 32–37. Annapolis, MD: Naval Institute Press, 1986.

Dilks, David, editor. *The Diaries of Sir Alexander Cadogan, 1938–1945.* New York: G. P. Putnam's Sons, 1971; first U.S. edition, 1972.

Friedman, William F. "Expansion of the Signal Intelligence Service from 1930–7 December 1941" (dated December 4, 1945). In *A Subject and Name Index to the MAGIC Documents: Summaries and Transcripts of the Top-Secret Diplomatic Communications of Japan, 1938–1945,* edited by Paul Kesaris, 17–31. Frederick, MD: University Publications of America, 1982. .

Fuchida, Mitsuo. "I Led the Air Attack on Pearl Harbor." In *Air Raid: Pearl Harbor: Recollections of a Day of Infamy,* edited by Paul Stillwell, 1–17. Annapolis, MD: Naval Institute Press, 1981.

Guillain, Robert. *I Saw Tokyo Burning: An Eyewitness Narrative from Pearl Harbor to Hiroshima.* Translated by William Byron. Garden City, New York: Doubleday, 1981.

Hart, Thomas C. (Admiral). "War on the Horizon." In *The Pacific War Remembered: An Oral History Collection,* edited by John T. Mason, Jr., 17–22. Annapolis, MD: Naval Institute Press, 1986.

Hinsley, F. H., and Alan Stripp. "Preface." In *Codebreakers: The Inside Story of Bletchley Park,* edited by F. H. Hinsley and Alan Stripp, v–viii. New York: Oxford University Press, 1993.

Holmes, W. J. *Double-edged Secrets: U.S. Naval Intelligence Operations in the Pacific During World War II.* Annapolis, MD: Naval Institute Press, 1979.

Joint Committee on the Investigation of the Pearl Harbor Attack. *Pearl Harbor Attack: Hearings before the Joint Committee on the Investigation of the Pearl Harbor Attack.* Washington, D.C.: U.S. Government Printing Office, 1946. 39 volumes, including the text of earlier governmental investigations. A 40th volume provides the panel's conclusions.

> Investigations included in the volumes are:
> Roberts Commission (December 22, 1941–January 23, 1942)
> Hart Inquiry (February 22, 1944–June 15, 1944)
> Army Pearl Harbor Board (July 20–October 20, 1944)
> Navy Court of Inquiry (July 24–October 19, 1944)
> Hewitt Investigation (May 15–July 11, 1945)
> Clausen investigation (November 23, 1944–September 12, 1945)
> Clarke Investigation (September 14–16, 1944; July 13–August 4, 1945)
> Joint Congressional Investigation (November 15, 1945–July 14, 1946)

Jones, R. V. *The Wizard War: British Scientific Intelligence, 1939–1945.* New York: Coward, McCann & Geoghegan, 1978.

Kimball, Warren F., editor. *Churchill & Roosevelt: The Complete Correspondence.* Volume One: *Alliance Emerging, October 1933–November 1942.* Princeton: Princeton University Press, 1984.

Layton, Edwin T. "Admiral Kimmel Deserved a Better Fate." In *Air Raid: Pearl Harbor: Recollections of a Day of Infamy,* edited by Paul Stillwell, 271–285. Annapolis, MD: Naval Institute Press, 1981.

_____, with Roger Pineau and John Costello. *"And I Was There:" Pearl Harbor and Midway—Breaking the Secrets.* New York: William Morrow and Company, 1985.

Leutze, James. *The London Journal of General Raymond E. Lee, 1940–1941.* Boston: Little, Brown, 1971.

Lowe, Michael. "Japanese Naval Codes." In *Codebreakers: The Inside Story of Bletchley Park,* edited by F. H. Hinsley and Alan Stripp, 257–263. New York: Oxford University Press, 1993.

McCormack, Alfred. "Origin, Functions and Problems of the Special Branch, M.I.S." In *A Subject and Name Index to the MAGIC Documents: Summaries and Transcripts of the Top-Secret Diplomatic Communications of Japan, 1938–1945,* edited by Paul Kesaris, 32–54. Frederick, MD: University Publications of America, 1982.

"Radio Security Station, Fourth Marine Regiment, Shanghia, China." Document SRH–179. As reprinted in *Listening to the Enemy: Key Documents on the Role of Communications Intelligence in the War with Japan,* edited by Ronald H. Spector, 28–39. Wilmington, DE: Scholarly Resources, 1987.

Rogers, Paul P. *The Good Years: MacArthur and Sutherland.* New York: Praeger, 1990.

Rusbridger, James, and Eric Nave. *Betrayal at Pearl Harbor: How Churchill Lured Roosevelt into World War II.* New York: Summit Books, 1991.

Safford, Laurence F. "A Brief History of Communications Intelligence in the United States" (written March 1952). As reprinted in *A Subject and Name Index to the MAGIC Documents: Summaries and Transcripts of the Top-Secret Diplomatic Communications of Japan, 1938–1945,* edited by Paul Kesaris, 1–16. Frederick, MD: University Publications of America, 1982.

Slusser, Robert M. "An American at Bletchley Park." In *Codebreakers: The Inside Story of Bletchley Park,* edited by F. H. Hinsley and Alan Stripp, 74–76. New York: Oxford University Press, 1993.

Spector, Ronald H., editor. *Listening to the Enemy: Key Documents on the Role of*

Communications Intelligence in the War with Japan. Wilmington, DE: Scholarly Resources, 1987.

Stripp, Alan. *Codebreaker in the Far East.* London: Frank Cass, 1989.

Thorpe, Elliott R. *East Wind, Rain: A Chief of Counter- Intelligence Remembers Peace and War in the Pacific, 1939–1949.* Boston: Gambit Incorporated, 1969.

Tolley, Kemp (Rear Admiral). "Army Snubs Navy in the Philippines." In *The Pacific War Remembered: An Oral History Collection*, edited by John T. Mason, Jr., 24–30. Annapolis, MD: Naval Institute Press, 1986.

van Der Rhoer, Edward. *Deadly Magic: A Personal Account of Communications Intelligence in World War II in the Pacific.* New York: Charles Scribner's Sons, 1978.

VanDyke, Gerald M. "Military Intelligence." In *Eyewitness to Infamy: An Oral History of Pearl Harbor*, edited by Paul J. Traveers, 27–31. Lanham, MD: Madison Books, 1991.

Welchman, Gordon. *The Hut Six Story: Breaking the Enigma Codes.* Harmondsworth: Penguin Books, 1982.

Winterbotham, F. W. *The Ultra Secret.* New York: Harper & Row, 1974. (The author headed Bletchley Park.)

Yardley, Herbert. *The Chinese Black Chamber: An Adventure in Espionage.* Boston: Houghton Mifflin, 1983.

Yardley, Herbert O. *The American Black Chamber.* Indianapolis: Bobbs-Merrill, 1931.

SECONDARY SOURCES

Andrew, Christopher. *Her Majesty's Secret Service: The Making of the British Intelligence Community.* 1985; New York: Viking/Elisabeth Sitton Books, 1986.

Bamford, James. "Introduction" to Herbert O. Yardley, *The Chinese Black Chamber: An Adventure in Espionage.* Boston: Houghton Mifflin, 1983.

Bath, Alan H. *Tracking the Axis Enemy: The Triumph of Anglo-American Naval Intelligence.* Lawrence, KS: University Press of Kansas, 1998.

Beesly, Patrick. *Very Special Intelligence: The Story of the Admiralty's Operational Intelligence Centre, 1939–1945.* Garden City, New York: Doubleday 1978.

Best, Antony. *Britain, Japan and Pearl Harbor: Avoiding War in East Asia, 1936–1941.* London: Routledge and London School of Economics, 1995.

Boyd, Carl. *Hitler's Japanese Confidant: General Oshima Hiroshi and Magic Intelligence, 1941–1945.* Lawrence, KS: University Press of Kansas, 1993.

Brown, Anthony C. *Bodyguard of Lies.* New York: Harper & Row, 1975.

_____. *"C": The Secret Life of Sir Stewart Graham Menzies—Spymaster to Winston Churchill.* New York: Macmillan, 1987.

_____. *The Last Hero: Wild Bill Donovan.* New York: New York Times Books, 1982.

Butow, R. J. C. *The John Doe Associates: Backdoor Diplomacy for Peace, 1941.* Stanford: Stanford University Press, 1974.

Clark, Ronald. *The Man Who Broke Purple: The Life of Colonel William F. Friedman, Who Deciphered the Japanese Code in World War II.* Boston: Little, Brown, 1977.

Collier, Basil. *Hidden Weapons: Allied Secret or Undercover Services in World War II.* London: Hamish Hamilton, 1982.

Costello, John. *Days of Infamy: MacArthur, Roosevelt, Churchill: The Shocking Truth Revealed—How Their Secret Deals and Strategic Blunders Caused Disasters at Pearl Harbor and the Philippines.* New York: Pocket Books, 1994

Crost, Lyn. *Honor by Fire: Japanese Americans at War in Europe and the Pacific.* Novato, CA: Presidio, 1994.

Drea, Edward J. *MacArthur's Ultra: Code-Breaking and the War against Japan, 1942–1945.* [N.p.]: University Press of Kansas, 1992.

Dunlop, Richard. *Donovan: America's Master Spy.* Chicago: Rand McNally, 1982.

Harper, Norman. *A Great and Powerful Friend: A Study of Australian American Relations between 1900 and 1975.* St. Lucia, Qld., Austrailia: University of Queensland Press, 1987.

Heinrichs, Waldo. *Threshold of War: Franklin D. Roosevelt & American Entry into World War II.* New York: Oxford University Press, 1988.

Hinsley, F. H., et al. *British Intelligence in the Second World War: Its Influence on Strategy and Operations* (volume 1). New York: Cambridge University Press, 1979.

_____. *British Intelligence in the Second World War: Its Influence on Strategy and Operations* (volume 2). New York: Cambridge University Press, 1981.

Horner, D. M. *High Command: Australia and Allied Strategy, 1939–1945.* Canberra, Australia: Australian War Memorial, 1982.

Johnson, Brian. *The Secret War.* New York: Methuen, 1978.

Kahn, David. *Kahn on Codes: Secrets of the New Cryptology.* New York: Macmillan, 1983.

_____. *Seizing the Enigma: The Race to Break the German U-Boat Codes, 1939–1945.* Boston: Houghton Mifflin, 1991.

Larrabee, Eric. *Commander in Chief: Franklin Delano Roosevelt, His Lieutenants, and Their War.* New York: Harper & Row, 1987.

Lash, Joseph P. *Roosevelt and Churchill, 1939–1941: The Partnership that Saved the West.* New York: W. W. Norton, 1976.

Lewin, Ronald. *The American Magic: Codes, Ciphers and the Defeat of Japan.* New York: Farrar, Straus, Grioux, 1982.

_____. *Ultra Goes to War.* London: Hutchinson & Company, 1978; paperback edition, New York: Pocket Books, 1980.

McLachlan, Donald. *Room 39: A Study in Naval Intelligence.* New York: Atheneum, 1968.

Miller, Nathan. *Spying for America: The Hidden History of U.S. Intelligence.* New York: Paragon House, 1989.

Morton, Louis. *Strategy and Command: The First Two Years.* In the *United States Army in World War II: The War in the Pacific* series. Washington, D.C.: Office of the Chief of Military History, Department of the Army, 1962.

Overy, Richard. *Why the Allies Won.* New York: W. W. Norton; 1996.

Packard, Wyman H. *A Century of U.S. Naval Intelligence.* A joint publication of the Office of Naval Intelligence and the Naval Historical Center. Washington: Department of the Navy, 1996.

Parrish, Thomas. *The Ultra Americans: The U.S. Role in Breaking the Nazi Codes.* New York: Stein and Day, 1986.

Prados, John. *Combined Fleet Decoded: The Secret History of American Intelligence and the Japanese Navy in World War II.* New York: Random House, 1995.

Prange, Gordon W., in collaboration with Donald M. Goldstein and Katherine V. Dillon. *At Dawn We Slept: The Untold Story of Pearl Harbor.* New York: McGraw-Hill, 1981.

_____. *December 7, 1941: The Day the Japanese Attacked Pearl Harbor.* New York: McGraw-Hill, 1988.

_____. *Pearl Harbor: The Verdict of History.* New York: McGraw-Hill, 1986.

Raines, Rebecca R. *Getting the Message Through: A Branch History of the U.S. Army Signal Corps.* Washington D.C.: Center of Military History, United States Army, 1996.

Reynolds, David. *The Creation of the Anglo-American Alliance, 1937–41: A Study in Competitive Co-operation.* Chapel Hill, [NC]: University of North Carolina Press, 1981.

Robertson, John. *Australia at War: 1939–1945.* Melbourne, Australia: William Heinemann, 1981.

Schaller, Michael. "General Douglas MacArthur and the Politics of the Pacific War." In *The Pacific War Revisited*, 17–34. Edited by Gunter Bischof and Robert L. Dupont. Baton Rouge, LA: Lousiana State University Press, 1997.

Slackman, Michael. *Target: Pearl Harbor.* Honolulu: University of Hawaii Press and Arizona Memorial Museum Associaiton, 1990.

Smith, Bradley F. *The Shadow Warriors.* New York: Basic Books, 1983.

_____. *Sharing Secrets with Stalin: How the Allies Traded Intelligence, 1941–1945.* Lawrence, KS: University Press of Kansas, 1996.

Smith, R. Harris. *OSS: The Secret History of America's First Central Intelligence Agency.* Berkeley: University of California Press, 1972.

Stafford, David. *Churchill and Secret Service.* Woodstock, New York: Overlook Press, 1997.

Stevenson, William. *A Man Called Intrepid: The Secret War.* New York: Harcourt Brace Jovanovich, 1976.

Troy, Thomas F. *Donovan and the CIA: A History of the Establishment of the Central Intelligence Agency.* [N.p.]: Central Intelligence Agency, 1975; declassified and slightly rewritten version, Frederick, MD: Aletheia Books/University Publications of America, 1981.

_____. *Wild Bill and Intrepid: Donovan, Stephenson, and the Origin of CIA.* New Haven, Connecticut: Yale University Press, 1996.

van der Vat, Dan. *The Pacific Campaign: World War II—The U.S.-Japanese Naval War, 1941–1945.* New York: Simon & Schuster, 1991.

Weintraub, Stanley. *Long Day's Journey into War: December 7, 1941.* New York: Dutton/Truman Talley Books, 1991.

West, Nigel. *MI6: British Secret Intelligence Service Operations, 1909–1945.* New York: Random House, 1983.

West, Nigel. *A Thread of Deceit: Espionage Myths of World War II.* New York: Random House, 1985.

Wohlstetter, Roberta. *Pearl Harbor—Warning and Decision.* Stanford, CA: Stanford University Press, 1962.

Yu, Maochun. *OSS in China: Prelude to Cold War.* New Haven: Yale University Press, 1996.

ARTICLE

Rabinovich, Abraham. "The Code Breakers." *Jerusalem Post* (International Edition), February 12, 1999, 20–22.

Index